THE
VEGAN ATHLETE

A Complete Guide to a Healthy, Plant-Based, Active Lifestyle

KARINA INKSTER
FOREWORD BY ROBERT CHEEKE

Skyhorse Publishing

Skyhorse Publishing books may be purchased in bulk at special discounts for sales promotion, corporate gifts, fund-raising, or educational purposes. Special editions can also be created to specifications. For details, contact the Special Sales Department, Skyhorse Publishing, 307 West 36th Street, 11th Floor, New York, NY 10018 or info@skyhorsepublishing.com.

Skyhorse® and Skyhorse Publishing® are registered trademarks of Skyhorse Publishing, Inc.®, a Delaware corporation.

Visit our website at www.skyhorsepublishing.com.

10 9 8 7 6 5 4 3 2 1

Library of Congress Cataloging-in-Publication Data is available on file.

Cover design by Daniel Brount
Cover photos by John C. Watson

Print ISBN: 978-1-5107-5921-3
Ebook ISBN: 978-1-5107-6161-2

Printed in China

CONTENTS

FOREWORD

The plant-based diet is coming of age at a time when a real cultural shift in food and lifestyle is taking place in North America before our eyes.

All around us we can see the impact from the growing number of people adopting a plant-based diet. From the increase in plant-based foods offered in grocery stores coast to coast, to the number of athletes, celebrities, doctors, family, friends, and neighbors who call themselves vegans, the world is changing in ways that benefit all of us.

Regardless of how a plant-based diet piqued your interest and compelled you to pick up this book, the planet and the animals thank you. In the social media–laden world we live in today, ideas are being spread and minds are being opened to new thoughts and worldviews at a faster rate than ever before. Each one of us has the power to influence a community, population, or society from the comfort of our smart phones, regardless of where we are, simply by sharing information.

We are witnessing a greater degree of health problems than ever before, environmental concerns are at an all-time high, and there is a palpable desire to change for the better. We are on the verge of something historic, a cultural shift during our lifetimes that we will be able to talk to future generations about, saying, "I remember when . . ."

Here, Karina's comprehensive approach to bridging the gaps between health, fitness, and great food creates a blueprint to follow to ensure success in health and in life. A plant-based diet not only supports the health of the individual but the health of the planet and all those with whom we share this precious place.

With tangible steps to get you on the right track in your quest to pursue a deeply meaningful change in health and fitness, combined with shopping and food preparation tips and one hundred innovative plant-based recipes, this is your new go-to resource for holistic wellness.

As a vegan athlete since 1995, I have two decades of experience in numerous sports backgrounds, including becoming a champion runner and champion bodybuilder. I am confident that my vegan athlete colleagues featured in this book will inspire you to elevate your own training to new heights. If you have been away from exercise for a while, perhaps you will be inspired to start anew, and you will have the guidance from those who have been down that road to direct you on your own path to success.

From eating right to fuel an active lifestyle, to the exercise benefits you can expect to experience, to healthy meal plans and recipes, this book covers it all. As a personal training specialist with a master's degree in Gerontology—specializing in health and aging—Karina will steer you in the right direction to optimal health. Karina has been following a plant-based diet and vegan lifestyle since she was a teenager. She walks her talk proudly and teaches you how to do the same.

Whatever it is that moves you, follow your passion and make it happen. Wishing you all the very best in health and fitness.

Robert Cheeke, bestselling author of *Vegan Bodybuilding & Fitness: The Complete Guide to Building Your Body on a Plant-Based Diet*; founder & president of VeganBodybuilding.com

VI   THE VEGAN ATHLETE

INTRODUCTION

The culture of food in North America is changing—and fast. Taking our continent by storm is a rapidly growing movement about food. Plant food, that is. More than 8 million North Americans choose to exclude meat from their diets, and an additional 25 million rarely eat meat. Many of these individuals consume no animal products whatsoever. Why do these vegans and vegetarians choose to forgo the steak, yogurt, or ice cream? Most commonly, they cite increasing and maintaining personal health. Add to this the steadily growing population of health and fitness enthusiasts who adopt plant-based diets to meet their performance goals, plus those looking to vegan diets for weight loss, and we've got a full-blown diet and lifestyle movement quickly expanding across the globe.

In line with being health conscious, individuals following or interested in plant-based diets know the importance of regular exercise to complement healthy eating. Ranging from elite amateur athletes to everyday fitness enthusiasts to inactive people who don't know where to begin, vegans and vegetarians need a practical, healthy-living guide tailored to their diets.

That's where *The Vegan Athlete* comes in.

This book is a comprehensive active-living guide and cookbook for current and aspiring vegans and vegetarians interested in making regular physical activity a part of their lives. I hope it motivates and inspires you to increase the quality (and length!) of your life by enjoying a whole foods, plant-based diet and engaging in regular exercise. If you're already enjoying a plant-based, active lifestyle, this book will support you in continuing to reach your health and fitness goals. With brand new recipes, at-home workouts, interviews with vegan athletes, and lifestyle tips, you're sure to add something new to your healthy-living repertoire. If you're new to vegan and/or active living, this book will get you started on the right foot.

The first edition of this book, published in 2014, was the first book in plant-based health to provide extensive lifestyle and fitness information, interviews with vegan athletes, as well as a collection of recipes. *The Vegan Athlete* contains healthy-living advice for everyone from beginners to amateur athletes, plus a well-rounded collection of one hundred mouth-watering recipes catering to the nutritional needs of active people. This book bridges the gap between diet and fitness, approaching health holistically and as a long-term lifestyle.

WHO SHOULD READ THIS BOOK?

This book is for you if you're interested in leading a healthy, active lifestyle that helps you feel good, look good, and live a long life free of illness. Sounds good, right? Trust me, it is. But why is it that so many of us lose our way when it comes to health and fitness? Why are so many of us overweight or even obese? Why do we feel so tired and lack energy? Why do we have so many health issues and diseases like diabetes, osteoporosis, heart disease, and cancer?

I think we all know the answers. Being active and eating right can be hard work. Unhealthy, sugary, or fatty foods are usually delicious and difficult to give up. Many people don't know where to start, especially given the overwhelming amount of health-related information available today. We're busier than ever in our daily lives, and so much is expected of us that taking time for our own health doesn't seem to fit into our schedules. Add to all this the personal barriers many of us face, like lacking the motivation or interest to start up an active lifestyle, and you've got a host of reasons why people are inactive, overweight, and disease-ridden.

If you're just starting out with eating a healthy diet and becoming more active, you might find it to be hard work. The longer you stick with it, though, the easier it becomes. Healthy living doesn't have to be difficult, overwhelming, or stressful. This book assumes that, like most people, you're very busy and have many commitments in your daily life. That's why you'll get plenty of healthy-living tips meant to simplify your life. The majority of the one hundred recipes in this book are meant to be prepared and cooked in thirty minutes or less. A few recipes require longer cooking time (which takes no effort on your part because you're just waiting), and a select few take extra preparation time in case you want to get fancier (e.g., Shepherd's Pie page 217). For the most part, however, I've created the recipes for busy people who want the most delicious and nourishing food by spending the least amount of time in the kitchen.

By the way, to me, "health" means not just eating the right kinds of foods, but leading an active lifestyle and enjoying good mental health, too. I hope this book encompasses this holistic view of health, providing insight (and perhaps a bit of motivation!) into how to enjoy a plant-based diet that supports and enhances regular physical activity, whether you're training for a marathon, going to weekly yoga classes, or building muscle mass at the gym.

So, congratulations to you for taking the step to read this book! It will get you well on your way to being armed with what you need to know to kick ass at living a healthy, enjoyable, fulfilling lifestyle.

DISCOVER YOUR "WHY"

We all know that working out and eating right just because someone else tells us to is not going to work—at least not for very long. "I guess I should because it's probably good for me" also doesn't usually work. We're not going to stick to a healthy lifestyle just because someone told us to or because we have a vague idea that exercise and good nutrition will make us healthier. We need our very own personal, *detailed* reasons.

Here are mine: I want to be strong and healthy for my life with my amazing husband. I want to sleep well, feel great, have lots of energy, challenge myself, have fun, and look great. Working out is meditative, clears my mind, and eases stress. Eating right (for me that's 100 percent vegan and mostly whole foods) keeps my energy high, my muscles fed, my skin and hair healthy, and my body lean.

In the words of one of my fitness role models, Miryah Scott:

"Treating your body right through proper eating and working out is about giving back to you, making time for you, conquering challenges, increasing your energy, boosting your self confidence and, most of all, it's about feeling good."

But first and foremost, I want to be an example for others who need help with their journeys to health.

We each need specific, concrete reasons as motivation to incorporate exercise and healthy eating into our daily lives. What are yours?

To get you thinking, here are seven reasons you should take care of your health:

1. You're going to live longer. Being active and eating a healthy diet mean you're much, much less likely to die at an early age. That's a pretty major benefit, if you ask me. And it's not just about you—think about all your friends and family members who want you to be around for as long as possible!

2. You're going to prevent horrible diseases like cancer and heart disease. It's not just about living longer—it's also about living *better*. What good is it to live an extra five or ten years if you spend that time in a hospital bed? Work out and eat right so you lower your chances of being diagnosed with everything from cancer and heart disease to osteoporosis and diabetes.

3. You'll have more energy. You'll function more effectively in day-to-day life. You'll be better at climbing stairs, doing housework, keeping up with the kids, carrying groceries, and everything else you do in a day. You'll also feel less tired and prevent the afternoon energy slump. All without caffeine!

4. You'll sleep better. People who exercise regularly tend to enjoy higher quality sleep than people who don't. That means less tiredness during the day, even if you spend the same amount of time sleeping (better quality sleep is more restful). Just remember, don't work out within a few hours of bedtime because your muscles, heart, and brain may be too stimulated to fall asleep. Morning, afternoon, or early evening exercise seems best for quality shut-eye.

5. Your bones and muscles will get stronger. Strong bones and muscles are extremely important. In later life, muscle strength—especially in the lower limbs—is highly predictive of falls. And falls are a big deal; up to 20 percent of falls in older age lead to death. Combine falls with weak bones from osteoporosis, and you've got a recipe for disability and loss of independence.

6. You'll maintain a healthy weight. Carrying excess weight is linked to developing heart disease, diabetes, osteoarthritis, cancer, respiratory problems, sleep apnea, varicose veins . . . need I go on? A healthy diet and regular exercise will help you maintain a lean figure for life.

7. Your sex life will improve. We feel better about ourselves when we work out regularly, and that leads to being and feeling better in the sack. Exercising regularly means better blood flow and circulation, and it releases feel-good chemicals in our brains called endorphins.

Exercise—especially resistance training—increases testosterone in both men and women. (Don't worry ladies, that's not a bad thing! We just don't have as much as men.) Increased testosterone is a key predictor of libido.

When we feel healthy, we don't tend to think about what it would be like being extremely sick or living with a chronic disease. For many people, it takes a rude awakening in the form of a heart attack, stroke, or cancer diagnosis to start thinking about optimizing their health. Better late than never, but why not start now?

As a bonus, caring about your health is fun! You get to try all sorts of new and delicious foods, try some new activities, and best of all—witness amazing changes in how you look, how you feel, and how long you live (although you won't witness that one 'til you're ninety).

BENEFITS OF AN ACTIVE, PLANT-BASED LIFESTYLE

Being active and being vegan each come with a host of health benefits. Add them together and you're setting yourself up for a long, fulfilling, and healthy life! The reward for exercising regularly and eating a plant-based diet isn't just increased individual health, though. You also may enjoy increased athletic performance, as well as a positive impact on our planet, including the environment and fellow humans.

Physical Health

As I'm sure you know, lifestyle-related diseases and conditions in North America are killing more of us than ever before. These conditions do sometimes have a genetic basis, but are greatly (if not mostly) influenced by our lifestyles. Even if a few of us do have genetic predispositions toward certain chronic diseases, our lifestyles are often the main determining factor in whether or not we're diagnosed with these conditions.

One in three Americans and one in four Canadians are obese (meaning a Body Mass Index of 30 or more). Along with obesity comes a laundry list of health consequences, including type 2 diabetes, cardiovascular disease, high blood pressure, osteoarthritis, numerous types of cancer, gallbladder disease, functional limitations, and disabilities.[1]

As a population, we're eating ourselves sick. But you don't have to be a part of this statistic! Choosing a balanced plant-based diet and exercising regularly—essentially, living a healthy, active lifestyle—is the absolute best way to ensure that you'll enjoy great health and a long, fulfilling life.

Keep in mind that eating any old plant-based diet does not automatically translate into eating a *healthy* diet. French fries, potato chips, white flour, beer, sugary candy, soft drinks, and a host of other extremely processed treat foods can be made entirely from plants. While treats certainly have their place in any well-rounded diet, a plant-based diet rich in unprocessed whole foods is the way to go. This book will show you how to create a diet like this.

More and more highly respected researchers and institutions are promoting a plant-based diet, based on studies supporting its health benefits.

For example, cardiologist and former Olympic rowing champion Dr. Caldwell Esselstyn is known for reversing heart disease in his high-risk patients. No surgery involved. Instead, he uses a plant-based, whole foods diet to reverse heart disease in his patients, some of whom had been given only a year to live (many lived for more than twenty years, and are still alive and well).

Dr. Dean Ornish—physician, founder of the Preventative Medicine Research Institute in California, and clinical professor of medicine at the University of California, San Fransisco—also has focused much of his research effort into reversing heart disease with a whole foods, plant-based diet. In 1990, results of one of his clinical trials showed that it was possible (and indeed, very effective) to reverse heart disease symptoms with a plant-based diet and an active lifestyle. These results were considered revolutionary at the time, because until that point it was believed to be impossible to stop the progression of heart disease symptoms.

One large-scale study from the Harvard School of Public Health followed more than 110,000 adults for more than twenty years. It found that eating red meat—in any amount—"significantly increases the risk of premature death." Published in the *Archives of Internal Medicine* in March 2012, the study found that consuming just one 3-ounce serving of unprocessed meat per day was linked to a 13 percent greater chance of dying during the course of the study. If this daily serving of meat is processed, like a hot dog or bacon, the risk of dying during the study was 20 percent greater.[2]

The largest comprehensive study of human nutrition ever conducted, called *The China Study*, found similar results. (By the way, I highly suggest reading the book of the same name, which explains the study's results in detail.) Using both clinical lab tests and population studies including many thousands of people, this research provides one of the best scientific arguments for the health benefits of a plant-based diet.

In a nutshell, principal investigator T. Colin Campbell and his associates found that casein, an animal protein found in products like cow's milk, promotes the growth of cancer. Astoundingly, increasing and lowering the dose of casein in lab studies could turn on and off the growth of cancer cells. Lowering the dose of casein and replacing it with plant protein greatly decreased cancer rates even in animals genetically predisposed to develop cancer!

The benefits of plant-based eating don't stop at cancer. Eating a healthy vegan diet may also protect you from obesity, diabetes, autoimmune diseases, as well as bone, eye, kidney, and brain diseases.

In light of this convincing, rapidly growing body of research that supports the incredible health benefits of eating a plant-based diet, many well-known institutions are making appropriate changes (albeit slowly).

For instance, the USDA's newest food guide, called "MyPlate," reclassifies the "meat and alternatives" section into a "protein" group, which includes many plant-based sources of high-quality protein as well as lean animal-based sources. This aims to show that we don't need meat to enjoy a healthy and balanced diet. However, nutrition experts at the Harvard School of Public Health take issue with some of the USDA's recommendations—many of which have been influenced by corporate pressure from the meat and dairy industries. Researchers at Harvard have created their own version of the "MyPlate" graphic based on the latest and highest-quality scientific evidence supporting the health benefits of a plant-based diet rich in vegetables, whole grains, healthy fats, and healthy proteins. Harvard's Healthy Eating Plate is "based exclusively on the best available science and was not subjected to political and commercial pressures from food industry lobbyists."[3]

Harvard's version replaces the USDA's dairy category with a water category, which includes tea and coffee. Experts at Harvard recommend limiting dairy, citing an increased risk for prostate and possibly ovarian cancer with high intakes of dairy. They also note that there is little, if any, evidence to support the notion that dairy consumption protects against osteoporosis. The USDA "MyPlate" doesn't distinguish between different types of protein. Harvard's version distinguishes between healthy protein (e.g., nuts, beans, fish, poultry) and proteins to be avoided (including red meat and processed meats). Harvard's version also depicts a bottle of healthy oil, which the USDA's version lacks. Plant-based oils are recommended for cooking and on salads in order to reduce unhealthy cholesterol in the body and to increase heart health. In 2019, Health Canada published a new food guide, no longer containing food groups or serving sizes. It almost completely eliminates dairy, and emphasizes eating "plenty of vegetables and fruits, whole grain foods, and protein foods. Choose protein foods that come from plants more often." This food guide also is not influenced by industry-commissioned reports, but rather by scientific evidence.

In sum, the message is straightforward. As T. Colin Campbell writes in *The China Study*, "People who ate the most animal-based foods got the most chronic disease. People who ate the most plant-based foods were the healthiest . . . There are virtually no nutrients in animal-based foods that are not better provided by plants."[4]

Athletic Performance

Over the past few years, the popularity of plant-based fitness has exploded. Professional athletes, amateurs, and beginners alike are turning to plant-based diets to increase performance, lose weight, build muscle, and increase day-to-day energy. Vegan sports supplements (e.g., the Vega brand) are extremely popular in mainstream stores across North America, and vegan fitness websites with tens of thousands of members (e.g., www.veganbodybuilding.com) are exploding onto the scene.

Since vegan fitness is a relatively new phenomenon (but growing steadily), there are few clinical research studies on the topic. Anecdotal evidence and expert opinion point toward a potential increase in athletic performance with a plant-based diet, but we'll need to wait for more high-quality, peer-reviewed research before we can say for certain.

One review paper published in 2019 focuses on endurance athletes. The researchers write, "Because . . . plant-based foods are rich in antioxidants, they help reduce oxidative stress. Diets emphasizing plant foods have also been shown to reduce indicators of inflammation. These features of plant-based diets may present safety and performance advantages for endurance athletes."*

Athletes from a wide range of disciplines have noted performance increases by adopting a plant-based diet. Tennis star Venus Williams, Olympic skier Seba Johnson, ultra-marathoner Scott Durek, former Ironman triathlete Brendan Brazier, MMA fighter Mac Danzig, ice hockey player Mike Zigomanis, and bodybuilder Jim Morris are all plant-based professional athletes (and there are many more).

Many elite amateur athletes are taking to veganism as well. One-hundred-two-year-old marathon runner Faujia Singh attributed his longevity and great health to his plant-based diet. In 2011, at the age of 100, he became the oldest person in the world to complete a marathon. Three days earlier, Ontario Masters Athletics reported that Singh achieved eight world age-group records in one day, consisting of the 200m, 400m, 800m, 1,500m, one mile, 1500m, 3,000m, and 5,000m distances.

In 2013, plant-based athlete Fiona Oakes won the women's portion of the North Pole Marathon. She's placed in the top 25 in some of the world's most prestigious marathons, including Berlin and London, and has broken numerous course records. She's also completed the gruelling Marathon des Sables, a 156-mile event across sand dunes and rough terrain in the blistering heat of the Sahara Desert. Participants carry all their own supplies for the duration of the race, except water. The equivalent of completing six marathons in six days, this race is often dubbed the "toughest race on Earth."

Sports nutritionists note that a plant-based diet might mean faster recovery times and maximized training, which leads to improved performance. This could be due to the high level of antioxidants and anti-inflammatory compounds found in vegan diets, which are thought to aid in athletic recovery.

---

* Barnard, N. D., et al. (2019). Plant-Based Diets for Cardiovascular Safety and Performance in Endurance Sports. Nutrients, 10(1). https://pubmed.ncbi.nlm.nih.gov/30634559

Animals, the Environment, and Our Fellow Human Beings

The benefits of veganism extend far beyond increased physical health. A vegan diet also has a far-reaching impact on animal welfare, our environment, and our fellow human beings. Each vegan has a different set of reasons for choosing the lifestyle, but we're all helping to make our planet a much better place, whether we know it or not.

One of the most common reasons people choose to exclude meat (or all animal products) from their diets is opposing the torture of animals in slaughterhouses and factory farms. Sir Paul McCartney's famous quote, "If slaughterhouses had glass walls, everyone would be a vegetarian," certainly rings true. People typically avoid learning about how animals are treated and the suffering involved in getting meat onto their plates. However, once we take responsibility to become aware of what happens behind those slaughterhouse walls, many of us stop eating meat on the spot.

By boycotting industries that cause inconceivable animal suffering, it's clear that eliminating meat, dairy, and eggs from our diets creates less harm and fosters more compassion in this world. From caged hens to overcrowded pig pens, from removing birds' beaks and pigs' tails without anaesthesia to confined and forcibly impregnated dairy cows—choosing a diet that doesn't support these practices is an ethical decision that allows many of us to live a life in accordance with our values.

We're also making a positive impact on the environment by eating fewer (or no) animal products.[5], [6] Here's a snapshot of the environmental damage you're not supporting by being vegan.

- Climate change: Animal agriculture generates more greenhouse gases than all transportation vehicles combined. There's no question this industry plays a major part in climate change and the resulting destruction of our planet.
- Pollution: Animal waste, which produces many times the tonnage of human waste, has no treatment requirements and few environmental regulations. No wonder animal waste is rated as one of the top ten sources of pollution in the world!
- Deforestation: Animal agriculture accounts for more than 80 percent of annual world deforestation. Expanding from the United States into Central America due to high demand for beef, cattle ranching has destroyed more rainforest than any other activity in this area.
- Loss of biodiversity: In the USA, livestock overgrazing has made extinct more plant species than any other cause. Native animals such as elk, unable to compete with cattle for available food, are disappearing quickly. Other animal species, including rattlesnakes, coyotes, and foxes, are regularly killed by ranchers in an effort to protect their herds.

This is just the beginning of the environmental destruction caused by animal agriculture. Sure, eating *less* meat will make a difference (that is, after all, science broadcaster and environmental activist David Suzuki's number one tip for saving our planet), but eating *no* meat is even more effective.

Of course, not all plant crops are created equal. Plant-based diets full of conventionally produced ingredients can also contribute to some of the above environmental problems, but perhaps not to the same degree. When in doubt, choose organic and local produce. These options are usually (but not always) less damaging to our planet, and thus more sustainable.

Just as plant-based diets have the potential to help save our environment, they also have the potential to help other humans. Are you familiar with the following astounding statistics?

- It takes 10 pounds of grain to produce 1 pound of meat, and almost 1,000 liters of water to produce 1 liter of milk. A third of arable crops in North America are used as animal feed.
- While foie gras farmers force-feed ducks through funnels to fatten them up, 60 million people per year die of starvation and related diseases.
- In the USA, livestock consume six and a half times more grain than the entire American population consumes directly. The Iowa-based Council for Agricultural Science and Technology estimates that if all this grain were to be consumed by humans directly, it would nourish five times as many people as it does after it is converted into meat, milk, and eggs.

There is, of course, no simple answer as to how resources like water and grain crops saved by eating fewer animal products should be used or distributed. But it's clear that we need to rethink our senseless misuse of food resources. Based solely on human impact, the humane option is clear: eat only plants.

The bottom line is that vegans and vegetarians are saving the world! We're reducing our own risk for countless chronic diseases, eating in accordance with our values, helping the human population, and saving the environment.

In 1998, at the age of eleven, I decided I wanted to stop contributing to the inhumane treatment of animals. I aimed to enjoy a diet that had as small an impact on the environment as possible and didn't support the horrors of animal agriculture. Thus, I decided to adopt a vegetarian diet. My parents were concerned that I wouldn't be eating a well-rounded diet, especially since I was still quite young, so they (in their typical academic fashion) asked me to do extensive research. And research I did. In addition to learning about vegetarian nutrition, I learned about the well-documented health benefits of excluding meat from our diets and about the far-reaching devastation animal agriculture wreaks on our planet. Being vegetarian came to mean more to me than just animal welfare—it was a life-enhancing, health-boosting, ethical decision.

In high school, at the age of sixteen, I started toying with the idea of becoming vegan. The dissonance I felt between my strong feelings about animal suffering and the fact that I was still supporting animal cruelty by eating dairy and eggs was becoming increasingly obvious. Becoming vegan was also a health decision. Suffering from various strange symptoms like constant sneezing and itchiness, pain in my joints, and debilitating migraines, I stumbled across a story of a woman in much the same situation. She cut out dairy from her diet and watched her symptoms disappear. So, of course, I tried the same! After a month of veganism, I felt fantastic and all my previously unexplained symptoms disappeared. At the end of the month I happened to drink a glass of milk and eat some milk chocolate. All my symptoms reappeared almost instantly. I immediately returned to veganism and have never looked back.

Many nonvegans see the plant-based lifestyle as limiting or restrictive, even devoid of enjoyment. This couldn't be further from the truth! There is no more powerful feeling than knowing my behavior aligns with my values. To me, veganism isn't a sacrifice, and it's not defined by what I leave out of my diet. By being vegan, I'm adding compassion, countless delicious foods I'd otherwise never heard of, and years to my life.

Here's my definition of veganism:

Veganism is a 100 percent plant-based diet and lifestyle in respect for and celebration of all life on Earth, as well as one's individual health and well-being. Veganism encompasses a sense of interconnectedness with the web of life, a form of activism, and a lifestyle. Vegans consume foods and use materials only from the *Plantae* (plant) or *Monera* (one-celled organisms) kingdoms. Thus, they do not eat anything without cell walls. Veganism typically involves understanding the use and management of resources, supporting sustainable agriculture, and knowing that human beings have responsibilities to one another, to animals, and to the environment that sustains all life-forms.

I've been strength training, swimming, jumping rope, and power yoga-ing my way to fitness since 2003. I've always been one to think about the future; I started strength training at the age of seventeen primarily to increase bone density so I could prevent osteoporosis in later life. Like my reasons for becoming vegetarian and vegan, my reasons for lifting weights have evolved over the years. Not only do I love feeling strong, having more energy, and sleeping better—I love how strength training makes me look!

My training program is very consistent throughout the year, and doesn't change much with the seasons. Due to horrible pollen allergies for most of the year, I don't do much outdoor exercise. I train between seven and eight times each week, across five to six days. My main workouts each week are three morning swims, and four evening strength training sessions, which consist of an upper body workout, a lower body workout, and two full-body workouts (often I'll add a third one to the end of my week), training my core each time. I always focus on the "gold standard"—compound moves like squats, deadlifts, lunges, push-ups, rows, and chin-ups.

Occasionally one of my swims will be replaced with an additional strength training session, where I focus on practicing specific moves I'm looking to improve (currently: weighted pull-ups and pistol squats). At the end of these sessions, I'll usually jump rope at a high intensity for 10 to 15 minutes.

In addition to being a Certified Personal Training Specialist, I hold a Master's degree in Gerontology with a specialization in health and aging—an educational background that lends itself well to health promotion, health psychology, and training motivation. I was the primary investigator of a year-long gerontological study addressing exercise classes offered for older adults throughout the Lower Mainland in BC, and I led a research initiative regarding active seniors in nonprofit organizations for the BC government's Seniors' Healthy Living Secretariat, a division of the Ministry of Healthy Living and Sport. I'm passionate about supporting others in leading healthy and active lives, and I have worked hard to overcome significant barriers to engaging in physical activity myself.

I deal with a potentially life-threatening condition called food-dependent exercise-induced anaphylaxis, which prohibits me from training after having eaten within eight hours, in case a food triggers a serious allergic reaction when coupled with exercise. I essentially schedule my life around this condition. I work out only in the mornings, after having eaten only oatmeal (which I know is a "safe" food).

Other barriers I face are severe seasonal allergies and asthma that limit my activity for six months each year, as well as weekly allergy shots after which I can't exercise—again, due to anaphylaxis risk.

My diet is 100 percent plant-based and I include as many whole foods as possible (foods that are in their natural states, as opposed to being processed). However, I don't deprive myself and I do indulge in small portions of treat foods such as dark chocolate (my favorite!). I eat a *lot* of food to fuel my active lifestyle, usually in many small meals throughout the day. I don't count calories on a regular basis, but I know from a few three-day food diaries that I consume an average of 2,500 calories per day. When I worked with clients in a gym (before switching completely to online work), I would consume upwards of 3,000 calories per day.

I think about food a lot, and it's not always in a good way! I have many food allergies I need to be constantly wary of, including a severe allergy to raw fruit. I have to cook all my fruit before eating it to denature the protein and thus render it safe for my body. This, as I'm sure you can imagine, takes a great deal of extra time. I'm also allergic to tree nuts, so I need to ensure I get sufficient healthy fats from other sources.

With careful and consistent planning, I make healthy, active living work for me. I always use the old cliché of "If I can do it, so can you!" with my clients and other people interested in healthy living. In addition to my numerous allergy challenges, during my years as a full-time graduate student working three jobs and planning my wedding, I still managed to train six days per week with careful planning and many 5 a.m. mornings. With very limited time for cooking, I learned to prepare healthy meals quickly, and now I help others to do the same. I understand the many challenges involved in maintaining an active lifestyle, and I aim to live by example in overcoming my own obstacles. I help my clients to enjoy working out and to fit regular exercise into their busy lives.

Feeling and seeing the results of my lifestyle are great fuel to keep it going. I feel great and want to keep it that way! I also want to help others—whether or not they're vegan—to achieve their own results, which is motivation for me to be my best.

In my journey to health and fitness, and in my challenge of overcoming my many obstacles to healthy living, I've learned that there's power in consistency. Small actions add up over time and can lead to huge results. I've also learned that enjoyment—an often-overlooked aspect of health and fitness—is one of the main keys to making a healthy lifestyle last. Healthy living becomes easy when it's something you enjoy and look forward to! I also find that one of the most powerful motivators to strive for continued health and fitness improvements is being able to inspire others. I believe we can each be a healthy role model, inspiring our children, friends, family, colleagues, and even strangers to live their best lives.

CHAPTER 1: WHY IS WORKING OUT IMPORTANT?

We all know that working out is important to our health. But why, exactly? (Other than the obvious factor of healthy weight maintenance, which I hope everyone knows about.) There are countless reasons exercise is important to your health! Although you need to be active consistently over a long period of time for the most health benefits, even one workout can make a difference. In case you're the impatient type, here are three immediate results you'll get from just one workout:

1. Twenty minutes of moderate physical activity has been shown to increase cognitive and attention abilities immediately thereafter. This effect can last up to an hour. So, instead of spending more time meeting your work deadline, schedule a quick workout instead. Your productivity will thank you for it.

2. Even just one workout can do wonders for your skin. As your heart rate increases during your workout, the surface of your skin gets treated to increased blood flow, leading to a nice, healthy glow.

3. Better sex! That's thanks to better blood flow after a good workout. One study on women found that a twenty-minute treadmill run increased genital arousal by 150 percent. This effect seems to last for about thirty minutes after finishing a workout.

In case those immediate results aren't enough to convince you to get moving, let's look at the benefits of adopting an active lifestyle over the long term. First, if you exercise regularly, you'll live longer. Studies have found that regular, moderate physical activity has a greater impact on longevity than does obesity. In fact, active overweight people in one study lived an average of 3.1 years longer than inactive, normal-weight people.[1]

Health isn't just about living longer, though. Regular exercise helps you to live longer, but it also helps you to live *better*.

One of my clients, a fifty-two-year-old single dad of three sons, calls exercise his "insurance policy" against age-related decline. He says, "Everyone talks about financial planning for retirement to ensure we have the funds to live life to the fullest. But what is all that if we don't have good health? I'm investing in good health [via personal training] as part of my healthy aging plan. I don't just want to be around for my kids and my future grandkids; I want to be healthy, active, and energetic! Exercise isn't just about losing weight or building muscle. It's also about functioning better in daily life and feeling better on a daily basis."

I completely agree. Some of the main reasons I exercise are to live a better day-to-day life and to function more effectively.

Living a healthy life now will bring you many, many benefits later. Some of us don't often think about what it'll be like when we're older (whatever "older" means to you—40? 60? 100?), but our future selves will thank us if we consider this more often. Being active is absolutely crucial in older age to maintaining independence, increasing quality of life, and decreasing disability. Between the ages of twenty-five and eighty, we lose approximately 40 to 50 percent of our strength.[2] The antidote to muscle and strength loss with age is, of course, regular exercise. We also lose bone density starting in our mid-thirties, which can result in osteoporosis and a high risk of bone fractures in later life (especially for women). Resistance training is your secret weapon of choice here.

While it's best to start living an active lifestyle as early as possible, "it's never too late" certainly rings true. Even for older adults who have been inactive their whole lives, starting an exercise program increases levels of agility, balance, flexibility, strength, and cardiovascular capacity—even for adults aged eighty and older.[3]

The physical health payoffs of regular exercise are clear. But did you know that regular exercise also has benefits for emotional and mental health? Regular physical activity seems to have a protective effect against developing depression. Studies have also found that regular exercise tends to have an antidepressant effect in people who already exhibit clinical depression.[4] Preliminary research shows that aerobic (i.e., cardio) exercise can decrease symptoms of anxiety, and that positive mood is found more often in people who exercise regularly than those who don't.[5]

CHAPTER 2: N.I.C.E.: FOUR PRINCIPLES OF GETTING RESULTS FROM EXERCISE

You may be just starting out with an exercise program, you may have exercised for a few months already, or perhaps you're a seasoned pro looking to increase your fitness know-how and prevent plateaus. How do you know whether what you're doing during your workouts is going to continue to get you results? How do you get fit in the first place? How do you increase your fitness level if you're already in shape? No matter your fitness level, the following four principles will guide you: novelty, intensity, consistency, and enjoyment (N.I.C.E.).

You need to keep doing new things, work out at a challenging intensity, exercise regularly over time, and have fun!

NOVELTY

In order to make progress, you need to keep your muscles guessing. This means you need to switch up your workouts and try new activities, rather than doing the same routine with the same weights at the gym, or running the same path for the same distance every morning. The key here is to find a balance between working on improving certain exercises (meaning you'll need to do the same exercises for a period of time) and changing them for further fitness development.

There are countless ways you can change what you're already doing. Run longer or faster, lift heavier weights for fewer reps or lighter weights for more reps, or swim sets of lengths at the pool at different paces. You'll prevent both plateaus—where you don't see fitness improvements, even though you're working out—and boredom.

Not only do you need to keep progressing with existing exercises (e.g., by using heavier weights or by performing more reps) and occasionally switch up the exercises you're doing, but you also need to vary the types of exercises you do. This will develop well-rounded fitness, help you to keep seeing results, prevent injury, and ensure you don't bore yourself to death. Competitive swimmer? Try rock climbing or a weight-training workout. Gym rat? Try an indoor cycling class (a.k.a. spin class). One of the reasons triathletes have relatively low injury rates compared to athletes from other disciplines is that they focus on three different sports, rather than just one, leaving time for muscle recovery between running, cycling, and swimming workouts.

INTENSITY

This one's a bit tricky and sometimes takes a lot of trial and error. Hiring a fitness professional to help you determine your ideal workout intensity will certainly simplify this process. Basically, you need to challenge yourself to get results (no surprise here), without injuring yourself. Lifting three-pound weights at the gym is not going to get you the lean and toned physique you want. Going for a ten-minute stroll every day is not likely going to get rid of those last ten pounds. You have to work hard for what you want!

So, what does being "active" mean, exactly? Don't worry, you don't have to sign yourself up for the next marathon or Ironman triathlon (although some day, why the heck not?). Everyone has a different definition for what *active* means, but let's go with the gold standard guidelines. According to North American guidelines from the US Department of Health and Human Services (HHS) and the Canadian Society for Exercise Physiology (CSEP), in order to get health benefits from exercise, we need to accumulate a minimum of 150 minutes of moderate- to vigorous-intensity aerobic exercise per week, in bouts of 10 minutes or more.[1], [2] Aerobic exercise targets your cardiovascular system and includes activities you can perform for extended periods of time, like jogging, playing tennis, swimming, or cycling. You can add up your physical activity minutes during your day, as long as you're active at a moderate level or higher. And what does "moderate" intensity mean? This is where the Talk Test comes in.

If you can maintain a conversation quite easily while you're exercising, you're at a low intensity. This is where you should start if you've never exercised before, or if you're warming up for more vigorous exercise.

Once you feel a bit out of breath and start taking a bit longer to respond to your conversation partner, you're at a moderate intensity. You should be able to maintain a conversation, but it'll be a bit more difficult than regular chatting, and you might take a few seconds before each sentence to catch your breath.

Vigorous intensity involves having difficulty maintaining a conversation. It's still possible, but it's very challenging.

If you can't maintain a conversation at all, your intensity level is high. This is reserved for fitness nuts who have worked out for a long time, and for professional athletes. Steer clear of this zone unless you have permission from a health professional!

In addition to 150 total minutes of aerobic exercise per week, American and Canadian recommendations suggest at least two days per week of muscle and bone strengthening activities focusing on the major muscle groups. This means resistance training. Whether you use dumbbells, weight-training machines, barbells, resistance bands, kettlebells, or your own body weight, resistance training improves your strength, muscle density, and bone density.

These guidelines apply to all adults over the age of eighteen, with an extra recommendation for adults aged sixty-five-plus. Older adults with poor mobility should perform physical activities that enhance balance and prevent falls. Tai Chi and yoga are popular forms of exercise that target balance.

The HHS and CSEP mention that these are minimum guidelines, and that more daily physical activity provides greater health benefits. I must add that this is up to a point. Extreme endurance athletes—or any extreme athletes for that matter—in some cases are at risk of harming their bodies. Some recent studies, for example, have suggested that long-term marathon runners are at risk of developing heart rhythm problems, as well as scarring and fibrosis of the heart.[3] This shouldn't scare you out of exercise, or even doing a marathon or two if you want to—cardiologists say it's OK to cross it off the bucket list, as long as you're not a full-time marathon runner. The point is to do everything in moderation. Ensure you balance your body with different types of fitness (cardio/aerobic activity, flexibility, strength, power), and give it enough rest between workouts for the most health benefits.

CONSISTENCY

You need to be absolutely consistent with your fitness plan, whether your goal is working out three days a week or six days a week. Creating a routine is extremely important for making healthy-living habits stick over the long term. You also need to be consistent with healthy eating in order to see and feel results from exercise. Stick to a workout schedule, stick to your healthy diet, be patient and persistent, and results will follow. Remember that small and consistent actions toward a goal will lead to incredible results over time.

Fitness professional and "trainer of trainers" Jonathan Goodman says, "In fitness, our job is to motivate and empower people to adhere to a program. The program itself is secondary."[4] Your actual workouts are secondary to sticking with your program over time to get results.

Did you know that only 15 percent of the Canadian population meets the physical activity guidelines mentioned earlier? Sedentary roles like office work are a major culprit. Here are four simple tips to help you sneak exercise into your workday. You don't have to exercise in one continuous bout to count toward the weekly recommendation, so these tips focus on shorter bouts of exercise throughout the day, which are usually easier to create for yourself while at work.

1. Set a timer on your computer or phone to ring every hour. Perform a very short exercise circuit each hour. For example, do ten push-ups, ten crunches, and ten bodyweight squats. That's eighty reps each after an eight-hour workday! In a former life as an office employee, I used to get all my coworkers to join me every hour.

2. Short walks throughout the day don't just increase your physical activity level, they can also increase your concentration and thus productivity. Take three brisk ten-minute walks during a workday, and you've achieved that day's physical activity recommendation.

3. Whether you work in an office building or you run your business from home, say "no" to escalators and elevators! Taking the stairs (at work, at the mall, on transit, etc.) instead will burn calories and increase your overall activity level.

4. Set up a simple piece of exercise equipment close to your workspace. Use it every time you pass it (e.g., when you get up to grab a snack or go to the bathroom). You can do shoulder presses with dumbbells, crunches on an exercise ball, biceps curls with a resistance band, or—my favorite—chin-ups on a pull-up bar that attaches to a doorframe.

Several short bursts of exercise are just as effective as one longer session. Even though we're all extremely busy people with countless different commitments, we can all prioritize health and make simple changes that'll have a lasting impact.

ENJOYMENT

If you're not enjoying your workouts, it's not likely you're going to keep at them for very long. It's a pretty obvious point, but one I think often gets forgotten. You're much more likely to stick to active living over the long term if you find an activity you like, so try out a whole bunch! There's no reason you should feel chained to the gym. Martial arts, racquet sports, swordplay, swimming, skiing, power lifting, stand-up paddling, rock climbing, yoga . . . you name it.

CHAPTER 3: PHYSICAL RECOVERY—JUST AS IMPORTANT AS EXERCISE

Muscle recovery is just as important as physical activity; they go hand in hand when it comes to taking care of your body and achieving your fitness goals. By focusing on both exercise and recovery, you'll be getting the most out of your healthy lifestyle.

When you work out at a challenging intensity, you're creating microscopic tears in your muscle fibers. Don't worry, that's a good thing! (Unless you overdo it, of course. See "Intensity" in the previous chapter.) This means your muscles need time between workouts to repair themselves. It's this between-workout time during which your muscles rebuild and gain density and strength. Your workout may last only 45 minutes, but it's what you do in the next 48 hours that can help or hinder getting the results you want. The general rule for weight training is to leave 48 hours between training the same muscle group. You could, for example, complete a full-body circuit on Mondays and Fridays, or even on Mondays, Wednesdays, and Fridays. Or you could train upper body on Mondays, lower body on Tuesdays, upper body on Thursdays, and lower body on Fridays. There are countless "training splits" as the fitness nuts call them—just find something that works both for your schedule and lifestyle and lets each muscle group rest for at least 48 hours. Keep in mind that more advanced trainees won't need as much recovery time. Long-term strength athletes will often train the same muscle groups daily.

With cardio activities such as running or swimming, there's less of a consensus among fitness professionals as to how long muscles take to recover. If you're training regularly, keep tabs on how your body feels and whether it's telling you it needs rest. Take at least one day off from intense exercise each week, and try to mix up your activities so you're not always doing the same thing.

TAKE A REST DAY

A rest day means a day without intense exercise in order to give your body time to recover from regular training. Rest days are appropriate for you if you work out at a moderate-to-high intensity four to six times per week. Someone who works out once a week for ten minutes does not need designated rest days. But someone training on most days of the week at a high intensity most certainly needs at least one rest day per week.

ACTIVE RECOVERY

If you regularly work out at a high intensity, active recovery days are often helpful. They're especially useful for those crazy fitness nuts who just can't deal with a day that involves no workout. In contrast to a rest day—where you're not doing any physical activity—active recovery means engaging in a low-intensity activity that differs from your regular workout activities.

For example, if you're a serious swimmer, your active recovery day might be going for an easy twenty-minute bike ride. If you lift weights at the gym regularly, your active recovery might be going for a walk. The idea is to do a very light, low-impact activity for a short period of time. Active recovery is a good way to relax, and to increase blood circulation. Increased circulation is thought to improve muscle recovery.[1]

MASSAGE AND MUSCLE TENSION RELEASE

Massage and muscle tension release techniques stimulate circulation into your muscles, which can help with recovery after workouts. Here are four different techniques to try.

Foam Roller

Using a foam roller is like getting a free sports massage. These long tubes of dense foam are fantastic tools for muscle tension relief. The denser (harder) the roller, the more in-depth the tension release, and the more discomfort you may feel if your muscles are very tight. If you're new to foam rolling, start with a softer roller and work your way up to a more firm version.

Foam rolling involves using your own body weight to massage your muscles. You sit or lie on the foam roller and simply roll back and forth. You can target almost any area of your body, including glutes, hamstrings, quads, calves, upper back, lats, and chest. You'll not only release muscle tension, but you'll also prevent injury, break up any scar tissue that may have formed in your muscles, and increase your range of motion. You might even feel a little less sore than you normally would in the days following a tough workout.

Foam rollers are great for releasing generalized tension in your body, but they also work wonders for muscle knot search-and-destroy missions. If you discover a muscle knot or trigger point while you're rolling, you can hold your position on the point for 30 seconds or more—until you feel it release. I like using a foam roller to find muscle knots and then using a tennis ball to release specific muscle knots.

Tennis Ball

Using a tennis ball can be very effective at releasing muscle tension. I find tennis balls are great for getting at very specific areas, like a particular muscle knot. This works well for back tension and lower body tension.

For tension in your back, stand against a wall with the tennis ball wedged between your back and the wall. Find the muscle knot you want to work on, and press your back into the ball. You can move around in little circles if you want, or side to side—whatever you find feels good and releases tension.

For tension in your lower body, like glutes, hips, or IT bands, sit or lie with the tennis ball under the muscle group in question, using your hands on the floor to take some of the weight off if necessary. Use your body weight to press into the ball. You can hold it stationary if you like, or move around from side to side. If your muscles are really tight, this can be quite painful! (But it feels fantastic once you're done.)

Muscle Stick

Imagine rolling back and forth over your muscles with a rolling pin. That's essentially what you do with a muscle stick. Muscle sticks are usually a bit smaller in diameter than a rolling pin, and many are broken into smaller moving parts to better contour to your muscles. The idea is the same as foam rolling—you use the stick to roll back and forth across your muscles, decreasing soreness and tension. I find the muscle stick to be useful during desk work, because I don't even have to get up from my chair to use it! The downside is you have to get someone else to roll your back for you, which is something you can easily do yourself on a foam roller. It's easier to adjust the level of pressure when you're using a muscle stick than when you're using a foam roller, and they're much more portable. Check out www.thestick.net for an example.

Massage Therapy

Massage therapy is an excellent way to recover your muscles and leave them feeling much less sore and stiff. You'll also increase circulation, joint mobility, and immune function while you're at it. Massage is a great method of preventing problems in the first place, including muscle knots, tension headaches, and various forms of injury. Most serious athletes have regular massages as part of their muscle recovery plans.

Stretching

Stretching directly after a workout can help your muscles to relax and to release tension. The clinical research jury is still out as to whether stretching can help to prevent muscle soreness in the days following a workout, but many people who work out regularly claim that it does. Make sure that you stretch when your muscles are warm, such as right after completing your workout, or after taking a hot shower. Stretching cold muscles—like at the beginning of a workout—can increase your risk of tears, strains, and pulls.

Stretching has many of the same benefits as yoga (not surprising, since they're both based on increasing flexibility), including increasing range of motion, preventing injury, and decreasing pain from muscle tightness.

YOGA

Research is beginning to support the effectiveness of yoga in decreasing delayed onset muscle soreness (DOMS).[2] DOMS is the soreness you feel in the day or two after a particularly challenging or new-to-you workout. Many of my personal training clients swear by yoga as an effective tool in decreasing their muscle soreness between workouts.

Yoga is also great for increasing flexibility and preventing injury. Many of us don't stretch for long enough (or at all!) after a workout to see any flexibility improvements over time. Yoga is a great way to get a healthy dose of flexibility and range of motion training. Also, many people find yoga more interesting than holding static stretches at the gym after a workout.

If you don't yet do yoga regularly, give it a try as a cross-training tool for your preferred physical activities. My two main activities are weight lifting and swimming, but I use yoga once a week to stretch and recover my muscles.

GET ENOUGH SHUT-EYE

Getting enough sleep is one of the most important things you can do to ensure your muscles recover and get stronger after a workout. During deep sleep stages, your pituitary gland releases growth hormone that facilitates muscle repair and tissue growth. Growth hormone deficiency often leads to an increased risk for obesity, decreased muscle mass, and a lowered capacity for exercise.[3]

The exact relationship between working out and sleep is still unclear, but a host of research studies has found a connection between sleep deprivation and decreased performance and recovery. Inadequate sleep is linked to low energy levels and increased levels of the hormones that break down muscle,[4] which is not something you want if you're looking to get—and keep—a lean body and a healthy metabolism!

Sleep is a prime time for the cells in our bodies to build new proteins (also known as protein synthesis).[5] Because protein is the building block of muscle, make sure you get your beauty sleep to keep your muscles healthy and functioning well.

Every person has his or her own sleep needs. There's no "gold standard" ideal amount of sleep to get each night, although most health authorities recommend between seven and nine hours per night. You may need to do some experimentation to figure out what your perfect sleep amount is. If you're waking up well rested each morning, it's a sign that you're getting enough sleep.

Not sure how much sleep you need? You can find out, but you need about two weeks of a very flexible schedule. Perhaps you can take a sleep vacation! Go to bed at the same time every night, and don't set an alarm. Just wake up naturally. You might sleep for longer than normal the first few nights if you're chronically sleep deprived and need to catch up on sleep, but take note of what time you wake up during the second week. You'll likely wake up at a similar time each morning, at which point you've discovered the amount of sleep your body needs.

For an easy five-minute test of reaction time, which can be an indicator of whether or not you're getting enough sleep, search for Harvard's "How Awake Are You?" online test.

Many of us are chronically sleep deprived. Here are nine tips to help you get the sleep your body needs:

How to Get Enough Sleep

- Keep a consistent sleep schedule. This means going to bed and waking up at the same time every day, including weekends and holidays. If you're getting enough sleep each night, this is easier than it might sound. I go to bed between 9:30 and 10:00 p.m. each night and get up between 6:00 and 6:30 a.m. every morning. Not only has this schedule helped me to get enough sleep each night (my sleep cycle isn't disrupted by sleeping in), but I also happen to really enjoy mornings, so I feel I get the most out of each day. Nothing like coming home on a Sunday morning having already eaten two breakfasts, worked out, and gone grocery shopping, to find my husband still sleeping!

- Try to minimize sleep-disrupting activities a few hours before bed. These include high-concentration activities, high-intensity exercise, and watching TV.

- Limit light exposure at night, including sunlight, indoor lighting, and screens. Try the "f.lux" app that changes the color of your screen display (for Windows, Mac, iPhone, and iPad) based on the time of day. When the sun sets in your corner of the world, the f.lux app makes your computer or phone screen look like your indoor lighting. When the sun comes up in the morning, it changes your screen back to its normal colors. Various research studies have found that "blue light" from screens may disrupt our sleep. By using an app like f.lux, you're minimizing your screen's blue light.

- Have a bedtime routine so that you can get into "sleep mode" before hitting the sack. This tells your body to start winding down.

- Avoid caffeine, alcohol, nicotine, and other substances that interfere with sleep.

- Don't have a clock visible while you're trying to fall asleep. Watching the clock while you're trying to fall asleep will probably make you feel stressed that you're not falling asleep, which won't help your efforts!

- Keep tabs on your food intake. Going to bed either really hungry or really full can make it difficult to fall—and stay—asleep.

- Invest in a good quality mattress and pillow set. Spending some decent money on a great mattress was one of the best investments my husband and I have made so far! We noticed an immediate improvement in sleep quality, which affected how alert we feel during the day.

- Make sure your room is comfortable for sleep: cool, dark, quiet, and devoid of clutter. Make use of blackout curtains and/or earplugs if you need them.

CHAPTER 4: WORKOUT PROGRAMS YOU CAN DO AT HOME

Just because you don't have a gym membership doesn't mean you can't get fit. And even if you do have a membership, you can perform these workouts at home with no equipment on days you don't make it to the gym. How's that for a high convenience factor? With the right moves, using just your body can be a challenging and highly effective workout. Labeled from "newbie" to "ridiculously advanced," there's a workout program for everyone!

Feel free to mix 'n' match these workouts. A beginner might go through the Kickstarter Strength Workout, then practice a few more advanced moves from other workout programs. Someone more advanced might start with the "It's a Bird, It's a Plane" workout and add the "Superhero Abs" workout for some added core work. If you're feeling particularly ambitious, try two of the ridiculously advanced workouts back-to-back.

Descriptions of each exercise are listed at the end of this chapter.

BODYWEIGHT WORKOUTS

The following seven workouts require only your own body, some floor space, and the occasional extra piece of common equipment like a chair or carpet. Many of my clients use workouts such as these while they're traveling to maintain—and increase—their fitness without access to a gym.

Kickstarter Strength Workout
Fitness level: Newbie
What you need: A bit of wall space, a bit of floor space, and a mat or carpet
The details: If you're just getting into fitness, this workout is for you. It aims to help you build a foundation of strength that you'll need for more advanced workouts. For your very first run-through, do one set of each exercise. If your muscles feel OK the next day (other than a bit of muscle soreness from working out, which is normal), increase your sets to 2, then 3, over a period of a few weeks.

- 10 wall push-ups
- 10 squats
- 10 reverse lunges
- 10 stick-ups
- 10 bird-dogs
- 10 crunches
- 10 supermans

Outdoor Park Workout

Fitness level: Newbie to intermediate

What you need: Some outdoor park space and a park bench

The details: I created this workout for sunny days when I take clients outdoors for their personal training sessions. In case of muddy, dewy, or otherwise non-ideal ground conditions, none of the moves require placing your hands on the ground or lying on the ground. Complete this routine as a circuit, moving from one exercise to the next, minimizing rest breaks as much as possible. Complete 20 reps of each move, or set a timer for 30 seconds for each move. Beginners complete 2 rounds of the program; intermediates complete 3 rounds.

- squats
- push-ups (hands on bench)
- butt kickers
- front kicks
- side kicks
- reverse lunges
- jackknife (on bench)
- standing bird dog
- triceps dips (hands on bench)
- mountain climbers (hands on bench)
- bench step-ups

Superhero Abs

Fitness level: Intermediate to advanced

What you need: A mat or carpeted area

The details: Get your core in top form with this effective workout. Complete 3 sets of each move. Intermediates complete 10 reps, and advanced exercisers complete 15 reps of each move. You can complete this routine as a standalone workout, or tack it on to the end of another workout.

- bicycle crunches
- V-ups
- hip raises
- Russian twists
- side plank with leg lift (both sides)
- plank (hold for as long as you can!)

It's a Bird, It's a Plane . . .

Fitness level: Intermediate to advanced

What you need: Floor space

The details: Here's a cardio workout that also targets your lower body and core. You'll be catching lots of air with all the jumping you'll be doing! Intermediates complete 15 reps of each move, and advanced exercisers complete 20 reps. Go through the program as a circuit, moving from one exercise to the next, taking as few rest breaks as possible. Repeat the circuit 5 times (or more if you're ridiculously advanced and not yet totally winded).

- high knees
- jumping jacks
- in-and-out jump squats
- butt kickers
- mountain climbers
- V-jumps
- front kicks
- side kicks

Strength Superpowers

Fitness level: Intermediate to advanced

What you need: Floor space

The details: Here's a full-body workout to increase your strength. This workout is composed of supersets, in which you alternate between 2 different exercises. Complete one set of move A, then one set of move B, then back to move A, then back to B. Intermediates complete each superset twice (10 reps of each move), and advanced exercisers complete each superset 3 times (10 to 15 reps of each move).

When doing planks, be sure to keep your abs engaged and hips in line with the rest of your body.

Superset 1:
- walking push-ups
- split squats (foot elevated)

Superset 2:
- close push-ups
- jump squats

Superset 3:
- V-ups
- inchworms

Superset 4:
- plank with alternating arm and leg raise
- single leg squats

Iron Man/Iron Woman

Fitness level: Ridiculously advanced

What you need: some floor space, bulletproof muscles, and a cardiovascular system of steel

The details: A collection of challenging bodyweight moves to try—if you dare! This workout is composed of supersets—complete a set of move A, then a set of move B, then back to move A, then back to B. Complete 3 sets of each superset (2 if you're not quite ridiculously advanced).

Superset 1:
- 10 superman plank walk-outs
- 10 burpees

Superset 2:
- 10 spider-man push-ups
- 10 jump lunges (switching legs mid-air)

Superset 3:
- 10 pike push-ups (feet elevated)
- 10 spider-mans in plank position

Superset 4:
- 20 mountain climbers
- 10 jump squats

Superset 5:
- bear crawl (10 forward and 10 backward)
- 10 V-ups

The Spider-Man

Fitness level: Ridiculously advanced

What you need: A bench, couch, or sturdy chair, and some floor space.

The details: If you want some serious bang for your buck when it comes to workout effectiveness, this is it. The entire workout takes only fifteen minutes, but you'll be working at a high level of intensity the whole time. You'll be timing yourself to see how many rounds of the workout you can complete before the time's up, so you can use this as a benchmark workout to track your performance progress. Summon your fitness superpowers and make sure you give this workout your all!

Set a timer for 15 minutes and see how many rounds of the following circuit you can complete. No breaks between moves!

- 10 spider-man push-ups
- 10 burpees
- 10 jump squats
- 10 reverse lunges (1 rep = both legs)
- 10 spider-mans in plank position (1 rep = both legs)
- 10 pike push-ups (feet elevated)
- 10 triceps dips
- 10 standing bird-dogs (each leg)
- 20 mountain climbers
- 20 jumping jacks

Spider-man push-ups strengthen all your core muscles as well as your chest, shoulders, and arms.

DECK OF CARDS WORKOUTS

If you're looking for an effective and fun home workout that's different every time, try a deck of cards workout. You'll use the same bodyweight moves from the workouts above, but you'll put them together much differently. The deck of cards becomes your personal trainer, dictating which moves and how many reps of each you'll complete. And you'll never do the same workout twice! How's that for *novelty* from the four principles of getting exercise results discussed earlier in this book?

Here's how it works. First, assign an exercise to each suit. For example, squats for hearts, push-ups for diamonds, burpees for clubs, and jumping jacks for spades. The number on each card tells you how many reps to do. In our example, a seven of diamonds would mean seven push-ups. Take as few breaks as possible during these workouts. I usually draw two or three cards at a time so I don't always have to stop moving.

Based on your fitness level, you can assign different reps to face cards and jokers. If you're just starting out, a face card might be five reps. If you're advanced, you could increase that to 20 reps. Aces are typically 11 reps.

You can also get an inexpensive deck of cards made specifically for fitness, with exercises and rep number options pictured on each card.

Deck of cards workouts are limited only by your own imagination. Here are some ideas to get you started using a regular deck of playing cards.

Evil Twin Deck of Cards Workout

Fitness level: Advanced (ridiculously advanced if you take no breaks)
What you need: Deck of cards, floor space
The details: Red cards are push-ups and black cards are squats. Face cards and jokers count for 10 reps, aces count for 11 reps. See if you can get through the entire deck!

Cardio Deck of Cards Workout

Fitness level: Intermediate to ridiculously advanced (depending upon break time)
What you need: Deck of cards, floor space
The details: Here's a challenging cardio workout you can do with minimal floor space and no equipment.
Hearts: front kicks (each side)
Diamonds: high knees (both feet = 1 rep)
Clubs: mountain climbers (both feet = 1 rep)
Spades: side kicks (each side)
Face cards: 10 V-jumps

Strength Deck of Cards Workout

Fitness level: Intermediate to ridiculously advanced (depending upon break time)

What you need: Deck of cards, floor space, bench or couch

The details: Based on classic strength moves, this workout will increase both your strength and your endurance.

Hearts: squats

Diamonds: push-ups

Clubs: reverse lunges (both legs = 1 rep)

Spades: inchworms

Kings: 10 triceps dips

Queens: 10 single-leg squats (each leg)

Jacks: 10 V-ups

Abs Deck of Cards Workout

Fitness level: Intermediate to ridiculously advanced (depending upon break time)

What you need: Deck of cards, carpeted area or mat

The details: Abs, abs, and more abs! Try a few rounds of this workout after you've completed a full-body program, or complete the whole deck of cards as a stand-alone abs workout.

Hearts: bicycle crunches (both sides = 1 rep)

Diamonds: Russian twists

Clubs: side plank with leg lifts (each side)

Spades: jackknife

Kings: 5 superman plank walk-outs

Queens: 10 hip raises

Jacks: 30-second plank

BODYWEIGHT EXERCISE LIST

Here are descriptions of the exercises found in the bodyweight workout programs, listed alphabetically. The muscle groups emphasized in each move are listed, as well as difficulty level. Difficulty level is based on ten reps to keep things as standardized as possible. Doing 100 squats in a row would be ridiculously advanced. Ten squats in a row? Not so ridiculous.

Bear Crawl

Emphasis: full body, focusing on core. Level: intermediate to advanced.

Start on your hands and knees, with your knees under your hips and hands under your shoulders. Rise up onto your toes, tighten your abs, and start embracing your inner bear! Reach forward with your right hand and left knee, landing your hand and toes on the ground at the same time. Then reach forward with your left hand and right knee, placing them onto the ground at the same time. Keep your core braced throughout, and your back flat and parallel to the ground. Try to resist moving your torso from side to side while crawling.

Bench Step-Up
Emphasis: lower body (quads, hamstrings, glutes). Level: intermediate.

Find a bench, step, or other piece of furniture you can step onto. Stand in front of it, then step onto it with your right foot. Keeping your back straight, step up until your right leg is straight, then return to the start position. Complete all reps on one side, then switch sides.

Bicycle Crunch
Emphasis: abs. Level: intermediate.

Lie on the floor with hands lightly touching the back of your head and legs bent at 90 degrees (feet off the floor). Tighten your abs and raise your upper back off the floor. Aim your left shoulder toward your right knee as you straighten your left leg. Then aim your right shoulder toward your left knee, straightening your right leg. This is one rep.Your legs will make a bicycle motion as your torso twists back and forth.

Bird-Dog
Emphasis: core (abs and lower back), glutes, upper back. Level: newbie to intermediate.

Start on all fours, with knees under your hips and hands under your shoulders. Contract your abdominal muscles. Lift your right hand and left leg off the floor, straightening both so they're in line with your torso (parallel to the floor). Return to the start position, and switch sides.

Burpee
Emphasis: full body and cardio. Level: advanced to ridiculously advanced.

Stand upright with arms at your sides. Squat down to place your hands on the floor, slightly wider than shoulder width. Kick your legs back into a plank position. With your upper body in place, jump your feet forward to the start position, then jump upward with both feet while returning to the original standing position. Burpees are meant to be completed as quickly as possible.

Butt Kickers
Emphasis: lower body and cardio. Level: intermediate.

Here's where you get to kick your own butt—literally! Start in a standing position. Pump your arms and run in place, touching your heel to your butt with every step. Two steps (one right and one left) count as one rep.

Close Push-Up

Emphasis: chest, triceps. Level: advanced to ridiculously advanced.

Get into a classic push-up position with your toes on the ground, hands under your shoulders. Now, move your hands closer together. Ideally you want your thumbs and forefingers touching, creating a diamond shape with your hands. Brace your abs, lower yourself to the floor until your chest almost touches the floor, then extend your arms back to the starting position.

Crunch

Emphasis: abs. Level: newbie to intermediate.

Lie on the floor with feet on the floor and legs bent. Place your hands behind your head. Tighten your abs and lift your upper torso from the floor, looking at the ceiling throughout. Lower back down until the backs of your shoulders touch the floor, and repeat.

Front Kick

Emphasis: lower body, core, and cardio. Level: newbie to advanced (depending upon speed and intensity).

Start in a "fighting stance" position with your right foot behind your left foot, your knees slightly bent, your arms up to guard, and your torso turned partially to the right. Lift your right foot off the ground by bending your right knee to about 90 degrees, then extend your leg to complete the kick. Bending at your knee and completing the kick are combined into a fluid motion. Return your right foot to the start position and repeat. To kick with your left leg, start in the "fighting stance" with your right leg forward.

High Knees

Emphasis: lower body and cardio. Level: intermediate to advanced.

Start in a standing position. Pump your arms and run in place, lifting your knees toward your chest as high as you can with each step. Two steps (one right and one left) count as one rep.

Hip Raise

Emphasis: abs (lower abs in particular). Level: intermediate to advanced.

Lie on the floor with arms at your sides, legs straight and raised to 90 degrees from the floor (if your hamstrings are tight, you can bend your knees slightly). Press your back into the floor and lift your hips off the floor as high as you can toward the ceiling. Slowly lower to the start position.

In-and-Out Jump Squat

Emphasis: lower body and cardio. Level: advanced to ridiculously advanced.

Start in a wide squat position, with hands clasped in front of you. Your back should be straight, knees bent at 90 degrees. Explosively jump into the air and land in a standing position with feet together. Jump into the air again and as you come down, lower into the initial squat position. That's one rep.

Inchworm

Emphasis: shoulders and core. Level: intermediate.

Start by standing with your feet together, bending forward to touch the ground with your hands on either side of your feet (bend your knees if you need to). Walk your hands out and away from your feet, lengthening your body into a push-up position. Once you've walked your hands as far as you can go, walk your hands back toward your feet to the starting position.

Jackknife

Emphasis: abs. Level: intermediate.

Lie on the floor with arms at your sides and legs straight. Simultaneously lift your torso (keeping your arms straight out in front of you and chest up) into a sit-up position and lift your legs, bending at the knees. Bring your knees as close to your chest as you can, then lower torso and legs to the start position.

Jump Lunge

Emphasis: lower body and cardio. Level: advanced to ridiculously advanced.

Start in a lunge position, with your right leg in front and left leg behind you, right knee bent at 90 degrees and left knee almost touching the floor. Explosively jump up, switch legs mid-air, and land in a lunge position with your left leg in front. Keep switching legs as you jump.

Jump Squat

Emphasis: lower body and cardio. Level: advanced to ridiculously advanced.

Start in a squat position, with knees bent at 90 degrees and hips bent behind you (ensure knees don't extend past your toes). Explosively jump into the air, and return back to the squat position as you descend. Repeat reps as quickly as possible.

Jumping Jack

Emphasis: cardio. Level: intermediate to advanced.

We all know these, right? Start in a standing position, with arms at your sides. Simultaneously jump your feet out to each side while raising your arms overhead. Jump to return to the start position. Repeat quickly.

Mountain Climber

Emphasis: cardio and core. Level: intermediate to advanced.

Start in a high plank position, with hands and toes touching the ground. Hands should be directly under your shoulders, and your torso and legs should form a straight line. Brace your abs and bend your right leg so your knee is close to your elbows, toes touching the ground. Keeping your upper body in place, jump your right leg back while jumping your left leg forward. Both feet should touch the ground at the same time. One jump with the right leg forward and one jump with the left leg forward counts as one rep.

Pike Push-Up

Emphasis: shoulders and upper chest (and less so, triceps). Level: advanced to ridiculously advanced.

Pike Push-Up

Elevate your feet by placing them on a bench or step. Start in a pike position, with your butt in the air, legs straight, and back straight (think of an upside-down "V"). Lower the top of your head toward the ground until almost touching, then press up to the start position. If you're not quite ready for the feet elevated version, you can do this move with your feet on the ground.

Plank with Alternating Arm and Leg Raise

Emphasis: core, glutes, upper back. Level: intermediate to advanced.

Start at the top of the push-up position, with your toes touching the ground, hands under your shoulders, and arms straight. Brace your abs, and lift your left arm and right leg off the ground, keeping them as straight as possible. Bring them parallel to the ground, then slowly lower. Now lift your right arm and left leg off the ground and repeat. Alternate sides for reps, keeping your abs tight throughout.

Plank

Emphasis: core. Level: newbie to ridiculously advanced (depending upon how long you hold this move).

Lie on your front on the floor. Place your forearms on the floor, with elbows directly under your shoulders. Place your legs together with your toes on the floor. Lift your body off the floor, ensuring you create a straight line all the way from your upper back to your ankles. Hold position.

Push-Up

Emphasis: chest, triceps, shoulders, core. Level: intermediate to advanced (newbie if you're doing knee push-ups).

Start in a high plank position, with hands and toes touching the ground. Keep your abs tight while bending your arms to bring your chest to the ground. Push up, straightening your arms until you return to the start position. Newbies can do this move with knees on the ground instead of toes.

Reverse Lunge

Emphasis: lower body (quads, hamstrings, glutes). Level: newbie to intermediate.

Stand upright with your arms by your sides. Take a big step backward with your right leg, dropping your right knee toward the ground and bending your left knee to 90 degrees. Keep your back straight and make sure you can see your left toes—you don't want your knee to extend past them. Push off with your right foot to return to the starting position. Repeat on the left side.

Russian Twist

Emphasis: abs. Level: intermediate.

Sit on the floor with knees bent, feet together, and feet lifted a few inches off the floor. Lean back with your torso to about 45 degrees from the floor. Clasp your hands together. Keeping your chest up throughout the movement, move your arms and torso to the right, touch the floor with your hands by your right hip, then turn to do the same on the left. That's one rep. Slow 'n' steady wins the race on this one!

Side Kick

Emphasis: lower body, core, and cardio. Level: newbie to advanced (depending upon speed and intensity).

Begin in a standing position, with feet a bit wider than hip width, knees bent just a little, and arms up to guard. Step your left foot toward your right to gain momentum, then lift your right leg, bending at the knee, and kick it out to the side. Return your right leg to the ground, then step your left foot back to the start position. Complete all reps on one side, then switch sides.

Side Plank with Leg Lift

Emphasis: core and lower body. Level: intermediate to advanced.

Lie on the floor on your right side. Prop yourself up with your right forearm on the floor. Stack your left foot onto your right, and ensure your right elbow is directly under your right shoulder. Lift up your body so only your right forearm and right foot are touching the floor. Keep your core engaged and your entire body in a straight line. Keeping both legs straight, raise your left leg toward the ceiling, then lower to the start position.

Single Leg Squat

Emphasis: lower body. Level: advanced to ridiculously advanced.

Stand with your feet hip-width apart. Lift your left leg, keeping it straight in front of you, and trying to get it as close to parallel to the ground as possible. Extend your arms out in front. Bending your right leg, squat down as close to the ground as possible, then return to standing upright. Repeat for reps, then switch sides.

Spider-Man (plank position)

Emphasis: core. Level: intermediate.

Start in a high plank position, with hands and toes touching the ground. Tighten your abs. Lift your right leg off the ground, bending at the knee and bringing the knee to the outside of your right elbow. Return to the start position and repeat with the left leg. That's one rep. Imagine you're Spider-Man climbing up a wall!

Spider-Man Push-Up

Emphasis: chest, triceps, shoulders, core. Level: ridiculously advanced.

Start in a high plank position, with hands and toes touching the ground. As you bend your arms and lower your chest to the ground, lift your right leg off the ground, bending at the knee and bringing the knee to the outside of your right elbow. Press up, straightening your arms as you return your leg to the start position. Repeat with the left leg.

Split Squat

Emphasis: lower body. Level: newbie (foot not elevated); intermediate (foot elevated).

Stand with hands on your hips, right foot forward and left foot back. Squat down by flexing your right knee and hip. Your right knee should form a 90-degree angle. Straighten both legs to return to the start position, complete reps, then switch sides. For the intermediate version, elevate your back foot by placing it on a bench or step.

Split Squat

Squat

Emphasis: lower body. Level: newbie.

Stand with your feet a bit wider than shoulder width, arms extended forward. Imagine sitting down into a chair—bend your legs until your thighs are parallel to the ground, squeeze your glutes, then come back up to standing. Keep your chest up and your back flat throughout the movement.

Standing Bird-Dog

Emphasis: Hamstrings and core. Level: newbie to intermediate.

Start in a standing position with arms at your sides, right foot a few inches off the ground. Lean forward, raising your right leg behind you and your left arm over your head. Keep your right arm against your torso. Your right leg, torso, and left arm should form a straight line, parallel to the ground. Hold for a second and slowly return to the start position. Complete reps, then switch sides.

Stick-Up

Emphasis: shoulders and upper body flexibility. Level: newbie.

Stand against a wall with heels, glutes, back, and head touching the wall. Start with hands at shoulder height, elbows bent and palms out. Mimicking a shoulder press movement, straighten your arms overhead until your elbows are locked. Ideally, the backs of your hands will be touching the wall throughout the movement, but if your muscles are tight, this may take time to achieve.

Superman

Emphasis: lower back. Level: newbie to intermediate.

Lie face down on the floor, with legs straight and arms extended overhead. Slowly raise legs and upper body off the floor, then return to the start position. Make sure you do this move smoothly and slowly.

Superman Plank Walk-Out

Emphasis: core and shoulders. Level: advanced to ridiculously advanced.

Start in a high plank position, with hands and toes touching the ground. Bracing your abs and taking small steps, walk your feet backwards as far as you can go while maintaining a flat back. Walk your feet back to the start position and repeat for reps.

Triceps Dip

Emphasis: triceps and shoulders. Level: intermediate to advanced.

Sit on the end of a bench (or couch, or sturdy chair) with hands placed on either side of your hips, legs extended in front of you. Lift your hips off the bench—this is the starting position. Lower your hips toward the ground while bending your elbows. Once you reach a 90-degree bend in your elbows, use your triceps and shoulder muscles to press back into the start position.

Triceps Dip

V-Jump

Emphasis: core and cardio. Level: intermediate.

Start in a high plank position, with feet together and hands and toes touching the ground. Tighten your abs and jump your feet out into a wide "V" shape, landing softly on your toes. Jump them back into the start position. That's one rep. Repeat as rapidly as possible.

V-Up

Emphasis: abs. Level: intermediate to advanced.

Lie on your back with legs straight and arms above your head. Keeping your arms and legs straight, raise your legs and torso into a "V" shape, reaching your hands toward your toes. Slowly lower to the start position.

Walking Push-Up

Emphasis: chest, triceps, shoulders, core. Level: advanced to ridiculously advanced.

Start in a high plank position, with hands and toes touching the ground, left hand under your left shoulder, and right hand positioned twelve inches (or more if you're advanced) in front. Complete a push-up by bending your arms, lowering your chest to the ground, and pressing back up, then place your left hand twelve inches in front of your right, walking your feet into place. Complete another push-up. Continue in this fashion for reps.

Wall Push-Up

Emphasis: chest, triceps, shoulders. Level: newbie.

Stand facing a wall with your toes about two feet from the wall. Place your hands on the wall at shoulder height, a bit wider than the width of your shoulders. Start the push-up by bending your elbows, bringing your face close to the wall. Straighten your arms to return to the start position. The further you place your feet from the wall, the more difficult this move becomes.

CHAPTER 5: BASICS OF THE PLANT-BASED DIET

I'm a fitness coach certified to provide basic nutrition information, but I'm not a dietitian. This book won't lay out a precise diet for you to follow. (No book should, anyway! That wouldn't take into account differing individual needs.) If you're looking for a specific diet plan tailored to your own goals, see a registered dietitian who can analyze the food you're currently eating and make suggestions for change. Seeing a dietitian might be especially important if you're a budding or amateur athlete, in order to assess your individual calorie and nutrient needs.

Keep in mind that although many people who call themselves nutritionists are extremely knowledgeable and well qualified, the term *nutritionist* does not have a standard definition. Anyone giving advice on nutrition—with appropriate training or not—can use the title *nutritionist*. Dietitians, however, generally have much more rigorous training and must hold a license and engage in continuous training to maintain it. Licensing requirements vary by country and by state, so it's best to ask individual nutritionists or dietitians for their background and credentials. Of course, bonus points for finding one who specializes in veganism and sports nutrition!

Being a fitness professional means being asked a lot of questions on a regular basis. My most common response to anything I'm asked is, "It depends." In health and fitness, there is very rarely a one-size-fits-all answer when it comes to the specifics of healthy living. Well-established general concepts backed by clinical research such as "exercise is good for you" or "eating lots of vegetables is important for good health" are common knowledge. The specifics, however, like exactly what types of exercise to do and for how long, or how many different vegetables to eat each day, are typically based on each individual's lifestyle, goals, genetics, and more.

Same goes for healthy eating. While there are some basic, well-researched fundamentals of a healthy plant-based diet, you'll need to figure out for yourself—perhaps with the help of a dietitian, doctor, fitness professional, etc.—what works best for you. For instance, everyone knows fresh fruit is healthy, but for someone like me who's deathly allergic to raw fruit, it clearly wouldn't be part of a healthy diet. (I eat all my fruit cooked.) Some people experience intolerances to certain foods, which involve uncomfortable gastrointestinal symptoms. In this case, trigger foods should obviously be avoided, even if they're universally considered healthy.

Allergies and intolerances aside, it may take some experimentation to discover which combination of plant foods works best for you, especially if you're active. Much of this depends on your fitness goals. Someone who has a very slim body type and wants to gain a lot of muscle will need to focus on eating lots of extra calories, many of which will come from protein. An endurance athlete, who will require lots of carbohydrates in his or her diet, may need to experiment with exactly which foods work best right before a race or athletic event.

The information in the following nutrition chapters is meant for active people who are following, or want to follow, a plant-based diet. It provides an overview of healthy vegan eating, but isn't meant to be a diet prescription for any individual. I'm aiming to give you ideas for what to try, what to buy, and how to prepare healthy plant-based foods, rather than prescribe a specific day-to-day diet plan.

WHAT IS HEALTHY EATING?

There's no standard definition of healthy eating—it's an umbrella term used to describe diets that are very nutrient-dense and nourishing for active individuals—but it can still be a useful way to talk about and classify foods and nutrition habits in a general sense. Healthy diets will typically have the following fundamental characteristics:

- Lots of vegetables and fruits
- Whole grains instead of refined grains
- Mostly whole, unprocessed foods
- Limited refined sugar, white flour, white rice, salt, and hydrogenated or trans fats
- Low in unhealthy fats, but healthy fats (e.g., unsaturated fats) are welcomed
- Roasting, grilling, sautéing, and steaming are preferred cooking methods (instead of shallow or deep frying)
- Limited alcohol

There will always be debates within the health and fitness industry about whether specific foods are healthy or not (which, by the way, depends upon each individual's fitness goals). Therefore, the term may not be very useful when it comes to deciding on a daily basis which foods are beneficial for you and which ones aren't. However, I think using *healthy eating* as a general term is a useful way to describe and think about diets that support long-term health and active lifestyles; much of it is based on common sense and common knowledge. In my view, healthy eating means enjoying a diet full of mostly whole, plant-based foods.

WHAT ARE WHOLE FOODS?

Healthy and nourishing vegan diets are based on whole foods. You've probably heard the term *whole foods* a million times (not counting the grocery chain of the same name), but what does it mean? Many terms in the food industry have no specific definition (think "natural" or "gourmet"), and this is no exception. Basically, whole foods are plant-based foods that are in their most natural states. They may be cooked, but they're minimally processed. Roasted carrots, cooked chickpeas, and salad greens are whole foods. Vegetarian "meats," refined sugar, and instant ramen are not.

The question here is, "How processed can something be and still be considered whole?" For instance, quinoa—an extremely nutritionally dense grain—has its bitter-tasting outer husk removed before it's ready to be sold. Rolled oats have been de-husked and rolled flat. Foods like these have been somewhat removed from their natural states, but they're considered close enough and are thus labeled whole foods.

Another thing to keep in mind is that the term *whole foods* always refers to nutrient-dense foods. Potato strips that happen to be deep fried into French fries are not considered whole. Theoretically, dried sugar cane could be considered whole, but most people wouldn't let it join the whole foods party because it's not particularly nutritious and should be limited in our diets.

You may find the occasional non-whole food in the recipes section of this book, like packaged flatbread. If you're adamant about sticking to an ultra-squeaky-clean, picture-perfect, pretty-much-unattainable diet, just skip over the few recipes that include ingredients like this. I'm a big fan of balance, which means the occasional food that isn't super nutrient dense is not a big deal. Remember, even professional figure competitors, bodybuilders, and athletes incorporate regular treat meals into their diet plans. I'm also a fan of convenience, especially as a busy business owner with many different hats to wear. As long as the vast majority of the foods you eat are fruits, vegetables, legumes, seeds, nuts, and whole grains, the occasional treat won't derail your health and fitness goals.

By the way, I think enjoyment is a very important aspect of healthy eating, just as I believe enjoyment is important in exercise. Trying new ingredients, creating new recipes, and finding foods you genuinely enjoy are key to ensuring you'll eat a nutritious diet for the long term. Of course, many of the foods we most enjoy are often classified as unhealthy, but even those "treat" foods like desserts and salty snacks have a place in every healthy, active vegan's diet—as long as you're moderating the amount! I'm not a fan of the word *cheat*, used so often to describe treats. I think it instills guilt rather than enjoyment. Instead, I use *treat* or *victory meal*. Eating nutrient-dense foods all week most certainly should be rewarded with a treat you can wholeheartedly enjoy. Food doesn't have to be either functional or enjoyable—it can be both.

HOW TO READ NUTRITION LABELS

In the interest of your own health, you should be curious about what's in your food. This would be obvious if you're making something from scratch, but even the most hardcore healthy eaters will eat foods that come in packages once in a while. Beware of marketing terms like "all natural" or "low fat." These don't mean the foods are better than products without those labels!

It's important to judge a food label as a whole, taking into consideration many different variables. Just because something is low in sugar, for example, doesn't mean it's healthy. You might be tempted to buy "low-fat" foods, but to make up for the lack of fat, these products often have lots of added sugar and/or salt.

Keep in mind that the information most relevant to you on a nutrition label is based upon your unique health goals and/or health conditions. If you're on a mission to lose weight, serving size and calorie content may be particularly important. If you're at risk for osteoporosis, calcium and vitamin D content are key. If you're looking to pack on muscle mass, you'll want to make sure you know the protein content of the foods you're eating.

> "Ingredients are listed by weight, in descending order of predominance. That means the first ingredient is always the most predominant in a food."

Also keep in mind that the carbohydrate and fat percentages you see on nutrition labels are based on a 2,000-calorie diet. Because we each need a different amount of calories to fuel our goals and lifestyles, make sure you take this into account and use the percentages only as a guideline. An inactive five-foot-one female who wants to lose 20 pounds most likely needs fewer than 2,000 calories per day. A six-foot-tall male elite triathlete will need much more than 2,000 calories per day.

As a general guideline, one serving of food with 5 percent or less of the daily value for a particular nutrient is considered low. One serving of food with 20 percent or more of a daily value is considered high.

The following label-reading tips will help you to decipher what's in your food, and whether it will support your health and fitness goals.

The Ingredient List

Perhaps most obviously, make sure you check out the ingredient list. Also take note of the order in which ingredients are listed. They're listed by weight, in descending order of predominance. That means the first ingredient is always the most predominant in a food, and the last ingredient is the least predominant.

Take the Starbucks reduced-fat banana chocolate chip coffee cake, for instance. I saw this item a few times over the course of four weeks in a client's food diary, so I decided to investigate its ingredients. Given its name, you'd think it would contain a decent amount of banana, right? Not so. Bananas are the thirty-fourth ingredient! Remember that products contain the highest proportion of the first ingredient. In this case, ingredient number one was sugar.

Serving Size and Calorie Content

At the very top of a standard nutrition label, you'll find the serving size and calorie content of the product in question. These can be deceiving sometimes, so make sure you take a close look! If you're buying a single-serving item like instant soup (yes, there are healthy instant soup options), sometimes a serving size is listed as only half the container. Nobody eats only half the soup! In this case you'd be getting twice the calories, and all the other nutrients, listed on the container.

I just pulled from my freezer a bag of my husband's potato and onion pierogies. One serving is 122 grams, or four pierogies. This contains 230 calories. Since my husband usually eats about 12 pierogies in a meal, that's 690 calories (three times 230)! He's not trying to lose weight so that's not a problem for him, but if you're aiming to eat fewer calories and lose weight, getting 920 calories from just one meal probably isn't the way to go.

Now I'm looking at my bag of frozen edamame (soybean pods). One serving is half a cup, and contains 90 calories. I usually eat at least one cup as a serving, so I'd need to double all the nutrients I see on the label to get a more accurate reading of what I'm consuming.

It's important to note that while calorie counting can be a helpful tool for increasing your health (whether it's weight loss or eating enough to support your physical activity), it's not the be-all and end-all answer.

I believe it has important value if used for relatively short periods of time in a health-enhancing manner, but I think calorie counting is—for the most part—unhealthy and unnecessary. There are physiological and psychological reasons for this.

Calorie counting is far from an exact science. The calorie counts we see on nutrition labels are based on a 100-year-old method that doesn't take into account how our bodies process different types of foods, or how the foods themselves were processed. For example, it takes our bodies much less energy to digest foods in liquid form (e.g., applesauce) than in solid form (e.g., fresh apples). Food labelling laws require calorie counts to be accurate within 20 percent. That's a lot of room for variation. When we consider how our bodies use and process different types of foods, nutrition label calorie counts can be off by up to 50 percent![1]

Other than living in a metabolic chamber, there's no way for the average person to know exactly how many calories he or she needs every day. It's all about experimentation, so I'd take each calorie count you get with a grain of salt. Try using this calculator (the most comprehensive I've seen): www.health-calc.com/diet/energy-expenditure-advanced. Make sure to look at the "total energy expenditure" number, and subtract ten to twenty percent if your goal is weight loss. Your basal metabolic rate is the rate at which your body uses energy while at rest, to support your vital functions. That number doesn't take into account the energy you use for anything other than simply being alive!

It can be helpful to have a general ballpark figure to work with (assuming it takes into account your weight, height, muscle mass vs. fat mass, activity level, gender, and age), but given how inaccurate calorie counting is, it's not the best way to increase health and/or lose weight.

Psychologically, I think constant calorie counting puts people at risk for developing unhealthy relationships with food. If you're doing calorie counting as a way to learn about your diet or to set a new baseline, that's OK. I had no idea I averaged 3,000 calories per day until I recorded my food for three days on a few different occasions. For me, it's always been a matter of eating enough, rather than eating too much. So I could potentially use the 3,000-calorie ballpark as a goal to hit each day to best fuel my workouts, muscle mass (which is difficult for me to keep if I don't eat enough), and turbo-speed metabolism. However, long-term calorie counting becomes exhausting, and I believe psychologically unhealthy. Once you know how much to eat by counting calories for a while, I suggest ditching the calories and listening to your body instead.

Fat Content

Directly below the calorie count you'll see a listing of fat content in grams. Remember that the percentage next to it is based on a 2,000-calorie diet. Not all fats are created equal, and not all fats are bad! On nutrition labels you'll see "Total fat" in grams, under which you'll find a breakdown of more specific fats. The only requirement when it comes to labeling laws is that saturated fats and trans fats be listed. It's best to avoid trans fats entirely and keep saturated fat consumption to below 10 percent of your total calories.

Some products might also list the healthy fat content, which are monounsaturated and polyunsaturated fats. These fats can lower your risk of heart disease and are also important to help your body absorb fat-soluble vitamins. If a nutrition label doesn't list these beneficial fats (which is common), how can you tell whether the product has more healthy or unhealthy fat content? (Other than looking at the ingredient list; for example, olive oil and avocado contain healthy fats, while partially hydrogenated vegetable oil and red meat contain not-so-healthy fats.)

Let's say you see a nutrition label with 10 grams of total fat. Under the total fat heading you see that the product contains 2 grams of saturated fat and 0 grams of trans fat. It doesn't list healthy fats, so you'll have to do a bit of simple math. 2 plus 0 gives you a total of 2 grams of less healthy fats. Subtract 2 from 10 and you get 8 grams of healthy fat. Two grams of unhealthy fats versus 8 grams of healthier fats mean the product in question is mostly healthy when it comes to fat content.

Now let's say you see another label with 10 grams of total fat, with 5 grams of saturated fats and 3.5 grams of trans fats. That's a total of 8.5 grams of less healthy fats, leaving only 1.5 grams of healthy fat. This would be a product to either stay away from entirely or enjoy as a treat in moderation. Keep in mind that there are plant-based sources of saturated fats, like coconut. These are generally considered healthier for us than animal-based saturated fats, but research is still ongoing.

Beware of products labeled as "low fat"! These products do contain fewer grams of fat per serving compared to their regular counterparts, but they're not necessarily more healthy. Decreasing the fat in a product usually means downgrading its flavor and texture, so low-fat products very often have added sugar and/or salt to make up for the lack of fat. In some cases, low-fat products actually contain more calories per serving than regular-fat products! The fewer calories from fat may work in favor of decreasing your heart disease risk, but if you're trying to lose weight or maintain leanness, these extra calories do add up. (Not to mention, sugar and salt overload carry their own risks!)

There's an added—and not as easy to detect—negative side to "low-fat" products. It's a psychological one. Seeing a "low-fat" label on a particular food is actually likely to make us overeat! When a food is labeled as "low fat," we're likely to increase perceptions of an appropriate serving size, and decrease consumption guilt.[2] Because we tend to feel less guilty about eating foods labeled as "low fat," we're more likely to overeat them.

The bottom line: when you see foods labeled as "low fat," you'll need to do a bit of extra sleuthing to determine whether you want these foods as part of your diet. Compare regular and low-fat versions of the same food to check for total calories, sodium content, sugar content, and any other differences. Very often, it makes sense to buy regular-fat products and watch your serving sizes instead of buying low-fat products that you're more likely to gorge on.

Cholesterol Content

Cholesterol is necessary for our bodies to function properly. Your body can make the cholesterol it needs without consuming any dietary cholesterol. In fact, minimizing dietary cholesterol intake appears to be very important in preventing stroke and heart disease. While cholesterol intake isn't the whole story when it comes to preventing these conditions, high cholesterol content in a food usually comes with high saturated fat content, which has long been considered a major risk factor for stroke and heart disease. Clinical research continues to study the links between heart disease and risk factors such as dietary cholesterol and saturated fats. People following entirely plant-based diets don't consume any cholesterol. The daily value of cholesterol you see on a food label represents the maximum suggested amount, so try to keep the percentage of daily value as low as you can. If you eat a 100 percent plant-based diet, you won't be ingesting any cholesterol at all.

Sodium Content

Similar to cholesterol, the sodium daily value is also based on a maximum suggested daily amount. Try to stick to low-sodium foods to prevent hypertension (high blood pressure), bloating, and excess water retention. The average North American consumes about 3,400 milligrams of sodium per day. That's more than double the amount we need for optimal functioning! The Canadian health recommendation for the daily upper limit of sodium—that is, the highest amount of sodium we can consume per day without adverse health effects—is 2,300 milligrams.[3] Interestingly, the daily value you see on a nutrition label is based on an upper limit of 2,400 milligrams. Even though this is on the higher end of what's considered healthy, it's only about a teaspoon of salt per day.

Carbohydrate Content

Like fat content, carbohydrate percentages you see on a nutrition label are based on a 2,000-calorie diet. Carbohydrate content is broken up into fiber and sugar. More of the former, and less of the latter is always a good rule to go by!

Fiber is important to feeling satiated after eating, and to a healthy digestive tract. A good rule of thumb is to aim for an absolute minimum of 25 grams of fiber per day. This is the gold standard used to calculate percentage of daily recommendation on food labels. For instance, you might see 5 grams of fiber in a certain food serving, and an accompanying 20 percent in the "percent of daily value" column.

Sugar content is also listed in grams. Protein bars, for example, which are foods usually marketed as healthy supplements for active people, often contain upwards of 20 grams of sugar in one bar. Most of us don't really know how much sugar 20 grams is, so here's how you can visualize how much sugar is in the foods you're buying.

One teaspoon of sugar weighs 4 grams. So, find the sugar content on a product's nutrition label, and divide the number you see by 4. That's how many teaspoons of sugar the product contains. I find it much easier to visualize sugar amounts this way, because we all know how much a teaspoon is. In the case of a protein bar that contains 20 grams of sugar, that's 5 teaspoons. For general health, it's best to stick to food products with sugar content in the single digits. Keep in mind that nutrition labels don't differentiate between *processed*, *added* sugars and *fruit* sugars. (Fruit sugars, of course, are a much better option than added sugars.) You'll need to look at the ingredient list to differentiate between the two.

The Starbucks reduced fat banana chocolate chip coffee cake I mentioned earlier happens to contain 50 grams of sugar. While it's true that some sugar content you see on a label may be from fruit sugars, remember that bananas are number 34 in the ingredients list and sugar is number one. That means the majority of sugar in this product comes from added, non-fruit sugar. Fifty grams of sugar is 12½ teaspoons. That's in only one piece of the coffee cake!

You'll notice that the fiber and sugar grams listed on a nutrition label usually don't add up to the total carbohydrate grams. The remainder is the amount of starch in a food. Let's say a product lists 10 total grams of carbohydrates with 6 grams of fiber and 2 grams of sugar. Subtract the fiber and sugar grams from the total carbohydrate content (10 minus 6 minus 2) to get a total of 2 grams of starch. Starch is an important fuel source for our bodies, so we should aim to eat foods that are higher in starch than in sugar. You've probably heard the term *starch* used with negative connotations by the diet industry. That's just a myth! Starches occur naturally in many healthy foods, like legumes, fruits, and vegetables. We need this major fuel source to survive.

Protein Content

Protein content on a nutrition label doesn't come with a percentage because we each have different protein needs, based on our lifestyles and our goals. Work with a dietitian to figure out your personal requirement. Multiply the protein content (which is listed in grams) by four to find out how many of the calories in a serving size come from protein. You can use this information—along with everything else on the label, of course—to determine where most of the calories in a product come from.

On the bag of frozen edamame I mentioned earlier, I see 10 grams of protein in one serving, with a total of 90 calories per serving. Ten times 4 is 40. So 40 out of 90 calories come from protein. That's more than 44 percent of calories coming from protein! No wonder edamame is one of the best muscle-building plant foods around. Because my main activity is weight training and I need a lot of protein to fuel and rebuild my muscles, I use protein content on nutrition labels to keep loose track of my daily protein total (although most of the food I eat doesn't come in packages).

Vitamins and Minerals

At the bottom of a nutrition label you'll see a listing of vitamins and minerals. Vitamins A and C, plus calcium and iron, are deemed so important to our health that they are the only vitamins and minerals that must be listed. Vitamins and minerals are listed as percentages instead of in milligrams or grams, because they're easier to understand than to memorize specific numbers for each nutrient. Keep in mind that vitamin and mineral percentages on nutrition labels are generalized and based on government recommendations for daily intakes. These might not be appropriate for you, however. Our vitamin and mineral requirements change with age and are different for men and women. For example, females aged 19 to 50 require 18 milligrams of iron daily, while females aged 51 and older, as well as males aged 19 and older, require 8 milligrams per day. Pregnant women need 27 milligrams of iron per day.[4]

Nutrition labels use 14 milligrams of daily iron as a benchmark, so keep this in mind when you assess whether you're getting enough iron. Say you read a nutrition label that shows the food contains 10 percent of the daily iron recommendation. Ten percent of 14 milligrams is 1.4 milligrams. If you're a female aged between 19 and 50 (with an iron requirement of 18 milligrams per day), 1.4 milligrams of iron is only 7.7 percent of your daily allowance. If you're pregnant, 1.4 milligrams of iron is only 5 percent of your daily requirement.

Work with a dietitian to ensure you get the vitamins and minerals you need, and get a blood test at least every year to make sure your nutrient levels are adequate.

TO CLEANSE, OR NOT TO CLEANSE

We've all heard of "cleanses" or "detox" diets. Maybe you've even tried one (or a few). Many people think that a good way to kickstart a healthy lifestyle change is to do a cleanse. Others look to cleanses for weight loss, increased energy, or to rid their bodies of toxins. Unfortunately, "cleansing" or "detoxing" is based on a misunderstanding of human physiology.

One of the best ways to find out whether a certain concept in the health and fitness field has any validity is to look up peer-reviewed journal articles on the topic. Peer-review is a process whereby a panel of professionals evaluate research to ensure it was conducted well and is up to professional standards. Scientific journals are specialized publications in which researchers publish findings from their studies. So, we're not talking about websites written by hobbyists, or even books written by PhDs. If there is no—or limited—good quality published research from clinical studies to support a certain claim, you can be pretty sure it's B.S., or you're ahead of the game and your topic hasn't been researched yet, but that's unlikely. Google Scholar (scholar.google.com) is a great resource for finding peer-reviewed journal articles.

In the case of dietary cleanses, which have been around for a long time, extensive research has been conducted. And guess what? Not only is there no evidence that detox diets actually do anything beneficial, but there's also no evidence to support the very basis of detoxing. Detoxing is based on a misunderstanding of how our bodies work. And, ironically enough, going on a detox diet can actually *increase* toxins in our bodies. Of course, nobody actually ever defines what a "toxin" is.

Melanie Hackett, who has a BSc in Biomedical Physiology and Kinesiology (and a whole host of other health-related certifications, and also happens to be my sister) is here to share her expertise and to set the record straight on so-called "cleanses" or "detox diets." Importantly, she has a specific definition of a toxic effect in the body caused by detox cleanses. Let's turn things over to her!

If you are interested in health you have probably heard of "cleansing" diets aimed at ridding your body of toxins by reducing what you consume to a very limited selection of healthy products for two or three weeks. Unfortunately, our physiology is not nearly that straightforward, and these diets simply don't do what they are intended for. In fact, more toxins are created during these diets! Of course, there are many different types of detox diets. Like all fad diets, most of these are merely a tool for companies to earn money off unwary consumers and aren't based on science at all. Even my mother, a very health-conscious and active sixty-one-year-old who generally looks for the science, used to do annual "cleansing" diets, consuming nothing but elderberry juice for several weeks in an attempt to "flush away" toxins. I will focus on these types of "cleanses."

> *"In general, if a diet is not healthy or is impossible to maintain permanently, it probably should not be done at all."*

In a normal human body with a healthy diet where caloric intake equals caloric expenditure, blood sugar levels are well regulated by insulin (and a second hormone, called glucagon). Insulin, released by the pancreas after a meal, takes the blood glucose and helps it enter all body cells, where it can be used as energy for all cell function. Extra glucose combines forming a substance called glycogen, which gets stored in muscle and the liver. These stores are crucial for maintaining blood glucose levels. They can be completely depleted after only a couple of hours of exercise at a heart rate 80 percent of your maximum heart rate, and they do not build back up unless a diet high in carbohydrates (fruits, veggies, quinoa, rice, whole grain bread, etc.) is eaten. These stores can also be depleted within a couple days of consuming much less than you are expending, or not having a diet consisting of about 60 percent carbohydrates.

When glycogen runs out, fatty acids and proteins are broken down instead in the liver. The by-products of this process are three types of ketone bodies, two of which the heart and brain use. The third is a waste product stressing the kidneys. Ketones also lower the pH of the blood. To correct this acidic blood, the respiratory system starts to hyperventilate to expel more carbon dioxide. In the blood, carbon dioxide combines with water and forms bicarbonate and a hydrogen ion. (The latter makes the blood more acidic.) If there is less carbon dioxide available, fewer hydrogen ions will be produced. However, less carbon dioxide also means less stimulus for breathing, and in extreme cases this can be fatal.

Excess ketones and the physiological effect they have can be considered toxic in the human body. These effects are pretty much identical to what happens both during starvation and during a diabetic coma when a diabetic's blood sugar is extremely high because the diabetic person lacks insulin to help shuttle the sugar from the blood to the starved cells. This is also what happens during the Atkins diet, one that should only be tried by morbidly obese people who are at alarming risk of fatality if they don't lose weight. In general, if a diet is not healthy or is impossible to maintain permanently, it probably should not be done at all.

Additionally, the net breakdown of proteins to provide energy (either in a high protein diet or when the body is starved of carbs) causes a negative nitrogen balance and taxes the liver, which tries to rid itself of the nitrogenous waste products that are produced. The immune system is weakened, and the levels of cortisol, our long-term stress hormone, may increase, further weakening the immune system.

The physiological effects discussed above merely state what toxins build up in the body and the negative effect on health during "detox" diets. This doesn't take into account the nutrient deficiencies that can occur during such limited diets, which have a cascade of harmful effects in the body.

Of course, some cleansing diets instruct you to eat lots of dark green veggies, a variety of plant-based foods, limited processed foods, legumes and nuts instead of meat, and a healthy caloric intake for you. To me, this sounds like a diet that might as well be maintained permanently.

Melanie Hackett
B.Sc. Biomedical Physiology and Kinesiology
Certificate in Health and Fitness Studies
Certificate in Human Nutrition

CHAPTER 6: SO, WHAT SHOULD I EAT?

We've discussed general principles of healthy plant-based eating such as whole foods and nutrition label reading. Now we're getting into the nitty-gritty details. The following sections will help you to build your own healthy plant-based diet. You'll get a comprehensive list of foods every active vegan needs in his or her kitchen, practical snack ideas, and a sample four-day food diary.

KITCHEN STAPLES FOR ACTIVE VEGANS

The following items are examples of what healthy, active vegans stash in their pantries. Most of the items in this section can be found at any supermarket, but a few specialty items may need to be tracked down at a health food store or natural grocery.

Vegetables
Fresh veggies

No healthy vegan on the planet is ever caught without a stockpile of veggies in the fridge. You just gotta have 'em—and lots of 'em—for a nutritious diet that will support your lifestyle. Make the produce aisle your first stop at each grocery store trip, and pile lots of different types into your cart, including dark leafy greens. Keep things exciting by switching it up. Kohlrabi? Kale? Daikon? Arugula?

Whenever possible and when the season is right, try to get your veggies from a local farmers' market. Not only will the produce likely contain higher levels of nutrients than veggies from supermarkets, given that they haven't been sitting around for as long as in-store produce, but they taste fresher and more flavorful. I also find the farmers' market experience to be more enjoyable than a trip to the "big box" grocery store!

Make sure you steam or stir-fry your veggies rather than boiling them to prevent leaching away a good portion of their nutrients. Cooking vegetables into a mushy state is a thing of the past (at least, it should be!); cook yours for only a few minutes, ensuring their colors are still vibrant and they've still got some "bite" to them.

Frozen veggies

Plan B after fresh veggies is to keep a small selection of frozen vegetables in your freezer so you can use them in a pinch. Frozen veggies typically have similar nutritional profiles to fresh vegetables, and can sometimes even contain higher levels of nutrients than fresh vegetables (especially when compared with fresh veggies from grocery stores rather than from local farmers' markets). Produce destined for freezing is picked when ripe and usually frozen within hours, "locking in" all its nutrients. Fresh produce, however, is often harvested before it's ripe, then shipped for long periods of time during which it loses nutritional value. If you're getting your produce from a farmers' market or local organics delivery company, though, you don't have to worry about nutrient loss.

Always choose in-season, local, and organic produce when possible, but resort to frozen fare for items not in season or when you just forgot to stop by the farmers' market on your way home from work. Frozen produce does have a slightly different texture and taste compared to fresh produce, but you're certainly not compromising your nutrition by using frozen goods.

Fruit
Fresh fruit
Keep a fresh fruit bowl stocked at all times with whatever is in season. Bananas, apples, pears, grapes, plums, oranges, grapefruit, kumquats, dragon fruit—you get the point. If you can, choose organic fruits to minimize your intake of residual pesticides.

Frozen fruit
Just like frozen veggies, this would be your second choice after fresh fruit. Frozen berries like strawberries and blueberries are popular choices when fresh berries are out of season, because they work very well in smoothies, crumbles, and fruit sauces.

Canned fruit
Canned fruit has a high convenience factor and a long shelf life. Try to stick to the "canned in its own juices" types, with no added sugar. Vitamin C content in canned fruit is much lower than in fresh fruit, and other nutrients may be decreased as well due to cooking the fruit during the canning process.

Grains & Pseudo Grains
Lots of highly processed grains such as white rice and white flour are not part of a whole foods, healthy eating plan. They are stripped of vitamin- and mineral-rich bran, and are also linked to increased risk for heart disease. White grains—composed of simple carbohydrates—cause an instant spike in blood sugar levels, similar to what happens when we consume white sugar. Whole grains, on the other hand, take longer to be broken down and digested, so they'll better regulate your blood sugar and keep you full longer.

Pseudo grains are, as the term implies, not actual grains. They're seeds, but used in similar ways as grains, for example as a base for stir-fried veggies. My favorite grain (oats) and pseudo grain (quinoa) are described here, but there are many, many more.

Oats

Oatmeal: the classic breakfast of champions. Steel-cut oats are much more nutritionally dense than instant oatmeal or rolled oats, so you should try using these whenever possible. Steel-cut oats are made of the whole oat kernel, retaining much of the plant's fiber. Use 4 parts water to each part steel-cut oats, and cook on the stove for about 20 minutes. In the microwave, make sure you use a large bowl to allow for bubbling, use the same ratio of water to oats, and heat on high for 10 minutes, stirring halfway through.

Rolled oats have had some of the bran removed, so they're lower in fiber than steel-cut oats. They've been rolled flat to ensure faster cooking times. I eat a bowl of oatmeal every single morning, and it takes only 3½ minutes to cook rolled oats in the microwave—probably even faster than waiting for the kettle to boil and using the packaged instant stuff. Use between 1½ and 2 parts water for 1 part rolled oats. You may need to experiment a bit to find your preferred consistency.

If your mornings usually involve rushing around in a frenzy and you don't eat breakfast until you get to work, pack Ziploc bags or Tupperware containers of oats and microwave them in a bowl at work. You can even cook oatmeal the night before and reheat at work. If you don't have access to a microwave at work, get yourself some quick-cooking oatmeal packages, ensuring you find a brand with no added sugar or salt. I used to pack these for super early days at work and prepare them at a reasonable breakfast hour—all you need is hot water.

Oatmeal serving suggestions: Add plant-based milk, berries, sliced apples, dried fruit, ground flax seeds, crushed nuts, and/or hemp hearts.

Quinoa

Actually a seed and not a true grain, quinoa (KEEN-wa) is a staple for plant-based active people everywhere. It offers a complete protein, meaning it contains all essential amino acids. It also has a high fiber content. Rinse and cook quinoa like rice: 1½ parts water to each part quinoa. You can even use your rice cooker! Use it as a base for stir fries, risottos, or casseroles, or enjoy it as a hearty salad ingredient. Quinoa is also sold as flakes, which you can use to make delicious breakfast bakes, and as flour, which you can use in gluten-free baking.

Pasta

Not just your usual assortment of wheat pasta—spaghetti, macaroni, you get the idea. Make sure you limit your use of regular pasta and choose whole wheat pasta whenever possible. Branch out and try some even healthier options! Check out the Asian foods and gluten-free aisles of your grocery store for some of these goodies:

- Rice noodles
- Bean thread noodles (a.k.a. glass noodles)
- Spelt pasta

- Brown rice pasta
- Japanese shirataki noodles (made from a type of yam)
- Tofu noodles
- High protein pasta (e.g., edamame, red lentil, or black bean). An excellent protein source for those of us who strength train!

Meat & Dairy Analogues

I call the foods in this section "analogues" because they're meant to be used just like their animal-based counterparts. Plant-based milks can be used just like cow's milk, and meat analogues are meant to be "replicas" of animal meats. Foods in this section are usually fairly processed, so use them sparingly.

Meat analogues

These are products that aim to make "fake meat" (usually from soy) that looks, feels, and tastes like animal meat. I'm generally not a fan of meat analogues, but they do have their uses. These products are usually highly processed, but they do contain large amounts of protein. These days, the options are endless. Tofurkey, veggie dogs, veggie burgers, any type of deli meat in soy form, breakfast links, breakfast patties, "chicken" strips and tenders, etc. I don't appreciate the fact that they imply they're substitutions for the "real thing" and that real meals should include animal products (quite the contrary!), but I do appreciate that they demonstrate the versatility of soy.

Another type of meat analogue—seitan—is made using wheat gluten, and is used extensively in East Asian and Buddhist vegetarian cuisine. An alternative to soy-based meat substitutes, seitan has a chewy texture eerily resembling meat.

Plant-based milks

I'm referring to lots of different plant-based milk types. Soy, rice, and almond milks are the most common, but you can also easily find oat, hemp, hazelnut, flax, and coconut milks. Throughout this book I'll be using the term "plant-based milk" to describe all of these options, so feel free to experiment.

Of the three most common plant-based milks, soy milk is the creamiest. I find it works well in lattes (almond and rice milks don't froth well when steamed), in cereal, tea and coffee, and in baked goods. Rice and almond milks are much lighter in texture and work particularly well if you're treating yourself by making light and airy baked goods such as cupcakes or angel food cake.

Legumes & Cultured Soy Products
Dried & canned legumes

If you're the planning-ahead type and can soak your beans, lentils, or peas overnight for cooking the next day, dried legumes are much more economical than cooked and canned legumes. Cooking beans and lentils from a dried state isn't feasible for everyone, though, given how much time it takes from start to finish. (Don't let the time aspect scare you away—you're not actually doing any work the whole time.)

To cook dried legumes, first place your legumes of choice into a fine colander or sieve. Rinse with water and remove any small stones or other natural debris you might find. Fill a large pot with water and soak your legumes overnight (8–10 hours). When ready to cook, drain the soaking water, fill the pot with fresh water (at least twice as much water as legumes), and bring to a boil. Reduce heat to low and simmer until cooked. Cooking time will depend on the type of legume you're cooking but is generally around an hour.

Keep a supply of canned (low or no sodium) beans, peas, and lentils on hand to use in recipes when you're not using dried legumes. Some ideas: kidney beans, chickpeas, lima beans, adzuki beans, navy beans, split peas, brown and green lentils.

Tofu

Low in calories, tofu (or bean curd) is an excellent source of protein and is readily available in any supermarket. There are countless varieties of tofu to choose from, so the type you choose will depend on the dish you're making and your personal preferences. Tofu is fairly tasteless by itself; it takes on the flavors of whatever it's being cooked with. My friend Holly suggests a very simple method of making delicious tofu that is crispy and browned on the outside—with no frying! Cut firm or extra firm tofu into ½-inch cubes, place on a baking sheet lined with parchment paper, and bake at 400°F for 20 minutes. Tofu made this way is fantastic in stir-fries.

Tempeh

Also a soy product, tempeh may be a bit more difficult to find than tofu. Tempeh is less processed and contains more protein, fiber, and other nutrients than tofu. Whole soybeans are used to make tempeh, rather than preprocessed soy milk, which is used to make tofu. Tempeh is more chewy than tofu and works well in stews, casseroles, stir fries, and more.

Oils

Stay away from hydrogenated oils and trans fats! These have been shown to increase the risk of developing heart disease.

There are many healthy oils to choose from. Indeed, we need to consume fats as part of a well-balanced diet; we just need to ensure they come from healthy sources.

Coconut oil is a healthier oil option. Not only is it extremely versatile in the kitchen, but it has many other uses, too. Coconut oil is solid at temperatures below about 77°F, with a consistency close to margarine or butter. Use it as a spread, or for cooking, as you would any other type of oil. You can also use coconut oil as an incredible moisturizer, hair conditioner, and massage oil.

Omega-rich hemp and flax oils are packed with nutrition. Their fatty acids are damaged when heated, so use these oils in salad dressings, in smoothies, as a topping for steamed veggies or baked yams, or anywhere else that doesn't require heating.

Extra-virgin olive oil is a healthier alternative to canola oil and is most often used for cooking. Try different types, depending on the recipe; light-flavored olive oil is best for baking, and more flavorful olive oil can be used for cooking and salad dressings.

Snacks & Readymade Foods

We all need quick and easy foods sometimes—we just need to make sure we're eating the right ones. Snacks can be a huge arena for excess sugar, salt, and loads of calories with no nutritional value. Make sure your cupboards are stocked with only healthy foods, and you won't be tempted to snack on sugary or otherwise unhealthy junk!

Cereals

Sugary cereal should be a very occasional treat, not a regular breakfast food. You don't have to be a tree-huggin' hippie to enjoy healthy granola. Look for other high-fiber cereals like bran flakes, and multigrain options abound. Try something new! Kamut puffs or psyllium bites, anyone? Just make sure they don't contain high amounts of sugar. Healthy cereals make a great super-easy breakfast, or anytime snacks between more hearty meals. Just add your plant-based milk of choice.

Pancake/waffle mix

Healthy options do exist: Go for the no-sugar, multigrain types. My favorite contains whole grain spelt and kamut flours, a good choice for those breakfast-for-dinner days, or a weekend morning when you have a bit of extra time to prepare breakfast. You can always add a tablespoon of agave nectar or maple syrup to the batter if you want to appease your sweet tooth. Top with maple syrup, fresh fruit, jam, or other fruit spreads.

Instant soups

The healthy kind! For hunger emergencies or small and simple meals at work, stock up on split pea, tomato pasta, lentil, etc., and skip the instant noodle soups with tons of MSG.

Protein powder

Not just for gym rats, protein shakes are a great emergency snack when you need something fast and filling between meals. It's best to get good quality protein from a variety of whole plant-based foods such as legumes and nuts, but a protein shake made with vegan protein is an easy-to-digest, healthy snack option and hunger fighter. I have a protein shake every night before bed to prevent waking up extremely hungry in the middle of the night. I also have a protein shake on weight-training days after my workouts to support my muscle-building efforts at the gym. I try to look for protein powder that does not contain soy, because I eat soy in other forms in my diet, and don't want to overdo soy intake. Vegan protein powders are exploding into the market and contain ingredients like brown rice, pea, and hemp. There are many, many types to choose from—shop around and try a variety of brands to find something you like.

Other healthy snacks

Of course there's some overlap here with other sections, such as fresh veggies, fruit, and cereals. Some ideas: Brown rice crackers, whole grain spelt crisps, raw veggies, various homemade vegetable spreads or pâtés, fresh and dried fruit, nuts, healthy readymade soups (e.g., Amy's soups or Happy Planet chili).

White Sugar Alternatives

We all know that a large amount of processed sugar is not part of a healthy diet. White sugar provides empty calories and wreaks havoc on our bodies, including suppressing the immune system, promoting tooth decay, and contributing to diabetes. Healthier eating may seem impossible, at first, for those of us with a sweet tooth. However, not only are there many healthier options to use as sweeteners, but it's also very common to experience a decrease in sugar cravings after sticking to a healthy diet for only a few weeks. It's best to limit even "healthy" sweeteners, because most still contain simple sugars that provide next to no nutrition. Also, for many people, eating sweet things leads to increased cravings for sweetness. Talk about a vicious cycle!

Sucanat

If you absolutely must use sugar as a sweetener, use this pure dried sugar cane with high molasses content instead of regular refined white sugar. It's delicious on oatmeal, in baking, and in hot beverages including tea and coffee. For baking, you can substitute it for granulated white sugar at the same volume (i.e., use 1 cup of sucanat to replace 1 cup of white sugar).

Agave nectar

Made from the agave plant (the same one from which tequila is made), this nectar is 1½ times as sweet as regular sugar and is slightly less viscous than honey. It's an excellent vegan alternative to honey and comes in a few different varieties. Light agave nectar doesn't have much taste to it; raw, amber, and dark agave have a bit of a caramel flavor. Dark agave is the least processed and contains the highest amount of minerals found in the agave plant.

Maple syrup

Maple syrup contains fewer calories than white sugar (by weight) and is less processed. This means it contains higher levels of trace minerals such as calcium and potassium, but it's still of minimal nutritional value and contains "empty" calories.

Stevia

From the sunflower family, stevia is a natural, no-calorie sweetener that is 300 times sweeter than sugar. This means if you're using it in tea or coffee, add an incredibly small amount! Just the tip of a teaspoon will suffice. Some people find stevia to have a slightly bitter aftertaste.

Brown rice syrup

Produced by combining brown rice with enzymes then cooking the resulting liquid to thicken it, brown rice syrup is a great option for baking and other desserts. It has a delicate flavor and is not as sweet as agave nectar (and usually not as pricey). Agave nectar and brown rice syrup have similar calorie profiles, but given that brown rice syrup is not as sweet as agave, you need to use more to achieve the same level of sweetness.

Coconut sugar

Made from the dried sap of coconut palm flower buds, coconut sugar has a lower glycemic index than white sugar. This means it likely won't spike your blood sugar as much as refined white sugar. Coconut sugar contains more vitamins and minerals than regular sugar, but don't let that fool you into eating large amounts. Coconut sugar should still be seen as an occasional treat—but one that is perhaps a bit better than standard granulated sugar.

Coffee & Tea

A moderate amount of coffee per day is correlated with a decreased risk for heart disease. Also, caffeine has been shown in many research studies to boost metabolism. As long as you're not overdoing coffee intake (sticking to one to two cups a day or less) and aren't using sweeteners or other add-ins, you'll reap the benefits of this liquid fuel. Drink your coffee black or with a small amount of unsweetened plant-based milk added. The French press is commonly regarded as the best method of making high-quality coffee at home.

When you're hit by a craving for sugary juice or a sweet carbonated drink (or anything else you're trying to limit, for that matter), have a cup of tea instead. You may be pleasantly surprised how drinking a delicious and healthful hot beverage can curb your less healthy cravings. Tea contains less caffeine than coffee, and herbal teas are caffeine free. Tea contains many plant antioxidants and beneficial amino acids, and a host of health benefits have been documented. In clinical research, black and green teas have been linked to decreased risk for heart disease and some cancers, lowered total and LDL ("unhealthy") cholesterol, increased oral health and immunity, and weight management.[1] [2]

It hopefully goes without saying that you should either drink tea plain, or use a nonsugar sweetener such as stevia. In black teas, try adding a few tablespoons of unsweetened soy milk.

Keep a few teabags at work, and stock up on your favorites for home. If you're a tea enthusiast (or tea enthusiast wannabe), I highly recommend stopping by your local tea shop and picking up a few essentials:

- Loose leaf tea: You'll immediately notice an improvement in flavor when you use loose leaf instead of tea bags. The tea leaves have more room to expand, and the tea quality is generally better.
- Tea strainer: I've been advised to not use metal "tea balls" for loose leaf teas, again because the tea does not have sufficient room to expand. Instead, use a mesh strainer or hanging basket-style sieve that inserts into a teapot or mug.
- Teapot: Get yourself a small teapot that holds about two cups of liquid—perfect for single servings or for sharing with someone worthy of your delicious teas. It's important to steep tea in a covered teapot so that it doesn't lose heat or flavor.

Green teas deserve special mention here. They contain high levels of antioxidants (cancer-fighting compounds) and have been shown to boost metabolism, meaning they may aid in fat loss. Matcha green tea is high-quality, finely powdered Japanese green tea known as an extra-powerful antioxidant. Because the whole leaf is ingested rather than just an infusion made from leaves, matcha, which contains caffeine like all green teas, is known to provide a longer energy boost than other teas, lasting up to a few hours. Perfect for increasing energy without coffee jitters!

A Plant-Based Athlete's Secret Weapons

Last but not least, keep on hand a selection of super-healthy extras to ramp up the nutritional value of your meals and snacks.

Flax seeds

Very high in Omega-3, flax seeds need to be ground before eating, otherwise they pass through the digestive system without providing any nutritional benefit. The best option to preserve nutritional content is to buy them whole and grind them yourself in small batches using a food processor. Store ground flaxseed in the freezer. Add ground flaxseed to smoothies, oatmeal, baked goods, or cereals.

Chia seeds

The Aztecs cultivated chia, which is native to Mexico and Guatemala, centuries ago. Only relatively recently has it cropped up as a "superfood" in North America, but better late than never! Extremely high in fiber and essential fatty acids, chia seeds are great in baked goods and on cereals and oatmeal. You don't need to grind these seeds like you do flax seeds, and you can add them to beverages—you'll barely notice their subtle taste. Mix a few teaspoons of chia seeds into your beverage of choice, and if you let it stand for a few minutes, the mixture will turn into a gel. Eat your coffee with a spoon, like pudding!

Omega 3-6-9 oil

To boost your intake of essential fatty acids, look for a plant-based omega 3-6-9 oil. You can use this in smoothies, in salad dressings, or just take it by the spoonful. Udo's Oil is a great plant-based option with a light flavor. These oils are not to be heated.

Hemp seeds & hemp hearts

Hemp contains an abundance of essential fatty acids—omega-3 and omega-6—which serve many important functions in our bodies. Omega-3 fatty acids are more difficult to get from food than their omega-6 counterparts, so finding a food rich in omega-3s is pretty much like striking gold. Shelled hemp seeds are called hemp hearts and have a softer texture than whole seeds. Both seeds and hearts make tasty garnishes on salads, steamed veggies, stir fries, and oatmeal.

BREAKFAST, SMALL MEAL, AND SNACK IDEAS

Clients and other people I speak with seem to find healthy breakfasts and snacks more challenging to create or to prepare than other types of foods. Since we're often in a rush in the mornings, and snacks are meant to be eaten between meals, we usually want these foods to require minimal preparation. Here you'll find a collection of ideas you can use for breakfasts, snacks, and small meals that each take just a few minutes to prepare.

Ten Breakfast Ideas

Here are ten healthy and simple breakfast options. People who don't eat breakfast are more likely to overeat later in the day, to make poor food choices for lunch, and to weigh more than people who eat breakfast regularly. It may be counterintuitive, but if you're looking to lose weight (or maintain your lean physique), don't skip breakfast. If you're not hungry in the mornings, have something easily digestible, like a small piece of fruit, glass of soy milk, or rice cakes with peanut butter; then eat something heartier later in the morning.

1. *Oatmeal.* I eat oatmeal every morning, and sometimes later in the day, too. Add soy milk, almond milk, applesauce, fresh fruit, berries, chopped nuts, and/or chia seeds. Place ⅓ cup of rolled oats into a bowl, and cover with water. You can experiment with the amount of water to get your desired consistency. Microwave on high for 3½ minutes.

2. *Granola.* Enjoy with soy yogurt, chopped fresh fruit, dried fruit, nuts, soy milk, and/or hemp hearts. Keep in mind that a lot of commercial granolas have tons of added sugar, so if you can't find a low-sugar version, try making your own (recipe on page 145).

3. *Cereal.* Cereals are generally not as hearty as oatmeal or granola, but there are some healthy vegan options available. Remember to steer clear of the sugary types! Try cereals from the *Kashi* brand, and look for high fiber content, such as bran with psyllium husks. As a snack or light breakfast I like kamut puffs with soy milk.

4. *Frozen waffles.* I eat two breakfasts a day; for my second breakfast after my workouts I usually enjoy *Nature's Path* brand "Flax Plus" frozen waffles with peanut butter. Again, beware of high sugar content. Check out your local health food store for no-sugar-alternative, grain-based options.

5. *Homemade pancakes or waffles.* These are best left for days when you have a few extra minutes to cook your breakfast. Search the web for healthy vegan recipes, or use a pancake and waffle mix to save time. Enjoy with homemade Berry Sauce (recipe on page 187), maple or agave syrup, and/or fresh fruit.

6. *Energy bars.* These are great for when you're short on time or eating on the go. Most store-bought energy bars are quite high in added sugars, but there are a few brands that are lower (e.g., *Simply Bars*). See recipe for Homemade Energy Bars on page 155. If you make a batch on weekends, you'll be set for the week.

7. *Absurdly Healthy Supercookies.* See page 276 for the recipe. Grab a few of these incredibly nutritious and filling cookies for a quick and easy breakfast. Enjoy with plant-based milk or top with peanut butter.

8. *Smoothies.* So many options! Smoothies are a delicious and easily digestible way to kickstart your day with nutrients. See recipes starting on page 249.

9. *Cream of wheat.* A delicious comfort food containing loads of iron. Add soy milk, almond milk, applesauce, fresh fruit, berries, chopped nuts, and/or chia seeds.

10. *Fruit salad.* Use whatever combination you like (e.g., chopped apples with mixed berries), and top with sliced almonds.

Snack and Small Meal Ideas: No Preparation Required

To get you thinking about how easy healthy plant-based eating can be, here's a list of healthy snacks that don't need any preparation. Keep a stash in your kitchen for when the munchies strike, or take some of them along to work.

- Dry roasted edamame (soy beans)
- Brown rice crackers
- Japanese rice crackers
- Small boxes of soy milk (unsweetened)
- Protein bars (e.g., *NuGo* or *Simply* bars)
- Store-bought hummus
- Small packages of nori (seaweed)
- Unsalted nuts
- Fresh fruit
- Precut baby carrots
- Cherry or grape tomatoes
- Store-bought kale chips
- Protein powder (mixed with water)
- Individual size soy, almond, or coconut yogurt
- *Happy Planet* smoothies

Snacks that Take Minimal Preparation

These snacks and small meals don't come directly out of a package or box but are very quick and easy to prepare.

Baked sweet potato or yam with mixed greens

Microwave a sweet potato or yam for 5 minutes on each side, or until soft. Make sure you prick it with a fork beforehand to prevent explosions! Add some mixed greens and perhaps a topping (e.g., hemp hearts, sesame seeds, chia seeds), and you're good to go. Snack's ready in 10 minutes, and you're spending 9½ of those minutes waiting for the sweet potato or yam to cook.

Rice-cooker rice, quinoa, and lentil combo

My friend Holly suggests cooking a combination of brown rice, quinoa, and red lentils in your rice cooker. You can use one third of each, or whatever proportion you like. Use twice the amount of water as dried goods, and feel free to add turmeric if you're using red lentils. Holly suggests serving this with fresh tomato and cilantro.

Baked beans with greens

Microwave a can of vegetarian baked beans in a bowl with a handful of baby spinach (or other greens like arugula or dandelion greens), then mix. Try adding grated or cubed smoked tofu for extra protein and flavor. Canned baked beans are not entirely a "whole food" because they contain sugar, but there are certainly worse things you could be snacking on!

Raw and/or steamed veggies

I always keep a container or two of steamed veggies in the fridge. They're easy to take on the go, and there's no excuse for unhealthy snacking if I've got these available. I top mine with hemp hearts.

Salads

I don't mean fancy entrée salads with radish roses and an eleven-ingredient vinaigrette. I mean two minutes of prep: put some mixed greens in a bowl (if you buy the prewashed kind, you don't even have to wash them) and add some simple extras. My favorites are mushrooms, sliced cucumber, and hemp hearts. If you want dressing, mix together one tablespoon olive oil and one tablespoon balsamic vinegar. Easy, right?

Homemade popcorn

Popping your own stovetop popcorn takes only a few minutes. Loaded with antioxidants, popcorn is a very healthy snack option. (It's the unhealthy toppings associated with popcorn that give it its bad rap). See page 163 in the recipe section to learn how to make your own popcorn.

Steamed edamame

You can buy frozen edamame (green soy bean pods)—preferably organic—and cook them in only a few minutes. They're a popular and high-protein vegan option at Japanese restaurants, but you'll save money by making your own.

ULTIMATE LIST OF PLANT FOODS

The following table lists delicious and healthy foods you should be consuming regularly as the bulk of your healthy diet that supports active living. There are many more foods in each category; the ones presented here are the most common and easiest to find.

Bulb & Stem Vegetables:

- Asparagus
- Celeriac
- Celery
- Fennel
- Garlic
- Kohlrabi
- Leek
- Onion
- Shallot

Flowers & Buds:

- Artichoke
- Broccoli
- Capers
- Cauliflower
- Rapini
- Squash blossoms

Seed-Bearing Vegetables (Botanically, these are fruits):

- Avocado
- Bitter melon
- Corn
- Peppers (e.g., bell peppers, chili pepper)
- Pumpkin
- Squash
- Cucumber
- Eggplant
- Okra
- Tomato
- Winter melon
- Zucchini

Root & Tuberous Vegetables:

- Bamboo shoot
- Beet
- Carrot
- Cassava
- Daikon
- Ginger
- Jerusalem artichoke (a.k.a. sunchoke)
- Jicama
- Parsnip
- Potato
- Radish
- Sweet potato
- Taro
- Turnip
- Water chestnut
- Yam

Green Leafy Vegetables:

- Arugula
- Beet greens
- Bok choy
- Cabbage (white, red, savoy, Napa)
- Chard
- Collard greens
- Dandelion greens
- Endive
- Kale
- Lettuce
- Lovage
- Mizuna
- Mustard greens
- Pea shoots
- Radicchio
- Spinach
- Swiss chard
- Watercress

Grains & Pseudo Grains:

- Amaranth
- Barley
- Buckwheat
- Bulghur wheat
- Kamut
- Millet
- Quinoa
- Rice (e.g., brown, wild, black, basmati, jasmine)
- Sorghum
- Spelt

Legumes:

Beans

- Adzuki
- Black
- Chickpeas
- Fava
- Kidney
- Mung
- Navy
- Pinto
- Soybeans

Lentils

- Brown
- Green
- Red

Peas

- Black-eyed
- Green (split)
- Yellow (split)

Seeds:

- Chia
- Flax
- Hemp
- Poppy
- Pumpkin
- Sacha inchi seeds (marketed as "Savi" seeds)
- Sesame
- Sunflower

Oils:

- Coconut oil
- Extra-virgin olive oil
- Flaxseed oil
- Hemp oil
- Pumpkin seed oil
- Sesame oil

Fruit:

- Apples
- Apricots
- Bananas
- Cherries
- Coconut
- Dates
- Dragonfruit
- Figs
- Grapefruit
- Grapes
- Guava
- Kiwis
- Kumquats
- Lemons
- Limes
- Lychees
- Mangos
- Melons (cantaloupe, honeydew, watermelon)
- Berries (blackberries, blueberries, huckleberries, cranberries, currants, raspberries, strawberries, etc.)
- Nectarines
- Olives
- Oranges
- Papayas
- Peaches
- Pears
- Pineapples
- Plums
- Pomegranates
- Quince
- Rhubarb
- Star fruit
- Tamarind
- Tangerine

Nuts:

- Almonds
- Brazil nuts
- Cashews
- Hazelnuts
- Macadamia nuts
- Peanuts (technically a legume!)
- Pecans
- Pine nuts
- Pistachios
- Walnuts

Sea Vegetables:

- Dulce
- Nori
- Kelp (e.g., kombu)
- Wakame

Fungi:

- Mushrooms (e.g., white/brown/cremini/portobello, shiitake, chanterelle, oyster, etc.)
- Yeast (e.g., nutritional yeast, baking yeast)

Algae:

- Spirulina
- Chlorella

Plants Used as Seasonings and Spices:

- Allspice
- Anise
- Basil
- Bay leaf
- Black peppercorns
- Caraway
- Cardamom
- Chamomile
- Chives
- Cilantro
- Cinnamon
- Cloves
- Coriander
- Cumin
- Dill
- Fenugreek
- Horseradish
- Lemongrass
- Licorice
- Marjoram
- Mint
- Mustard seed
- Nutmeg
- Oregano
- Parsley
- Rosemary
- Saffron
- Sage
- Star anise
- Tarragon
- Thyme
- Turmeric
- Vanilla
- Wasabi

SAMPLE FOUR-DAY FOOD DIARY

In case you're curious about what, exactly, other active vegans eat, here's a four-day food diary of my diet. Remember that I might eat more than the average 5-foot-6, 125-pound female. I'm very active and am genetically a "hardgainer." That means my body type is naturally lean and I have to work very hard to gain and maintain muscle mass. Add these factors to my hummingbird-speed metabolism, and I usually consume around 2,500 calories per day. Women who aren't as active, have different body types, or are working to lose weight would eat much less than that! In any case, my diary isn't meant to be a diet prescription. Rather, it's just an illustration of one person's plant-based diet that supports an active lifestyle. The following food logs were recorded when I was training clients at the gym, before I transitioned to online coaching. Hence the slightly higher caloric intake!

Karina's Food Diary

Day 1

6:15 a.m.	½ cup (dry)	Oatmeal with soy milk
7:40 a.m.	1 (tall glass)	Protein shake (1 scoop) plus ½ cup soy milk
8:30 a.m.	2	Flax waffles with peanut butter
9:00 a.m.	1½ cups	Assam tea with ~5 tablespoons soy milk
11:15 a.m.	2 cups	Homemade split pea soup
	2 cups	Mixed greens
	200ml	Soy milk (*Natura* brand)
2:40 p.m.	1 giant	Yam (baked in the microwave)
	1 medium	Zucchini
	~10 small	Rice crackers
	2 medium	Mushrooms
	5 pieces	Chickpea falafel
6:00 p.m.	200ml	Soy milk (*So Good* brand)
	~10 small	Rice crackers
8:00 p.m.	2 cups	Miso, seaweed, enoki mushroom, chili, noodle soup
	3 squares	70 percent dark chocolate
10:00 p.m.	1 scoop	Protein shake

Day 2

7:30 a.m.	½ cup (dry)	Oatmeal with ¼ cup soy milk
10:30 a.m.	2	Flax waffles with peanut butter
	1½ cups	Assam tea with ~5 tablespoons soy milk
12:30 p.m.	¾ cup	Granola with hemp seeds and flax seeds
	¾ cup	Soy milk
2:00 p.m.	¾ cup	Steamed carrots
	~30	Steamed green beans
	6 pieces	Chickpea falafel
3:00 p.m.	1 square	70 percent dark chocolate
	Medium	Soy decaf latte
5:30 p.m.	2 pieces	Chickpea falafel
	~20	Steamed green beans
	½ cup	Steamed carrots

8:30 p.m.	2 cups	Tofu yellow curry (with carrots, mushrooms, brocolli, cauliflower, cabbage, etc.)
	1 cup	Jasmine rice
	1 cup	Soy milk
10:10 p.m.	1 scoop	Protein shake

Day 3

7:45 a.m.	¾ cup (dry)	Oatmeal with soy milk
10:00 a.m.	200ml	Soy milk
10:30 a.m.	1 scoop	Protein shake
11:30 a.m.	2	Flax waffles with peanut butter
	1½ cups	Assam tea with ~5 tablespoons soy milk
2:30 p.m.	250 grams	Veggie beefless "tips"
	1 cup	Mixed greens
4:00 p.m.	1 slice	Homemade limoncello cake (no frosting)
	½ cup	Ginger kombucha
7:00 p.m.	1½ cups	Stir-fried carrot, onion, broccolini, bok choy
	¾ cup	Veggie "chicken" in orange sauce
	½ cup	Basmati rice cooked in vegetable stock
	¼ cup	Caramelized onions
	2 tablespoons	Hemp hearts
10:00 p.m.	1 scoop	Protein shake
	2 teaspoons	Chia seeds

Day 4

7:00 a.m.	½ cup (dry)	Oatmeal with soy milk
9:45 a.m.	1	Grapefruit (broiled)
10:00 a.m.	1½ cups	Chai latte: homemade slow cooker tea and spice concentrate plus ½ cup soy milk
12:00 p.m.	1 cup	Hemp/flax seed granola
	1 cup	Soy milk
1:45 p.m.	1 cup	Fajita filling (tofu, carrots, spices, broccoli, onion, green onion)
	½ cup	Kidney beans and black beans

	1	Flax tortilla
	1 cup	Baby kale
	3 pieces	Chickpea falafel
	10 pieces	Roasted seaweed
2:30 p.m.	1 cup	Chai latte: homemade slow cooker tea and spice concentrate plus ½ cup soy milk
4:40 p.m.	1 cup	Fajita filling (tofu, carrots, spices, broccoli, onion, green onion)
	1 cup	Baby kale
	½ cup	Kidney beans and black beans
	8	*Late July* brand crackers
7:00 p.m.	200ml	Soy milk
8:30 p.m.	Giant	Salad: Baby kale, lots of chickpeas, purple cabbage, mushrooms, hemp hearts
	1 tablespoon each	Olive oil and balsamic vinegar
10:00 p.m.	6	*Late July* brand crackers
10:45 p.m.	1 serving	Vega protein shake

CHAPTER 7: THINKING AHEAD: TIME- AND SANITY-SAVING NUTRITION TIPS FOR WORK, TRAVEL, AND HOME

Staying on track with a healthy diet becomes a bit more challenging when you're not in the comfort of your own home. However, with the right know-how and a bit of practice, it'll become second nature. This chapter shows you how you can easily maintain a healthy, plant-based diet that will fuel your active lifestyle when you're at work, traveling, or otherwise on the go. I'll also share some daily food preparation tips that will simplify your nutrition—and your life.

VEGAN FOOD PREP

Many athletes like the convenience of having food ready to go during the week, without having to cook on a daily basis. Batch-cooking once or twice a week can save a lot of time, and it ensures you're one step ahead of yourself when it comes to nutrition. (Hungry? Great! There's food already prepped. You don't have to raid the kitchen or cook while you're famished.)

Vegan food prepping is simple: find recipes you like, and make large batches. It helps if you have a large freezer, but it's not required.

Here's what I do for my own food prep:
Once a month:
- Giant batch of chickpea protein balls (kept in freezer)
- Thirty containers with smoothie ingredients (frozen strawberries, blueberries, and blackberries; chia, hemp, and flax seeds; flax oil; peanut butter; and rolled oats). For my daily smoothie, I'll defrost the ingredients in the microwave for 30 seconds, add soy milk, and blend

Every two weeks:
- Twelve to eighteen flatbread pizzas (kept in the freezer)
- Big batch of red lentil dhal (half is frozen for the following week)
- Homemade granola (for fruit/yogurt parfaits; see below)

Every week:
- Four almond/coconut yogurt parfaits with blueberries, raspberries, and pomegranate seeds (my husband eats these with granola)

- Buddha bowl ingredients (see Buddha bowl section below for more info).
- Tofu scramble with mushrooms, kale, onion, and carrot.
- Tabouleh salad: cucumber, cherry tomato, parsley, green onion.

PREPARING HEALTHY PLANT-BASED FOOD FOR WORK AND TRAVEL

Having to resort to buying your lunches while at work not only limits your healthy meal options, but also cuts into your bank account. Once packing food for the day becomes routine, you won't even notice the small amount of effort it takes. You could, for example, pack leftovers from the previous day's dinner, complemented with fresh fruit, veggies and hummus, trail mix, protein bars, or brown rice crackers.

For the four days a week that I used to train clients in person, I spent between eight and eleven hours at the gym each day. As someone who needed about 3,000 calories per day, my food preparation was very important! I was lucky enough to have available a microwave, kettle, and sink for trainers to use, as well as a large grocery store right next door. Everyone at the studio knew my signature meals: either a yam, zucchini, and mushrooms cooked in the microwave plus an *Eating Right* split pea soup made with hot water from the kettle, or a big bowl of microwaved frozen veggies with chickpeas, hemp hearts, and a bit of soy sauce I kept in the communal fridge. If you have a microwave or kettle at work, make use of them!

Packing food for travel can be a bit more complicated, depending upon how you're traveling and for how long you'll be away. With some careful planning, though, you'll always have available many plant-based options. I never leave for a trip—even for a single night—without a large bag of food in tow. Here are the nonperishables I packed for a recent two-night trip:

- 4 *Simply Protein* bars
- Ziploc bag with oats to make oatmeal in the microwave
- Ziploc bag with 3 servings of protein powder
- Matcha powder
- 3 200mL soy milk boxes
- 2 instant miso soup packets
- 1 box brown rice crackers
- Loose leaf peppermint and green tea
- 3 homemade fruit leathers

Often I look for hotels, condos, or Airbnbs with full kitchens so I can supplement what I bring with fresh foods. On this particular trip my husband and I stayed at an Airbnb with a fridge and full kitchen in the suite, so I also packed perishable items:

- 1 package shirataki tofu noodles (to add to the miso soup listed above)
- Natural peanut butter (for rice crackers listed above)
- 3 cups prepared *Tofu Scramble* (see page 143 for recipe)
- 3 cups homemade Applesauce (see page 273 for recipe)
- Kale, mushrooms, and cucumber for salad
- Hemp hearts in a Ziploc bag
- Ground flax seed in a Ziploc bag
- 4 *Absurdly Healthy Supercookies* (see page 276 for recipe)

If I weren't extremely allergic to raw fruit and tree nuts, I would have also packed apples, bananas, cashews, almonds, and other fruits and nuts.

Sound like a lot of work to prepare to this extent? The first few times I packed food like this, it was a bit of a hassle, but it soon became easy. It now takes what seems like almost no extra time. While doing my regular grocery shopping I instinctively buy extra foods I'll need for travel, then I stuff them into my luggage, and I'm ready. The small amount of preparation involved is completely worth it when you know you'll have healthy food options while on the go.

If you're travelling by plane, make sure you Google the airports you'll be at to find out what food options you may have there. There are usually a few vegan options at airports, even if they're just salads or soups. Know what's available, and plan accordingly.

> *"The small amount of preparation involved is completely worth it when you know you'll have healthy food options while on the go."*

One of my best friends, Holly, was a mining engineer for a decade. We met in eighth grade gym class, bonding over the fact that we were both vegetarian. We later both made the transition to veganism. Before she started a career coaching business, Holly spent much of her work time traveling. She worked two weeks on, two weeks off. That meant she worked very long hours for two weeks in a small mining town in Quebec, then had two weeks off in our hometown of Vancouver, BC. Rinse and repeat. Often she'd travel to other mining sites around the globe, with accommodation that often had no cooking facilities. She became an expert in eating healthy vegan foods while traveling, with limited cooking options. Here are some of Holly's tips for savvy plant-based travelers who want to stay healthy. Take it away, Holly!

- I usually shop for groceries instead of trying to find something I can eat at a restaurant. There are some awesome options from the grocery store if you have access to a fridge and microwave.
- If I'm not going for very long (just a few days), I try to minimize the amount of things I have to buy. I'll try to go to Tim Hortons or some similar joint and pick up some plastic utensils and cardboard coffee cups (larger size is better). I use them and then (attempt to) wash them with the hotel-provided soap.

- If I'm going for more than about a week, I'll usually buy a set of cheap Tupperware or a bowl (to microwave food in), a knife (so much better than a plastic knife), a fork, a spoon, a plate (to cut things on), a sponge, and the cheapest dish detergent I can find. I usually buy those things at Walmart so I don't cut into my daily budget too much.
- If you're staying somewhere with no fridge or microwave, you can usually still kind of "cook" if you get hot water at coffee shops or convenience stores. If it's winter, you can buy perishable food and store it in the trunk of your car (I do this all the time)!
- I usually bring protein bars with me because protein options are tough to come by when you're vegan and traveling in remote areas of Canada. They can be fairly high in calories depending upon the brand, so I usually eat a third at breakfast, and the other two thirds at brunch and linner [that's Holly's combination of lunch and dinner]. [Karina's note: *Simply Protein* bars are low in calories and sugar, but high in protein!]
- Here's a list of foods you can buy at the grocery store that can basically be eaten without any cutting or cooking:
  - Mini soy milk packs (unsweetened!)
  - Dessert tofu packages
  - Soy nuts and roasted edamame
  - Hummus
  - Healthy dried soups (e.g., black bean, pea, miso, etc.)
  - Asian-type dried noodle soups (e.g., Annie's has udon noodle soup in different flavors)
  - Pita, bagels, or bread
  - Rice crackers
  - Arrowroot cookies
  - Low sugar cereal (but you need a bowl or disposable coffee cup)
  - Snow peas
  - Cherry tomatoes
  - Regular tomatoes (eat them like apples)
  - Red, orange, or yellow bell peppers (eat them like apples, too)
  - Mini applesauce cups
  - Prewashed spring mix salads, arugula, or spinach. You can buy dressing, or sometimes there are mini packs. If neither of those is appealing, you can mix your hummus into the salad.
  - Mini carrots
- Here's a list of foods that you can cook with a microwave, fridge, and access to a knife. The key to these is that they can be microwaved in a reasonable amount of time.
  - Vegan "chicken" breasts or strips
  - Amy's brand frozen shepherd's pie or lasagna
  - *Uncle Ben's* instant brown rice cups

- Broccoli or cauliflower
- Zucchini
- Green beans
- Bell peppers (any color)
- Green onions
- Canned soups or chilis (you need to pack or buy a can opener)
- Canned baked beans (check for lard/pork!)
- Lemons [Karina's note: how about cooking some broccoli, cauliflower, mini carrots, and bell peppers in the microwave, then drizzling with fresh lemon juice?]

EATING OUT: RESTAURANTS AND DINNER PARTIES

One of the few struggles I face in being vegan (let alone one who tries to eat a very nutritious diet) is not wanting to make dinner hosts feel imposed upon. Before going for dinner hosted at a friend's house, I'll always eat a small meal so I don't show up ravenous. Often I'm eating with family and friends and I know what will be prepared, but it's always a good idea to bring a dish of your own to share. That way, not only will you have something to fall back on in case you have limited options, but you'll also spread some vegan love and deliciousness, showing that vegan food doesn't have to be exclusively for health nuts who eat only "weird" food. (But we all knew that already, right?)

Because I've been vegan since 2003—more than half my life at the time of this book's publication!—everyone I know is well acquainted with my dietary habits. In my case, it's more challenging to deal with my many food allergies than it is to deal with the fact that I'm vegan. One of my strong suits is creating delicious vegan desserts, so that's what I'll most often bring to share, after making sure I'll have a healthy main course option to eat. I know from experience that bringing mouth-watering vegan desserts to share—even simple ones like dark chocolate–dipped strawberries—is always appreciated and spreads the word about plant-based diets at the same time! I often bring veggie burgers and/or salads to barbeques, or a simple side dish like roasted veggies to other dinner gatherings.

I lived most of my life in Vancouver, BC, where eating out on a vegan diet is very easy. If you're a new vegan it might take some experimentation and learning about options, but many larger cities have vegan-friendly restaurants. If you find yourself in a city with limited vegan options or at a restaurant that isn't particularly veg-friendly (or a small town like the one in which I live now), don't be afraid to ask the chef to make you something off-menu.

If you're searching for a restaurant that will have many plant-based options, non-Western fare is often a good bet. Asian restaurants will have brown rice, steamed vegetables, edamame, or rice noodles. Sushi joints—one of my favorite types of restaurant—are great for vegans. More and more sushi restaurants now carry brown rice as a healthy option. You could order miso soup if it doesn't contain fish, any number of vegetable rolls or cones, gomae (spinach salad with peanut dressing), tofu teriyaki, etc. Thai restaurants almost always have vegan options; just ask that your meal be made 100 percent vegetarian (there's often fish in dishes like vegetable curry). Italian restaurants will have tomato-based sauces, salads, and more—just make sure to tell them to hold the cheese. You can even go to a steak house and get a satisfying vegan meal! I had some of the most delicious veggie fajitas I've ever eaten at a local steak house once, made with portobello mushrooms and lettuce wraps. If there's nothing like that on the menu, have them make you a baked potato, big salad with balsamic vinaigrette, and/or steamed veggies. Check out www.happycow.net for vegetarian- and vegan-friendly restaurant listings from around the world. Although it may take some extra planning and working off the menu, going out for dinner—either at someone's house or at a restaurant—doesn't have to be difficult on a healthy, vegan diet.

DAILY FOOD PREPARATION TIPS TO SIMPLIFY YOUR LIFE

It's Thursday night, and you've just come home from work. It's been a long week and a particularly stressful day, so you haven't had much time to cook, or even to eat. You're ravenous, but the only foods in your house are unhealthy snacks staring you down from the cupboards. Of course, those would derail your healthy eating plans. With a few tweaks to your food-making routine, you can prevent situations like this and be better equipped to tackle hunger with healthy eats. (What are all those treats doing in your cupboard in the first place, anyway?!) Here are a few simple food preparation tips that may save you some time and keep you prepared for healthy, plant-based eating throughout the day.

Make Large Amounts of Food

This is a very simple strategy, but it is one of the best ways you can minimize spent time in the kitchen while maximizing the amount of ready-made meals you have available.

- Double a recipe and use leftovers for lunch or dinner the following day, or with dishes like soups and stews, freeze leftovers for later use.
- When you prepare even something simple, make extra servings to eat later. When I make a salad, I store two or three additional servings in Tupperware containers for the next day or two. It takes almost no extra time, and saves having to pull out the cutting board and prepare all the veggies the next time I want a salad.
- Reserve one day a week when you can spend some extra time in the kitchen. Cook a few different dishes (or a large batch of one dish) to have ready for the week. Also prepare a few snacks like homemade trail mix or hummus. You could even put together Ziploc containers or bags of smoothie ingredients and store them in the freezer. When you need a smoothie, all you have to do is empty the bag and blend. These methods of food preparation are well known among both professional and amateur athletes—we're all busy

people and need to prepare ourselves for the week ahead using the least amount of time possible.

The Wonderful World of Slow Cookers

This is one kitchen appliance I'd highly recommend purchasing, if you don't have one already. Not only are slow cooker recipes ridiculously easy and time-efficient, but they also taste extra delicious after simmering for several hours. You can throw together your meal before work in 10 to 15 minutes and come home to a ready-made dinner!

Slow cookers simplify recipes that would otherwise take more effort. Try any soup or stew recipe in this book in your slow cooker. Just throw in all the ingredients and set to "low" for about 6 hours, or "high" for about 4 hours. Add ingredients such as greens, fresh herbs, and pasta during the last 30 minutes of cooking.

Note that food at the bottom of the slow cooker cooks faster than food at the top. You can layer foods, such as lentils and split peas at the bottom, yams and potatoes near the middle, and broccoli at the top. Also, no peeking! Lifting the lid leads to temperature loss, and you'll need to add on twenty minutes or so of cooking time for each peek. Instead, spin the lid to disperse condensation and take a peek in that way if you need to.

Plan Your Meals

A little forethought can go a long way when it comes to healthy plant-based eating.

- Create a menu plan for the week and make sure you have all ingredients available. If you're making and using leftovers (and you should!), you need to prepare only three or four meals per week. My sister-in-law uses a blackboard on her apartment wall to plan meals, so she and my brother-in-law can easily see the whole week's plan and what will be needed. I use a dedicated list in my "Reminders" app on my phone. All you need to plan is what you're making on which day, and which ingredients to buy on your weekly grocery trip.
- Pack your meals for work the night before so you don't have to worry about it in the morning. Pack a lunch bag and keep it in the fridge. You could even throw together all the ingredients for a morning smoothie; all you need to do is blend it in the morning.

Grocery Delivery Companies

When I lived in Vancouver, I'd take five minutes each week to order groceries online. Every Wednesday afternoon, I'd find my box of groceries outside my apartment door, packed and delivered by my local organics company (www.spud.ca). It really doesn't get much easier than that! Search Google for grocery delivery companies in your area. You'll save yourself a lot of time, and you're also being more eco-friendly by saving car trips to the grocery store, supporting sustainable and organic agriculture, and buying locally.

Prices at organics delivery companies are generally not more than what you'd pay at the grocery store, although of course this varies by company. The company I used offered free delivery with orders over thirty-five dollars, and I saved money by not paying for gas.

I still headed to my grocery store on a regular basis, but having my organics delivery each week with fresh produce, staples like flours and grains, and household items, saved me a lot of time.

Now that my husband and I live in Powell River, BC, we use our local grocery store's online ordering feature. We keep a running grocery list throughout the week in the store's app. We submit our order on Friday nights, and Saturday mornings we pick up our order, with store staff even bringing it to our car!

CHAPTER 8: NUTRITION FOR VEGAN ATHLETES

If you're very active and eat a plant-based diet, this chapter is for you. I'll go over a few challenges often encountered by athletes who are newly vegan, and then we'll take a look at six specific nutrients you'll need to consider. Next, I'll cover everyone's favorite vegan nutrition topic—protein!—followed by a discussion of supplements you may want to consider.

OVERALL FOOD VOLUME

Whole, plant-based foods are typically very nutrient-dense, and not very calorie-dense. You can eat a salad the size of your torso for only a few hundred calories! To fuel a very active lifestyle, you'll need to ensure you're consuming enough calories for your specific goals.

You may notice that on a vegan diet, you need to eat a larger volume of food to get the same number of calories you used to get as an omnivore. Use an app like MyFitnessPal or Cronometer to track your calories for a while, just to be sure.

Losing Weight Unintentionally?

Sometimes, athletes who go vegan will lose weight unintentionally. As mentioned, whole, plant-based foods are typically not as calorie-dense as most animal products (which is good news if your goal is to *lose* weight!). If you're concerned about losing weight, it may help to keep track of your calories for the first few weeks of your transition. This way, you can know for sure if you're hitting your mark or if you're at a deficit.

Hungry All the Time?

If you're consistently hitting your calorie goal—and you're still feeling hungry—check that you're consuming enough protein and healthy fats for your particular goals. Protein, especially, is very satiating, so focus on ingredients like seitan, tofu, and tempeh. Fiber is also very satiating, so fill your plate with whole grains, legumes, and veggies.

NUTRIENTS OF NOTE FOR VEGAN ATHLETES

A well-planned, whole foods, plant-based diet is extremely beneficial to your health. A few nutrients found abundantly in animal-based foods may need special attention, to ensure you're consuming enough of them on a plant-based diet—especially if you're active.

To make extra sure you're not only consuming but also *absorbing* enough of the nutrients you need, make sure to get regular blood tests, at least annually. You'll be able to check for nutrients like B12, iron, zinc, and vitamin D. If it turns out you're low in any of these, work with your healthcare provider and/or a registered dietitian on supplementation. (Note: being low in nutrients like iron and B12 is *not* a vegan-specific issue. Many people are low in these nutrients, whether they're vegan or not.)

Six Extra-Important Micronutrients
Iron

Iron is necessary for producing red blood cells, and it helps to carry oxygen throughout the body. It's more difficult for the body to absorb plant-based sources of iron. Make sure you're regularly including lots of iron-rich foods in your diet, like soy products, dried apricots, fortified grain products, blackstrap molasses, beans, lentils, artichokes, and dark leafy greens.

RDA: 8 milligrams per day for men and women over age 50, and 18 milligrams for women aged 19-50.

Note: Don't take iron supplements without medical supervision! Iron is not something our bodies can excrete if we get too much of it.

B12

All vegans should take a B12 supplement—either a sublingual pill or a liquid. Vitamin B12 is produced by bacteria. In centuries past, we'd get B12 from soil particles on our food, but this is no longer the case. (By the way, the reason animal products contain B12 is because those animals themselves were given B12 supplements, not because there's B12 inherent in meat, eggs, etc.)

Vitamin B12 is crucial for keeping blood and nerve cells healthy, and helping the body to use fats. B12 deficiency is extremely dangerous and can result in nerve damage. So don't take any chances—take your supplement! Typical supplement doses are in the 500 to 1000 microgram range. Adults need only 2.4 micrograms per day, but we don't absorb all the B12 in our supplements (or food). Don't worry about taking too much—your body will just excrete what it doesn't need.

In addition to your supplement, great sources of this vitamin include nutritional yeast, fortified non-dairy milks like soy and almond, and fortified meat alternatives.

RDA: 2.4 micrograms per day for all adults.

Calcium

Calcium is necessary for healthy bones, and helps muscles to contract. Plant-based sources of calcium include almonds, tahini (sesame butter), figs, tofu, collard greens, and fortified non-dairy beverages. Did you know that a glass of fortified soy milk has more calcium than a glass of cow's milk? One cup of cow's milk typically contains 30 percent of the RDA, whereas one cup of fortified soy milk (e.g., the Silk brand) contains 45 percent of the RDA.

Unlike nutrients like B12, iron, and vitamin D, you can't measure your body's calcium levels via blood work. To ensure you're getting enough calcium, track your food for at least a few days using MyFitnessPal or Cronometer.

RDA: 1000 milligrams per day, and 1200 milligrams per day for women aged 50+ and men aged 70+. The World Health Organization recommends 500 milligrams per day.

Vitamin D

Vitamin D is essential for strong bones and teeth, helping the body to absorb and use calcium and phosphorous. Find Vitamin D in fortified cereals and non-dairy beverages, and, of course, by spending time in sunlight. For most people living in the northern hemisphere, a vitamin D supplement is necessary to get optimal levels.

RDA: 600 International Units (15 micrograms) per day for adults under 70, and 800 International Units (20 micrograms) per day for adults over 70.

Omega-3 fatty acids

Omega-3 fatty acids play a crucial role in brain function, reduce inflammation, and may help prevent heart disease. Plant foods rich in omega-3's include flaxseed oil and ground flaxseed, walnuts, sacha inchi seeds, chia seeds, and hemp hearts.

DHA is a type of omega-3 fatty acid. You probably know that fish oil is a good source of omega-3's, but did you know that the omega-3 in fish comes from the algae they eat? Why not get your nutrition straight from the source?! You can get algal DHA oil to use as a supplement. Research is still ongoing, so there's no consensus on daily dosage. Follow the manufacturer's instructions, and/or check with your healthcare provider.

RDA: There are no set standards for omega-3 intake. Most organizations recommend a minimum of 250-500 milligrams of combined EPA and DHA daily for most adults.

Zinc

We need zinc for proper immune system function, growth and development across the body, wound healing, and more.

Vegan foods high in zinc include pumpkin seeds, almonds, peanuts, peas, fortified oatmeal and cereals, and sesame seeds.

RDA: 8 milligrams per day for women, and 11 milligrams per day for men.

Nutrition Considerations for Vegan Athletes

I interviewed registered dietitian Susan Levin for insight into special considerations vegan athletes (or vegans who are very active) may need to make when it comes to nutrition. Ms. Levin has a specialty certification in sports dietetics. She is the director of nutrition education for the Physicians Committee for Responsible Medicine, a Washington, D.C.-based nonprofit organization dedicated to promoting preventive medicine—especially better nutrition—and higher standards in research. She researchers and writes about the connection between plant-based diets and a reduced risk of chronic diseases. She also assists in teaching nutrition and health classes to participants in clinical studies that explore the links between diet and various medical conditions. Ms. Levin is an avid runner and a VegRUN.org coach.

Other than an overall increase in calories, how should a vegan athlete's diet differ from someone who is less active? Are there any particular nutrients to take note of for endurance athletes versus strength athletes?

For starters, an athlete's dietary needs may not change that much regardless of dietary preference, depending on the level of activity. So if you follow a vegan diet and start exercising the minimal recommended amount, your natural hunger cues tend to take care of your increased needs. For athletes who train regularly, carbohydrates should always be the bulk of the diet. Endurance and strength training both call for increased protein, but only slightly for endurance training (from 0.8 grams per kilogram of body weight to 1.3 to 1.5 grams per kilogram of body weight per day). For strength training, those needs range from approximately 1.2 to 1.8 grams per kilogram of body weight per day. Athletes should keep in mind that most of us consume about twice our needs in protein without even trying. Protein is not hard to get!

Because plant foods are nutrient-dense as opposed to calorie-dense, a vegan athlete who trains intensely and regularly may find that he or she needs to eat more often in order to maintain weight and to prevent weight loss. For these athletes, smoothies and shakes are good options to supplement the diet throughout training.

Any thoughts on how a vegan diet could potentially benefit the performance or recovery of athletes? Peer-reviewed research is sparse on this subject, but public interest seems to be growing.

I think a lot of athletes approach training as a time to teach the body how to get faster or stronger through repetition of a specific exercise. What training really is, is a time to figure out how the body excels at a particular event. That means, among other things, figuring out how to fuel for optimal performance. Many professional athletes have realized, through trial and error, that a vegan diet allows them to train more often because of the shorter recovery time needed.

There are several theories as to why a vegan diet would be better than other diets. Training is actually a stress on the body and its immune function. A vegan diet full of fruits, vegetables, grains, and legumes provides a clear immune boost with its high antioxidant content (and avoidance of pro-inflammatory products found in meat and dairy products). This immune boost could be what allows vegan athletes to train and recover in rapid succession.

Plant-based fitness is burgeoning among professional and amateur athletes alike. Any thoughts on this trend overall?
I'm thrilled to see the trend, because adopting a nutrition or exercise plan should support all aspects of health, not just one like weight loss or strength. That's what I love about the combination of a vegan diet and exercise—it supports heart health, cancer prevention, diabetes prevention, healthy body weight, less joint pain, improved mood, less risk of dementia, and the list goes on and on. I only see the trend continuing as more people experience the benefits firsthand.

BUT . . . WHAT ABOUT PROTEIN?

The myth that vegans don't get enough protein is still—unfortunately—prevalent. In this section I'll go over why that's completely false, how much protein you actually need, and how easy it is to get your protein needs met on a plant-based diet.

All foods contain amino acids, the building blocks of protein, and most foods contain at least some ready-made protein.

How Much Protein Do I Need?

There are no one-size-fits-all protein recommendations like there are for nutrients like iron, B12, and zinc. Your protein needs depend on many factors like your body weight, overall activity level, and the type of training you do.

Government health organizations recommend that most people get between 10 percent and 35 percent of their total calories from protein. On the low end (which includes sedentary people), that's about 46 grams per day for women and 56 grams per day for men. This is extremely simple to achieve. Did you know 100 grams of rolled oats contains 16 grams of protein? Or that one cup of tempeh has between 30 and 40 grams of protein?

Highly active people, especially those who strength train, require higher protein intakes than sedentary people. Based on Susan Levin's recommendations from the previous section, a female who weighs 140 pounds (63.5 kilos) and strength trains regularly would need 114 grams of protein per day, at the high end of the scale. If she eats 2000 calories per day, that's 23 percent of her total calorie intake coming from protein, which is easy to achieve on a plant-based diet.

My friend and colleague Dr. Anastasia Zinchenko (PhD in biochemistry, competitive bodybuilder, and powerlifter) has conducted her own research into vegan athletes' protein needs. She found that slightly higher protein intakes may be optimal: between 1.8 and 2.5 grams of protein per kilogram of body weight per day. Her research focused on advanced strength athletes who train most days of the week, so if you're just getting into strength training or are at an intermediate level, you likely won't need as much protein.

MYTH: If you eat enough calories, you'll automatically get enough protein.

"If you eat enough calories, you'll get enough protein without even thinking about it!" is something I hear quite often in the vegan world. For sedentary people, this is likely accurate. But if you strength train, you'll need to pay attention to your protein intake. If you're inactive, you need 0.8 grams of protein per kilogram of bodyweight per day. For a 150-pound person, this works out to 54 grams of protein per day. That's tofu scramble for breakfast, a black bean burrito for lunch, and dry-roasted edamame as a snack. You've hit your protein goal even before having dinner!

If you're a 150-pound strength athlete, you'll need between 122 and 170 grams of protein per day. A day's worth of protein for this athlete may include a tofu scramble with seitan strips for breakfast; a smoothie made with hemp hearts, chia and flax seeds, and protein powder for a snack; a lunch of edamame pasta with tomato sauce and veggie ground round, and a black bean burrito for dinner. Hitting your daily protein goal is definitely attainable as a strength athlete—it just takes a bit more thought when it comes to mealtime.

So, Where Do I Get My Protein?

There are many excellent plant-based sources of protein! Here are just a few:

- Edamame (soy beans, either steamed or dry roasted)
- Seitan
- Quinoa
- Beans (e.g., kidney, navy, fava, pinto, cannellini, chickpea)
- Lentils (e.g., red, green, brown, French)
- Nuts (e.g., almonds, hazelnuts, pistachios, cashews, walnuts)
- Seeds (e.g., hemp, flax, chia, sesame, sacha inchi, pumpkin, sunflower)
- Nut butter (e.g., peanut or almond)
- Non-dairy milks (soy has the highest protein content)
- Tofu
- Tempeh

The tables below list vegan, whole food protein sources, starting with balanced protein sources (high protein levels and relatively low carb and fat levels). I'll then list protein sources that are higher in carbs, followed by protein sources higher in fat.

Balanced protein sources (per 100 grams)

	Calories	Carbs (g)	Protein (g)	Fat (g)
Almond flour (fat reduced)	315	4	40	11
Black bean pasta	165	15	22.5	2
Coconut flour (fat reduced)	368	22	17	16
Firm tofu	96	2.5	12	5
Miso	180	23	11	11
Nutritional yeast	390	45	50	5
Seitan	111	4	21	2
Soy flour	424	16	40	20
Tempeh	193	9	19	11
Textured vegetable protein	362	38	50	1
Vital wheat gluten	390	13	76	2

Protein sources higher in carbs (per 100 grams uncooked)

	Calories	Carbs (g)	Protein (g)	Fat (g)
Amaranth	371	65	14	7
Black kidney beans	252	44	22	1.4
Butter beans	338	63	21	1
Chickpeas	364	61	19	6
Lentils	353	60	26	1
Mung beans	347	63	24	1
Oats	379	69	13	7
Quinoa	368	64	14	6
Split peas	341	60	25	1

Protein sources higher in fats (per 100 grams)

	Calories	Carbs (g)	Protein (g)	Fat (g)
Almond butter	650	6.5	25.5	58
Almonds	612	7	21	63

Cashews	590	31	20	67
Chia seeds	418	20	21	46
Flax seeds	480	6	23	41
Hemp seeds	514	15	30	41
Peanut butter	579	12	30	56
Pistachios	571	28	21	38
Pumpkin seeds	541	18	25	51
Sunflower seeds	584	20	21	54
Tahini	678	11	27	56
Black sesame seeds	518	21.5	22	38

Don't I Need Whey Protein?

The short answer: nope.

Whey (derived from dairy) has long been a protein shake staple for many strength athletes, but this is changing—and quickly.

Whey contains slightly higher amounts of branched chain amino acids, which can help with muscle-building, than most plant-based protein powders. However, this doesn't seem to translate into any measurable differences in real life: most studies on the subject found that subjects gained similar amounts of muscle and strength whether they were supplementing with whey or a plant-based protein (usually pea).

For example, a 2015 study[*] published in the *Journal of the International Society of Sports Nutrition* had participants (men aged 18 to 35) pair their strength training with either whey or pea protein supplementation. All participants increased the size of their biceps muscles, with no differences between groups.

A 2019 study[†] measured a variety of variables, including body composition, muscle thickness, force production, workout performance, and strength. There were no significant differences between groups in any of these variables between participants who supplemented with pea protein versus those who supplemented with whey.

If you're concerned about getting all your essential amino acids, a 70 percent pea and 30 percent rice protein blend is very similar in amino acid profile to whey protein.

---

[*]   Babult, N., et al. (2015). Pea proteins oral supplementation promotes muscle thickness gains during resistance training: a double-blind, randomized, placebo-controlled clinical trial vs. whey protein. Journal of the International Society of Sports Nutrition, 12(3). Accessed February 12, 2020 at https://jissn.biomedcentral.com/articles/10.1186/s12970-014-0064-5.

[†]   Banaszek, A., et a. (2019). The Effects of Whey vs. Pea Protein on Physical Adaptations Following 8-Weeks of High-Intensity Functional Training (HIFT): A Pilot Study. Sports (Basel), 7(1), 12. Accessed February 12, 2020 at https://www.ncbi.nlm.nih.gov/pmc/articles/PMC6358922/.

What's the Deal with Soy? Won't It Give Me Man-Boobs and Cancer?

There's no need to worry about soy, unless you're legitimately allergic to it. Soy is one of the best protein sources we vegans have access to, so go for it! Fears about soy messing with your hormones, leading to man-boobs, or causing cancer are completely unfounded. When you look at the research that's been done on soy intake, it's associated with health benefits and cancer prevention, rather than the opposite.

Let's call in an expert: registered dietitian and director of nutrition education for the Physicians Committee for Responsible Medicine, Susan Levin.

Take it away, Susan!

I'm not exactly sure how soy got its bad rap. It's one of those nutrition mysteries, like when protein became an elusive, hard-to-find nutrient or when milk became synonymous with bone health. I guess hammering away at untruths for long enough can actually be effective. I could insert an allusion to US elections here, but I'll refrain(-ish). Regardless of how the misinformation started or even how it was spread, the evidence does not support reason to fear soy products. So let's break it down by categories and follow the trail of science.

Cancer

Let's start with one of the biggest misconceptions—soy products increase your risk for cancer, specifically breast cancer. Soybeans and many other foods contain isoflavones, natural compounds whose chemical structure is vaguely similar to estrogens. Some people have called these compounds "phytoestrogens" ("phyto" comes from the Greek word for "plant").

In 2008, researchers combined the results of eight prior studies on the relationship between soy products and breast cancer, finding that women who had the most soy—in the form of soy milk, tofu, etc.—were 29 percent less likely to develop breast cancer, compared with women who ate little or no soy products.* In 2014, researchers looked again, this time combining the results of 35 prior studies. Again, soy had a preventive effect, cutting breast cancer risk by 41 percent.†

So soy products appear to reduce the likelihood that breast cancer will strike. But what about women who have had cancer already? Some women who have been treated for breast cancer avoid soy products, on the theory that soybeans contain estrogens that can make cancer grow. However, in 2012, researchers analyzed the results from 9,514 breast cancer survivors. It turned out that women consuming the

---

*   Wu AH, Yu, MC, Tseng CC, Pike MC. Epidemiology of soy exposures and breast cancer risk. Br J Cancer. 2008;98(1):9-14.

†   Chen M, Rao Y, Zheng Y, et al. Association between soy isoflavone intake and breast cancer risk for pre- and post-menopausal women: a meta-analysis of epidemiological studies. PLoS One. 2014;9(2):e89288.

most soy products had roughly 30 percent less likelihood that their cancer would recur, compared with women who consumed little or no soy.[*]

Male hormones

Soy products have no adverse effects on men and may help prevent cancer in men. A meta-analysis based on more than 50 treatment groups, showed that neither soy products nor isoflavone supplements from soy affect testosterone levels in men.[†] An analysis of 14 studies published in the *American Journal of Clinical Nutrition* showed that increased intake of soy resulted in a 26 percent reduction in prostate cancer risk.[‡] Researchers found a 30 percent risk reduction with nonfermented soy products such as soymilk and tofu.

Thyroid health

Clinical studies show that soy products do not cause hypothyroidism.[§] However, soy isoflavones may take up some of the iodine that the body would normally use to make thyroid hormone.[¶] The same is true of fiber supplements and some medications. In theory, then, people who consume soy might need slightly more iodine in their diets. Soy products can also reduce the absorption of medicines used to treat hypothyroidism. People who use these medicines should check with their health care providers to see if their doses need to be adjusted.

Summary

Soy products are in no way essential. They are very handy for replacing meat, milk, and many other foods, and, if anything, soy products reduce the risk that cancer will ever start and, in women who have been treated for breast cancer already, reduce the risk that cancer will come back. They do not appear to have adverse effects on the thyroid gland, but may reduce the absorption of thyroid medications. The benefits of soy products appear to relate to traditional soy products, not to concentrated soy proteins.

---

[*] Nechuta SJ, Caan BJ, Chen WY, et al. Soy food intake after diagnosis of breast cancer and survival: an in-depth analysis of combined evidence from cohort studies of US and Chinese women. Am J Clin Nutr. 2012;96(1):123-132.
[†] Hamilton-Reeves JM, Vazquez G, Duval SJ, Phipps WR, Kurzer MS, Messina MJ. Clinical studies show no effects of soy protein or isoflavones on reproductive hormones in men: results of a meta-analysis. Fertil Steril. 2010;94:997-1007.
[‡] Yan L, Spitznagel EL. Soy consumption and prostate cancer risk in men: a revisit of a meta-analysis. Am J Clin Nutr. 2009;89:1155-1163.
[§] Messina M, Redmond G. Effects of soy protein and soybean isoflavones on thyroid function in healthy adults and hypothyroid patients: a review of the relevant literature. Thyroid. 2006;16:249-258.
[¶] Divi RL, Chang HC, Doerge DR. Anti-thyroid isoflavones from soybean: isolation, characterization, and mechanisms of action. Biochem Pharmacol. 1997;54:1087-1096.

WHAT SUPPLEMENTS SHOULD I TAKE AS A VEGAN STRENGTH ATHLETE?

We've already covered a few vitamins and minerals you may want to consider supplementing, so this section focuses on supplements specific to athletic performance.

Creatine Monohydrate

Creatine is one of the most well-studied supplements on the market. While our bodies make their own creatine (it's a substance found naturally in muscle cells), we vegans don't get any from our diets. So while you won't be deficient if you don't supplement, taking creatine can improve your short-duration, high-intensity athletic performance—such as sprinting or lifting weights. There may also be cognitive benefits, like slowing down the rate of cognitive degeneration we experience as we age, but more research is required here.

Creatine helps our muscles produce energy, which means it can help us to increase the intensity of our workouts. It's stored in our muscles for longer-term use, which means it doesn't matter when you take it—you don't have to time it around your training.

Creatine as a supplement is synthetically manufactured, so it's not derived from animal products. A daily dose of between 3 and 5 grams of creatine is generally recommended. Make sure you use a powder, rather than capsules, as capsules often contain gelatin (made from animal bones, cartilage, and skin).

Protein Powder

Plant-based protein powder can provide a convenient muscle-building boost (especially because it gives you lots of protein with almost no carbs and fats), but it's not a good idea to rely on it as your main protein source.

The key to a healthy diet is a varied diet, and only by eating a variety of foods can you obtain the wide range of amino acids—the building blocks of protein—you need to thrive. The good news is that all plant foods contain amino acids; they're just present in different proportions. For example, pumpkin seeds and seaweed are high in leucine (required for muscle growth), oats are high in tryptophan (vital to a healthy nervous system), and sunflower seeds are high in methionine (necessary for building cartilage). A protein-shake-and-veggies diet is not going to provide you with enough amino acid variety, so make sure you eat a range of different protein sources. Try to get the bulk of your protein from foods like tempeh, tofu, seitan, black and kidney beans, nutritional yeast, nuts, and seeds. If you need to top off your protein, one or two shakes a day is fine.

The availability of plant-based protein powders has exploded in recent years, so you've got a lot of options: pea, brown rice, pumpkin seed, hemp, soy, and more. Try to get a powder that contains minimal added ingredients, so it's giving you *just* protein (and not also carbs and fats). It's generally recommended to blend powder types so that you get a wider range of amino acids, like using brown rice and pea protein together.

Note: Sorry to break it to you, but there's no such thing as a delicious plant-based protein powder. If you find one that tastes good, it'll more than likely have many additional ingredients in it, possibly even including sugar. Protein powder is the only thing I consume purely for utilitarian purposes.

BCAAs

I included this one in the list because it's extremely popular . . . and ineffective. So don't waste your money! Branched chain amino acids (BCAAs) help us gain muscle and prevent muscle loss when we're fasting—or so we're told by the companies selling them.

BCAAs are comprised of leucine, isoleucine, and valine: 3 essential amino acids (which can't be made by our bodies). However, we can't build muscle unless *all 20* amino acids are present. Your priority should be making sure that your overall protein intake is appropriate for your goals, rather than focusing on just three amino acids.

For people whose protein intakes are extremely low, supplementing with BCAAs *may* be helpful. In this case, though, the first order of business should be increasing overall protein intake, rather than taking a supplement.

CHAPTER 9: INTERVIEWS WITH PLANT-BASED ATHLETES

I've interviewed twenty athletes who eat an exclusively plant-based diet. From dancers and marathon runners to strongmen and bodybuilders, we'll cover a wide range of athletic disciplines. These athletes share their best active living and nutrition tips with you. Whether you're a complete beginner or a seasoned pro, these tips and ideas will help you keep getting results from your health and fitness endeavors, while simplifying your life at the same time. Many of the athletes interviewed here are qualified fitness and/or nutrition professionals, but keep in mind that their suggestions should be taken as ideas to try out, instead of prescriptions for your particular goals and lifestyle. It's always best to see a fitness coach of your own who can help you formulate a plan based on your current fitness level and training priorities.

Each athlete has a unique perspective on eating, training, and vegan ethics. However, I noticed several themes emerging across many different responses. For example, eating five to six small meals throughout the day instead of three larger meals is often suggested in order to stay energized and fuelled for training, as well as to prevent overeating due to hunger. Quality workouts require quality fuel. Also, every athlete I interviewed—no exceptions—packs food for work, travel, and just generally on the go. People who are serious about eating a healthy diet and maintaining an optimal level of physical functioning take responsibility for what they eat. When we're outside of our own homes, we need to be prepared with nutritionally dense meals and snacks.

Many athletes mentioned the role of a plant-based diet in accelerating recovery after training. Athletes, fitness professionals, and nutrition experts are catching on to this idea, but it requires further research studies before we can say for certain. Thwarting stereotypes of skinny, weak vegans—especially for the bodybuilders interviewed here—was another dominant theme. One of my interviewees can deadlift 525 pounds and another runs 100-plus-mile races!

When it comes to giving advice to people just starting out in fitness, many of the vegan athletes I interviewed suggested starting small and focusing on consistency. In the beginning, it's very important to focus on creating habits that will last, like moving your body for at least 20 minutes 3 or 4 times a week—regardless of the particular activity. The importance of enjoying the physical activities you engage in was also often mentioned.

Lastly, these athletes all describe a high quality of life based on their vegan diets. They're able to live in accordance with their values, fuel their preferred physical activities, and better both themselves and the world.

ROBERT CHEEKE

Robert Cheeke is one of the world's foremost plant-based bodybuilders, and wrote the foreword to this book. A vegan since 1995, Robert founded the popular website www.veganbodybuilding. com, authored *Vegan Bodybuilding and Fitness*, and is a Team Vega Ambassador for Sequel Naturals. Thousands of vegans and vegetarians the world over are motivated and inspired by Robert's impressive physique, his remarkable work ethic, and his dedication to improving lives and spreading the message of vegan compassion. For more about Robert and his work, visit www.veganbodybuilding.com. Join him on Facebook at www.facebook.com/ VeganBodybuildingAndFitness and on Twitter at @RobertCheeke.

What are some ways in which your active, plant-based lifestyle contributes to your quality of life? What does it do for you? How does it enhance your life?

The combination of eating plant-based whole foods and exercising regularly is a sure way to support a healthy lifestyle, creating an environment for a good quality of life. That is true for many who fully embrace both nutrition and exercise, and it certainly rings true in my life. I don't like to use the word *busy*, because we all make choices that determine the use of our time—which we should be held accountable for—but I will say I lead a very active life. An energy-producing diet of quality plant foods supports my active lifestyle, and exercising regularly enables me to stay fit, feel young and agile, and add a whole lot of fun to my life. I work on a lot of different projects at once, and I believe both of these lifestyle choices support my ability to take on such an action-packed workload.

Please share your best nutrition tips for vegans who are interested in healthy diets to support their active lifestyles.

When I think of nutrition tips for others, these are the primary things that come to mind:

A. Avoid processed foods as much as possible, consuming only whole plant foods.

B. Realize that most people eat only the same ten foods week after week for their entire lives. Don't fall into that category. Go out of your way to eat a variety of foods, especially a lot of greens, vegetables, and fruits.

C. Eat small meals throughout the day. Constantly nourishing yourself rather than eating a few large meals with long periods of time in between will help you to avoid overeating or undereating. It will also keep you energized throughout the day.

D. Save money by buying bulk foods, eating unprocessed foods, and preparing meals at home instead of eating out.

E. Whole fruits, diverse fruit salads, fresh veggies and hummus, and mixed nuts all make great snacks that take little or no time to prepare and are nutrient dense.

As a plant-based athlete, what sorts of foods do you prepare or pack when you travel?

As an athlete, you always want to be prepared with plenty of fuel so you can be ready to exercise anytime. As a vegan, this is very easy. Fruit is the best fuel source I know of and is plentiful year-round anywhere you have access to a grocery store. I keep a gym bag that contains fruits such as apples, oranges, bananas, and berries, as well as energy and protein bars with me everywhere I go. I'm very fortunate to be working for a wonderful plant-based nutrition company, Vega, and I have access to all the Vega whole-food products including various bars, snacks, and performance drinks. Carrying fruits and Vega with me on road trips, flights, and other travels enables me to eat throughout the day and eliminates the excuse of not having time or food to exercise and recover, grow and build.

You're recognized the world over as a positive, inspirational representation of vegan health and fitness. How do you think your life would have been different, had you not decided to become vegan?

I honestly don't know what my life would be like had I not chosen to become vegan at age fifteen. As an athlete back then, my vegan lifestyle supported my athletic career, prompted me to start my own company, Vegan Bodybuilding & Fitness, and helped me to establish numerous projects stemming from that. My artistic side has been expressed through my documentary and my first book as well as through my website, and all of these platforms are centered around the vegan fitness lifestyle.

My professional job working for Vega also stemmed from my vegan fitness lifestyle. It was through filming my documentary in 2005, which featured Vega's formulator, Brendan Brazier, that I landed my job with Vega that same year. I've been there ever since in a job I enjoy, and I haven't had to search for a new line of work in nearly a decade. A lot of my friends are out of work and struggling to find jobs right now. If not for my unique lifestyle and the situations I created for myself through vegan fitness, perhaps I'd be in the same boat, working a random job for a random company doing something totally normal and not unique. I prefer to be unique and enjoy what I do, and I have the vegan lifestyle to thank for that.

Please share your best active living tips for vegans and vegetarians who are just beginning to exercise, or those who want to be more active.

The best way to make progress and become more fit is to take action and exercise regularly. There is a big difference between wanting and doing. One is an inaction that gets you nowhere and the other is an action that gets you on your way to where you want to go. Keep a training journal to hold yourself accountable, so you're aware of what your training schedule is really like. Without accurate documentation we're likely to think that we're training a lot more often than we really are. That distorted view of reality doesn't help us achieve our goals. Even if reality is hard for us to accept, it is a helpful tool for us on our road to improvement. Simply find ways to maximize the 1,440 minutes you have each day to include some form of exercise daily. That might mean spending less time on the internet or it might require more diligent time management, but these are progressive steps toward being more active and helping to make exercise feel like second nature.

Another tip is to find a form of exercise that is very enjoyable to you. If you don't like riding a bike, chances are good that you won't ride it very often. If you love to dance, dance often. If you'd rather read a history novel than run, don't run. If you'd rather play basketball than watch basketball on TV, play more often. One area a lot of people struggle with is the concept that exercise equates to going to the gym or running on a treadmill. Exercise is anything that elevates your heart rate while your body is in motion. From sex to skateboarding, you've got many options.

What has been the greatest diet- or nutrition-related challenge for you as a plant-based athlete?

The greatest diet-related challenge for me is actually a unique one. The most challenging aspect I've come across is determining which specific vegan diet is the most conducive to my personal and athletic goals. I have followed a standard vegan diet, a soy- and gluten-free vegan diet, a supplement-free vegan diet, a vegan diet with lots of sports supplements, a high-fruit vegan diet, and probably a few other variations as well. I am still determining which one is best for me as far as digestion, how I feel, energy levels, convenience, cost effectiveness, etc. There are a lot of business opportunities to endorse vegan products, but there is also something to be said for just eating healthy plant-based whole foods and getting all nutrition (aside from vitamin B12) from them. I'm still experimenting with my own type of vegan diet.

What are some athletic achievements you'd like to highlight?

Ever since I started exploring Buddhism and Jainism a little over a year ago, I have been less and less interested in achievements. I don't really see the value in comparing myself to others. We're all different. Some of us are faster or stronger than others, but I don't think that makes one person better than another because of it. Some are simply faster and stronger and some are not as fast or strong, but likely have a whole lot to offer in many other areas of life. I used to love competition and when I was a runner I enjoyed winning and succeeding in races. As a bodybuilder I embraced it too, and experienced victory just about as often as defeat. The outcome didn't change what I appreciated about the sports: the hard work and dedication that went into being able to perform at a high level. I think the true essence of sports is to play, not to win. A lot of people use the expression, "In it to win it." I used it many times myself. Now I'm just here to appreciate the art and individual and team expression displayed in athletics. Basically, I want to play and have fun and hope that others have fun in sports too.

Vegans often talk about how our diets allow us to live in accordance with our values. What do you value in life? What's important to you? How do you share this with others?

I've long enjoyed the expression, "deep-rooted belief system" when describing what veganism means to me. I became vegan in 1995 because of a concern for the well-being of animals. I didn't want to cause suffering to innocent animals, and a vegan lifestyle fell in line with my belief system. I value consideration above all else. I look at how considerate others are before I evaluate any other aspect of their character. A considerate person does not mistreat others, does not take advantage of others and does not willingly or knowingly cause needless suffering to others for any reason.

A vegan lifestyle encompasses much more than diet, but diet is an integral part of a compassionate value system. I value peace and compassion, freedom of expression and individualism, and I value kindness perhaps above all. I make an effort to not only live a vegan lifestyle, but a very kind and compassionate lifestyle extending well beyond the inherent underlying issues within the vegan culture, including compassion for all. From the language I choose to use (and choose not to use) to the actions I will or will not take, I strive to live in accordance with a deep-rooted belief system that all of us should be treated kindly as often as possible.

MELODY SCHOENFELD

Melody Schoenfeld, MA, CSCS, has more than twenty-four years of personal training experience. She was 2019's NSCA Personal Trainer of the Year and Personal Fitness Professional's February 2020 Trainer of the Month. She is the owner of Flawless Fitness, a small personal training studio, and Evil Munky Enterprises, a small custom fitness equipment manufacturing business. Melody holds a Master's degree in Health Psychology. She has held state and American records in all three lifts in powerlifting, has competed in strongman events, and performs old-time strongman feats of strength such as tearing phone books and bending steel bars. Her expertise in health and fitness has been featured on numerous television programs throughout the United States, and she has been published and quoted in many publications such as *Shape*, *Oxygen*, and *Men's Fitness*. Melody has several articles published within the *Strength and Conditioning Journal*, and is the author of *Pleasure Not Meating You: A Science-Based Approach to the Vegan Lifestyle (and Some Recipes, Too)*, and her second book will be published this year.

What are some ways in which your active, vegan lifestyle contributes to your quality of life? What does it do for you? How does it enhance your life?

Honestly, what it mostly does for me is make me feel good that I'm living within my moral code. I'm vegan because it's important to me to do the least harm possible to the planet and the creatures on it, and veganism fits in with that goal for me. When I was eating animal products, I had a very hard time rationalizing it in my mind. I know there's no perfect road, but I'm doing the best I can, and I feel good about that.

Please share your best nutrition tips for vegans who are interested in healthy diets to support their active lifestyles.

First of all, you almost definitely need to supplement. B12 (found in many fortified foods) and a vegan DHA/EPA supplement are the most important. I recommend creatine and taurine for vegan athletes. If you're deficient in iron, you may need to add that (talk to your doctor); many athletes lose more iron than non-athletes. Magnesium, vitamin D, and calcium are often deficient—not just in vegans, but in most people.

Second, not all proteins are the same. Different vegan proteins have different amino acid profiles, and it's important to get a wide variety of protein sources each day to make sure your bases are covered. Although the jury is still out in the scientific world of exactly how much protein vegan athletes need, most evidence points to us needing around twice what an omnivore would require. This could change as research on the subject improves, but for now, err on the side of getting more protein than recommended for regular athletes in your class. I try to make sure I get in as much protein as possible at every meal—I do a protein shake for breakfast (21g) with high-protein flax milk (an extra 8g) and a scoop of water lentil powder (an extra 4g). Lunch usually includes sprouted whole grain bread, a big pile of Tofurky slices, a low-sugar vegan protein bar (18g), and some fruit. Dinner varies day to day but always includes more than one kind of vegan protein source (tofu, tempeh, beans, hempseed, bean sprouts, pea sprouts, nutritional yeast, quinoa, etc.). If I'm feeling like I still haven't gotten enough protein, I'll grab another bar or shake if I'm in a hurry.

Third, make sure you're getting enough calories to fuel your sport. Many vegans don't eat enough, and their health suffers as a result.

As a plant-based athlete, what sorts of foods do you prepare or pack when you travel?

My favorite thing about traveling is trying new vegan restaurants (or vegan options at restaurants)! So I tend to eat out a lot. But if those options aren't available, or if I'm pressed for time, I usually grab protein bars, salads, and various healthy meals and snacks at local supermarkets or health food stores.

How do you think your life would have been different, had you not decided to become vegan?

I think I'd just continue to have a hard time reconciling my beliefs with my food. That's really uncomfortable for me.

Do you have any active living tips to share with vegans who are just beginning to exercise, or those who want to be more active?

Feel free to start small. You don't have to do everything at once to get benefits, so try breaking it up throughout the day. Give yourself a goal of, say, 30 minutes of something that gets your heart rate up by the end of the day. So you could do a 5-minute quick walk or jog around the block in the morning, climb stairs for three 5-minute sets during your lunch hour, and have a 10-minute dance party in your living room when you get home. As your fitness improves, add more time to your cardio challenges (i.e., 45 minutes by end-of-day), and try doing more at once (either time-wise, such as 8 minutes instead of 5 at a time, or exertion-wise, such as adding sprints or hills to a walk/jog) if time and ability allow.

With weight training, I really recommend getting at least one session with a really good personal trainer if finances allow in order to be sure you execute moves properly, or use video/YouTube instruction from a trusted source. There are a lot of not-so-good "fit pros" out there, so be sure to check your sources before taking their advice.

Never, ever do something that hurts. Exercise is not comfortable, but there's a big difference between the burn you feel from working your muscles and the pain from an injury. There is absolutely no reason to do a movement that injures you—there are always other options. It isn't "no pain, no gain." It's "no pain, no pain."

What has been the greatest diet- or nutrition-related challenge for you as a plant-based athlete?

The biggest challenge for me was probably quitting eating massive amounts of sugar, although that isn't technically related to my plant-based diet. Anyway, it was one of the hardest diet changes I've ever made, but I got through it! I honestly haven't had too many issues as a plant-based athlete, even when traveling.

How do you promote muscle recovery?

I listen to my body and taper back when I need to. I try to prioritize getting to sleep at a decent hour in relation to my wakeup time, and when I can't get enough sleep at night, I try to take a nap if possible (I'm lucky enough to have a break midday that allows me to do that). If I've been training hard for several months, I often take a week off. I do not train when I'm sick, and I don't ever try to train through pain. I'm a big fan of epsom salt soaks when possible.

What are some athletic achievements you'd like to highlight?

I've held state and American records in all 3 lifts in powerlifting.

I came in second in my class in California's Strongest Woman in 2016 (I pulled a 385-pound deadlift off 18-inch blocks in that competition, which I am especially proud of, considering I weigh between 105 and 110 pounds, depending on what I ate that day).

I perform old-time strongman feats of strength such as bending structural steel bars, nails, and horseshoes, rolling up frying pans, tearing phone books, license plates, and decks of cards, and so forth.

JEFF GOLFMAN

Allow me to introduce the energetic, race-running, eco-entrepreneur, and powerhouse that is raw vegan athlete Jeff Golfman. I had the opportunity to interview him during one of his visits to Vancouver. Jeff is a man of many talents, but I'll focus on his athletic and raw vegan sides here. Check out his website at www.thecoolvegetarian.com to learn more about his eco-business and philanthropic projects.

Jeff enjoys a 100 percent raw vegan diet, has practiced yoga daily for seventeen years, and runs six days per week. He competes in countless races, including 5, 10, and 20 km (in many of which he's come first overall). Some of his amazing personal best times include 10 km in 44:44 and 13.1 miles (21 km) in 1:41:00. The week before our interview, he placed second in his age group in a 20 km race. Impressive!

Jeff says his raw vegan diet provides him with an incredible quality of life. Compared to his previous diet (he's been vegetarian for more than two decades), his 100 percent raw diet provides him with increased energy, better stress management and sleep quality, improved digestion, diminished effects of aging, and the list goes on.

The benefits of a plant-based, whole foods, and in Jeff's case completely raw diet are clear, but how does he do it? Jeff's on a plane several times per week on business. What about eating raw while traveling?

Jeff always packs a food stash, including ground flax, hemp, and chia seeds; celery salt (dehydrated ground celery); a seasoning mix of herbs; and a few fresh lemons. It's easy enough to order a fruit- or vegetable-based salad at any restaurant, to which he can add any of the aforementioned goodies to complete the meal. Complement this with his usual array of smoothies, juices, and other uncooked vegan fare, and you've got a well-rounded 100 percent vegan diet that goes easy on the planet and is ridiculously healthy.

Jeff makes his lifestyle seem very simple and accessible to anyone. He does, after all, strongly believe that we vegans should be "bringing it down to the street" and engaging with others in the community to spread the message that being vegan is easy, anyone can do it, and it's not reserved for celebrities like Ellen DeGeneres who can afford a personal chef. Jeff works sixty to eighty hours a week and travels extensively, but still prioritizes his athletic training and the diet that supports it. He's clearly reaping the benefits of ultra healthy eating, and loving it.

How does someone interested in veganism start out? Jeff suggests "not going from zero to hero overnight." It takes time to make lasting lifestyle changes, and depending on one's previous diet it might be a shock to the body, too! Jeff emphasizes the importance of eating enough calories from healthy sources, drinking enough water, and seeking out easily digestible sources of (healthy) fat and calories.

Interested in becoming more active? Much like his advice to new vegans, Jeff notes that people new to active living should start gradually, rather than immediately going all out and risking injury. He suggests starting with leg and core work, and factoring in cross-training (something that benefits all athletes). Cross-training means doing something different from your usual workout, to prevent injury and to achieve more well-rounded physical fitness. For example, if you're a runner, you can supplement your running workouts with weight training. Same goes for a weight lifter, who might want to cross-train with plyometrics or swimming.

MANNY ESCALANTE

Manny Escalante, from Arvada, California, is a multisport athlete. He focuses on endurance running and bodybuilding but also loves water sports and anything he can do outdoors with his two dogs!

What are some ways in which your active, plant-based lifestyle contributes to your quality of life? What does it do for you? How does it enhance your life?

An active lifestyle gives me more energy and self-confidence. I look at completing each workout as a "win" for the day. Being vegan and active allows me to trump the myths that vegans are frail and sickly.

Please share your best nutrition tips for vegans who are interested in healthy diets to support their active lifestyles.

Don't be afraid to experiment, and know that you will not always like every food. Make sure to follow a well-balanced diet to support your needs. Being vegan can be just as unhealthy as not being vegan, so make smart, nutritionally dense food choices.

As a plant-based athlete, what sorts of foods do you prepare or pack when you travel?

I always take some "just in case" foods. My favorites are protein bars (Clif Builder, Pure Protein), fruit, nuts, and Primal Foods Jerky. When I fly somewhere I look for a local store to pick up hummus and some meat alternatives to supplement whatever else I am eating during the day.

What sorts of considerations must you make when eating at restaurants—not only as a vegan, but also as an athlete? Any suggestions for fellow plant-based athletes?

I make do wherever I go. I do not want people to feel that when you are vegan you cannot go out anywhere. I ask a lot of questions of the servers and can always have something to eat at restaurants. I know that later in the day I may need to eat again in order to have a well-balanced meal, but I am OK with putting in that effort. I usually check out veganeatingout.com, and the PETA website, which lists some good vegan foods available at various places.

Please share your best active living tips for vegans and vegetarians who are just beginning to exercise, or those who want to be more active.

Find what you love and do it regularly. It may take a while to find what that is, but stay active doing various things until something clicks. Make sure you do some form of strength training, cardio, and flexibility training. You cannot do just one all of the time. Start slow and do it consistently. Put exercise in your schedule or it will never happen. I recommend that you have a plan. Hiring a fitness professional (i.e., personal trainer) to help you to develop it is often best.

What has been the greatest diet- or nutrition-related challenge for you as a plant-based athlete?

Stay in tune with what your body is telling you as you begin the transition. Often cravings will arise and they may be a call for nutrients, not the product. Early in my vegan career, I thought I wanted tuna, but the cravings quickly vanished when I added more fats to my diet. Maybe I was missing some omega-3s (which flaxseed contains).

What are some athletic achievements you'd like to highlight?
- 35-mile run, Big Bear, California
- Long Beach Marathon, barefoot
- 2nd place, vegan bodybuilding show

MATTHEW WOODMAN

Matthew Woodman is one of the top runners in the UK (and that's quite a feat, given how many runners there are!). He's constantly winning races or placing in the top ten, all fueled by his healthy vegan diet.

What are some ways in which your active, plant-based lifestyle contributes to your quality of life? What does it do for you? How does it enhance your life?

I believe a vegan diet and not having animal consumption on my conscience give me a healthier quality of life.

Please share your best nutrition tips for vegans who are interested in healthy diets to support their active lifestyles.

Don't worry about protein, calcium, or iron! You will obtain all these from a balanced vegan diet.

Have dried fruit, seeds, avocados, etc., on hand to snack on.

Listen to your body—if you are hungry, then eat! Don't count calories—each person's metabolism and activity levels vary.

Eat five or six meals a day rather than three.

As a plant-based athlete, what sorts of foods do you prepare or pack when you travel?

Flapjacks, apples, bananas, dark chocolate, dried fruit (prunes/dates/figs), crisps/chips.

How do you think your life would have been different, had you not decided to become vegan?

I do not think I would have been in such good health, and I would exhibit more obvious signs of aging.

Please share your best active living tips for those vegans and vegetarians who are just beginning to exercise, or those who want to be more active.

Do something you enjoy rather than what everyone else does or what is the flavor of the month. Do activities that fit in with your lifestyle. Don't be too hard on yourself if you miss training days. You won't always be fit and strong during every exercise session. I believe that varying your training sessions is very important, as the body responds better and it keeps things fresh.

Be realistic—if you haven't trained for many years, you're not going to change that overnight. Focus on long-term and sustainable goals.

Cross-train. I am a strong believer of the benefits of doing more than one form of exercise. I run, weight train, and also regularly circuit train.

What has been the greatest diet- or nutrition-related challenge for you as a plant-based athlete?

I have encountered no challenges or difficulties.

What are some athletic achievements you'd like to highlight?

I am one of the top vegan runners in the UK. I nearly always place in the top 3/5/10 at races. I have won some races too—the Stebbing 10-mile race, Ricky Road Run, 9.3 miles and 5K on the Rides trail race—all in 2011 for example.

I have respectable race times, and I ranked in the top 650 road runners in the UK. (There are many tens of thousands of road runners in the UK!):

5 miles – 27.10
10 miles – 54.40
Half-marathon – 1.15.22

I was also honored to be asked to give a talk on vegan nutrition and exercise at Paris World Vegan Day in 2011.

MEGAN STORMS

Megan Storms has qualified and completed the Boston Marathon (more than once!) and won first place in her age group in a 70.3-mile distance triathlon. She also routinely places in her age group at 10K races, half marathons, and full marathons. She contributes to her triathlon coach's podcast, "Zen and the Art of Triathlon," by discussing plant-based foods for athletes. Check out her website at www.veganrunningmom.com.

What are some ways in which your active, plant-based lifestyle contributes to your quality of life? What does it do for you? How does it enhance your life?

Being a vegan helps me in so, so many ways. I am happier, healthier, and more ambitious than I ever was before becoming a vegan. I have boundless energy and require less downtime than most people. I feel younger at thirty-six than I did at twenty-one! I can run and play with my kids without losing my breath. I can actually keep up with them!

I recover faster with my clean diet. I can exercise more than my omnivorous counterparts, as I rarely am sore or tired.

As a plant-based athlete, what sorts of foods do you prepare or pack when you travel?

I am a pro at packing salads. I take them with me most days and also pack them for my husband. I also try to always carry some fruit, nuts, and bars on me for quick snacks. When we travel I pack more of the same type of items but also bring along things like peanut butter and jelly sandwiches, cut-up veggies, dry cereal, and air-popped popcorn for snacking.

How do you think your life would have been different, had you not decided to become vegan?

If I had not become vegan I imagine I would be far less fit and would be carrying around extra weight. I also feel I would not be as happy. There is a certain joy I have attained knowing I am compassionate to all creatures and that I am doing a good part in helping our environment with my eating choices.

Please share your best active living tips for those vegans and vegetarians who are just beginning to exercise, or those who want to be more active.

Take it one step at a time. If you are just starting out and are walking, for example, then make it a goal to walk ten minutes longer or a mile longer each week. Make attainable goals. Register for a race or walk to have motivation. Listen to music, podcasts, or audio books while exercising to make it more enjoyable if you like. Just remember to be safe and be sure you can hear traffic, etc. Be kind to yourself and remember that by exercising you will have more energy in the long run. It takes time to form habits and to enjoy being in motion!

What has been the greatest diet- or nutrition-related challenge for you as a plant-based athlete?

I would say the biggest challenge for me has been figuring out what I can eat before a big event. I am a marathoner and a triathlete so I participate in events that are long-lasting. I train for many hours at a time as well some days. Figuring out what my stomach can tolerate took some experimentation. Ultimately I have found I need to eat very basic things the night before an event, such as homemade gluten-free waffles or potatoes. The morning of an event I eat oatmeal with some fruit and nut butter. I have eliminated gluten from my diet and find it benefits my GI tract "happiness."

MICHELLE RISLEY

Weight lifter and all-around fitness badass Michelle Risley lives in Atlanta, Georgia. As a hospital pharmacist she works long hours but doesn't let that get in the way of living a healthy, active lifestyle.

What are some ways in which your active, plant-based lifestyle contributes to your quality of life? What does it do for you? How does it enhance your life?

It enables me to be an active, energetic, and very healthy forty-seven-year-old. I have the energy to do the things I want to do, as well as keep up with a very vigorous workout schedule. I am currently in the best shape of my life. I know, beyond a shadow of a doubt, that if I wasn't eating a whole-foods, vegan diet, I wouldn't be able to sustain my workout schedule, while also working night shifts at the hospital.

The thing that keeps me most motivated to stay in shape is to be a role model. I want to show others that you don't have to fall apart and gain weight as you get older. I also want to be an example that you don't have to eat crazy amounts of animal proteins to gain muscle and stay lean. I want to be a walking, talking billboard for what being vegan can look like.

Over the past five years, I have become more involved with animal rights. By being a fit, strong, lean vegan, I don't really have to say much to get people asking me questions. People often ask me how I eat and what I do to stay in such amazing shape. This often becomes the opening to a conversation about my being vegan because of my love and compassion for animals, which is the primary reason I went vegan to begin with. So for me, this has become the easiest way to advocate for animals.

Please share your best nutrition tips for vegans who are interested in healthy diets to support their active lifestyles.

Just because you're vegan doesn't mean you're healthy! Get back to basics with food. Build the majority of your diet from whole foods. Get away from all of the processed junk out there. Basically, if it comes in a bag, box, jar, or can, and has more than two to three ingredients or ingredients you can't pronounce or you don't know what they are, don't eat it! Or at least eat it in small quantities, as a treat. Prepare most of your meals at home. That way, you know exactly what you're eating and how it was prepared. When eating out, choose wisely. And try this tip: always eat a small meal or snack before you go out to eat.

As a plant-based athlete, what sorts of foods do you prepare or pack when you travel?

I never leave home without a small cooler containing two to three small meals and snacks. I always pack my meals for my shifts at work. I work ten-plus hour shifts at a hospital, which means I take three meals and two snacks with me. Never get caught without having healthy food with you! Eat often. It's much better for your body and your metabolism to eat small meals and snacks throughout the day. I eat every three hours.

What sorts of considerations must you make when eating at restaurants—not only as a vegan, but also as an athlete? Any suggestions for fellow plant-based athletes?

As mentioned earlier, I eat a small meal or snack before I go out. That way, I am not too hungry or tempted to eat something that I would only regret later. And even if I decide to splurge a little and have wine and/or dessert, I am much more inclined to have only a small quantity. On days that I know I will be eating out later, I have less carbs and fat leading up to that restaurant meal. That way, I know I won't go over my macro ranges. If I end up not eating enough carbs or fat by the end of the day, I just have a bigger meal before bed to make up for it.

Please share your best active living tips for those vegans and vegetarians who are just beginning to exercise, or those who want to be more active.

If you've never exercised before, it's best to check with your health practitioner to make sure you are healthy enough for exercise and/or to know your limitations. It would also be prudent to hire a qualified trainer to help you get started. But be forewarned that many will probably tell you that you can't reach your goals if you're vegan. Stay true to your convictions!

Tell them that if you hire them, they have to agree to work within your dietary choices. My trainer is a huge carnivore. But he knows that I would fire him faster than he could say the word *vegan* if he tried to pressure me to eat differently. Finding a qualified vegan trainer would be optimal. But that's not always possible. [Self-promotional message from Karina: check out www.karinainkster.com for vegan fitness and nutrition coaching.]

What has been the greatest diet- or nutrition-related challenge for you as a plant-based athlete?

It took a little time for me to figure out how to best get enough protein without getting too many carbohydrates or too much fat in the process. I learned that I just had to plan my meals and snacks ahead of time, taking into consideration my macro ranges and limits. If I didn't plan ahead, I usually ended up eating most of my fat and carbs for the day way before I had enough protein.

What are some athletic achievements you'd like to highlight?

Although I wasn't able to compete in a figure competition as planned, I did get down to 8 percent body fat without losing very much muscle, and was very close to being "stage ready." So I know for sure that it is possible to be vegan, gain and retain muscle, and get very lean!

MIKE MAHLER

Mike Mahler is a strength trainer and hormone optimization researcher based in Las Vegas, Nevada. Mike has been in the fitness industry for over twelve years and has taught workshops, including over a 100 kettlebell workshops, all over the US and overseas. His current focus is on the field of hormone optimization via nutrition, training, nutrition supplements, and lifestyle. Mike is also the author of *Live Life Aggressively! What Self-Help Gurus Should Be Telling You*.

Mike is a respected writer, having written over 100 articles for publications such as *Muscle & Fitness, Men's Fitness, Hardcore Muscle Magazine, Planet Muscle, Testosterone Magazine, Ironman Magazine, Ironman Magazine Japan*, and *Exercise Magazine For Men*. Mike has also been featured in *Muscle & Fitness, Men's Fitness UK, UPN News*, and *CBS News*.

What are some ways in which your active, plant-based lifestyle contributes to your quality of life? What does it do for you? How does it enhance your life?

I love animals and eating a vegan diet plays a big role in my spiritual and ethical values. I like knowing that I can be strong, healthy, and have an optimal hormone profile on a vegan diet. I do not have to compromise my values.

I thrive very well on vegan food and feel that I am able to extract a great deal of energy from the food I eat without having to utilize a great deal of energy. I wake up refreshed and ready to go, and attack workouts and projects.

Please share your best nutrition tips for vegans who are interested in healthy diets to support their active lifestyles.

I think it is important to avoid overly processed food. Stick to real vegan food and get complete protein from combining legumes with nuts and seeds. This combination has a nice balance of protein, fat, and low glycemic carbohydrates. Make sure to have a salad every day and eat some raw fruits and veggies. Coconut oil is a must for vegans, as it is loaded with medium-chain fatty acids for energy and is a saturated fat that helps with hormone optimization and a healthy metabolism.

As a plant-based athlete, what sorts of foods do you prepare or pack when you travel?

I like to keep it simple, so trail mixes of almonds, walnuts, pistachios, pumpkin seeds, goji berries, and cashews work really well. I also make homemade protein bars to take on the road made from pea and rice protein powder, flaxseed powder, almond butter, and spices.

What sorts of considerations must you make when eating at restaurants—not only as a vegan, but also as an athlete? Any suggestions for fellow plant-based athletes?

Avoid white flour, white rice, and sugar, and focus on clean food such as veggies, legumes, nuts, and seeds. Start each meal with a salad and finish each meal with a hot cup of tea.

Please share your best active living tips for those vegans and vegetarians who are just beginning to exercise, or those who want to be more active.

Start with what you will be able to be consistent with. Do not try to take on too much too soon. Walking a mile a day is a good start. When you have that down, start throwing in some bodyweight exercises such as push-ups, squats, planks, etc., to build a baseline level of strength. Then move on to weight training and focus on compound exercises that provide the most benefit, such as squats, deadlifts, bent-over rows, and military presses.

What has been the greatest diet- or nutrition-related challenge for you as a plant-based athlete?

At first it was difficult to figure out how to get a good amount of protein. Many advise to combine legumes with brown rice or grains, but such a combination is way too high in carbohydrates. Combining legumes with nuts and seeds, for example, works much better.

It takes some trial and error to figure how to dial it in for each individual. Making sure to avoid excessive amounts of carbohydrates can be an issue, so one has to be diligent with the right combinations.

What are some athletic achievements you'd like to highlight?

Here are some of my workout accomplishments:

Deadlifting 525 pounds

Bench press 315 pounds for 6 reps, and 365 pounds for 1 rep

One-arm kettlebell snatch 105 pounds for 17 reps each arm

One-arm kettlebell military press 10 reps with a 97-pound bell

Double kettlebell clean and military press 19 reps with 2 70-pound bells

44-inch box jump for 3 reps

DAVID O'MEARA

David O'Meara is a world-renowned coach, speaker, author, and athlete. He has made a career of inspiring amateur and professional athletes of all ages. He has also trained both coaches and Fortune 500 executives on his trips around the world in Europe, Asia, and Africa.

David has been the keynote speaker at world sports conferences, financial institutions, leadership organizations, and educational conferences. He is the author of three books: *Creating Amazement*; *Play Better, Live Better*; and *Tennis Unlimited*. David is a certified personal trainer and fitness counselor based in Sarasota, Florida.

What are some ways in which your active, plant-based lifestyle contributes to your quality of life? What does it do for you? How does it enhance your life?

With a vegan diet I'm able to age more gracefully, sleep more soundly, increase blood flow, maintain consistent levels of energy, and achieve high athletic performance.

Please share your best nutrition tips for vegans who are interested in healthy diets to support their active lifestyles.

A raw salad a day keeps the doctor away. Start your day with a plant-based protein shake followed by nuts and fruit. Eat five small meals per day instead of three big ones.

As a plant-based athlete, what sorts of foods do you prepare or pack when you travel?

When I travel, I pack Vega One all-in-one nutritional shake packets to start my day, Vega Sport Protein Bars for a snack, and Vega Sport Performance Protein packets for recovery after my workouts. I also pack a peanut butter sandwich and fruit for lunch on the flight.

How do you think your life would have been different, had you not decided to become vegan?

My father died of colon cancer at fifty-six years old. So I knew at an early age that my nutritional intake would be a priority in my life based on my genetic predisposition. I needed to alter the standard American diet that I grew up on and switch to a plant-based diet that would ease digestion. If I had not decided to become vegan in my early twenties, I would not have been as athletic later in life, I'd probably be fatter, and I would definitely not be waking up with a bounce in my step every morning.

Please share your best active living tips for those vegans and vegetarians who are just beginning to exercise, or those who want to be more active.

- Mobilize before your sport, don't stretch.
- Stretch after your sport, don't just get in the car.
- Nourish your body with your nutritional intake, don't just stimulate.
- Use resistance training properly, don't body build. This can be learned at www.BodyProtection.com.
- If you can run, then run.
- Life is better on the move, so stay active six days a week.

What has been the greatest diet- or nutrition-related challenge for you as a plant-based athlete?

I have traveled to every continent except Antarctica, and my greatest diet-related challenge is finding healthy vegan options in all the corners of the world. However, international awareness on the benefits of vegan eating has been increasing in the last 25 years, so it is definitely getting easier and less strange.

What are some athletic achievements you'd like to highlight?

In the last five years, I have completed world tours that people think are just "crazy challenges." These tours are based on breaking the mile in less than five minutes, repeatedly. Speed, strength, endurance, and recovery are required. It is up for debate which of the tours was the most challenging, but you can look for yourself at www.OneMileRunner.com and decide. Now turning fifty years old and still breaking five minutes in the mile, I feel very fortunate to have discovered the values and benefits of my vegan lifestyle over three decades.

AUSTIN BARBISCH

Austin Barbisch is a competitive bodybuilder, endurance runner, licensed massage therapist, and personal trainer. He has placed incredibly well at both sports, including a first place win for a 115-mile race!

What are some ways in which your active, vegan lifestyle contributes to your quality of life? What does it do for you? How does it enhance your life?

With a vegan diet, I have experienced much better recovery time after exercise. I run ultra-marathons in the cooler months and compete in bodybuilding shows the rest of the year. Since switching to plant-based eating, my running mileage has improved with no detrimental effect, so I show up in better condition for my races. As for the bodybuilding aspect, my strength has gone up with my lean muscle, and I find it much easier to diet down while keeping this muscle mass. I have taken 35 minutes off my best 100-mile race time, and placed higher in my bodybuilding shows. The coating that I used to have on my tongue is gone, and my knees and shoulders ache less after heavy lifting and long training runs and races as well. I also need less sleep. I have been feeling completely rested after six and a half hours of sleep, compared to eight hours when I ate animal products. That works out to 22.8 more days of conscious life each year!

Please share your best nutrition tips for vegans who are interested in healthy diets to support their active lifestyles.

I usually start my day with a "proto-mocha-latte." This is a breakfast concoction that I have been relying on for the last ten-plus years to start my day. It is composed of two to four cups of coffee, a cup of almond milk, and protein powder. Sometimes I add a half cup of oatmeal for additional carbs. I snack throughout the day on various nuts and fruits. I also try to get one or two nice big salads into the day (mixed greens, chopped apples, pears, steamed cauliflower, broccoli, nuts, and a good dressing tossed with lots of nutritional yeast). I usually make a smoothie with protein powder, frozen bananas, strawberries, blueberries, and some type of green like kale, spinach, or frozen broccoli after my workouts.

As a plant-based athlete, what sorts of foods do you prepare or pack when you travel?

I usually carry a container of various nuts and fruits. Sometimes I also bring a shaker with protein powder in it, ready to mix with water, nut milk, or coffee.

How do you think your life would have been different, had you not decided to become vegan?

I switched to a plant-based diet for ethical reasons. I have always loved animals and had seen factory farming atrocities in the media long ago, but somehow managed to displace that reality from my everyday life. I met a few vegan friends and started to realize that in order to live in ethical truth, just being kind to my neighbor was not going to cut it. Being vegan makes me feel like I am doing something kind for the world and the beautiful life forms running, flying, and swimming on it. If my instincts don't lead me to kill an animal, then I have no place eating one. I feel that my compassion for the world would not have developed as far had I not discovered veganism. I would also not be as athletically competitive.

Do you have any active living tips to share with vegans and vegetarians who are just beginning to exercise or those who want to be more active?

Herbivores can thrive if they keep a variety of plant-based foods in their diet and stay active in their chosen sport. Recovery from strenuous exercise seems to improve with this diet, so they can probably work out harder and longer as their bodies becomes more alkaline.

What has been the greatest diet- or nutrition-related challenge for you as a plant-based athlete?

The first two months of going vegan made for a confusing time at most restaurants. Many servers are not aware of all animal products, so I've just formed a list of questions in my head. I'm also gluten free, so I am sometimes very limited in choices. I now think it's fun to work around a menu to create something interesting. I do not miss meat or dairy anywhere near as much as I thought I would. I have no problem getting nutrient-rich complex carbohydrates and proteins on a vegan diet, so my physical and mental performance is far better.

How do you promote muscle recovery?

I make sure to take in at least three or four servings of protein-rich meals a day (quinoa, lentils, tempeh, tofu, or protein powder). I do a fair amount of stretching, but not as much as I probably should. I am a licensed massage therapist, so I am a huge advocate for its ability to help flush away metabolic waste and separate muscular adhesions for improved kinetic efficiency. I run three to four times a week during ultra-marathon training. I feel this keeps me from overtraining and reduces injury. When bodybuilding, I lift about five times a week (each day is a separate body part) and take two days off, so I end up working each body part (chest, shoulders, legs, back and arms) only one time a week for full recovery.

What are some athletic achievements you'd like to highlight?

Bodybuilding/Physique (on a vegan diet):

April 13, 2013 MRI Texas shredder
  2nd place masters bodybuilding
  3rd place masters physique

April 27, 2013 INBF Drop Zone
  2nd place open bodybuilding
  2nd place masters bodybuilding
  2nd place open physique

Pre-vegan:

July, 2011 Southwestern Natural Bodybuilding show
  3rd Place: men masters bodybuilding

Running (on a vegan diet):

February 2, 2013
  The Rocky Raccoon 100 Mile
  Time: 22 h 35 min

December 3, 2012
  Run Like the Wind 24 hour race
  1st place; 115.32 miles

Pre-vegan:

December 3, 2011
  Run Like the Wind 12 hour race
  1st place; 60.76 miles

December 2010
  Run Like the Wind 12 hour race
  2nd place; 59.32 miles

June 2011
  Hells Hills 50-mile race
  Time: 11 h 34 min

November 2010
  San Antonio Rock and Roll Marathon
  Time: 3 h 19 min

April 2011
  Nueces 50-mile race
  Time: 12 h 4 min

2007 Prickly Pear 50K
  Time: 5 h 14 min

February 2011
  The Rocky Raccoon 100-mile race
  Time: 23 h 10 min

ANDREA BERMAN

Andrea is a software engineer by day, and a fitness and life coach the rest of the time. She's a self-proclaimed lifelong geek whose hobbies up until after her college years were mainly sedentary. Andrea spent the year after finishing college losing over one hundred pounds, most of which she had gained very rapidly during her last two years of college. She kept them off for many years until becoming inactive and encountering several struggles with food intolerances (as well as learning how to become vegan). In 2010 Andrea became a certified Beachbody Coach. Since then, she's committed to getting her life on track and helping others to be happy and healthy. She's also certified in P90X, INSANITY, and life coaching. At the time of our interview she was studying for her personal trainer certification.

What are some ways in which your active, vegan lifestyle contributes to your quality of life? What does it do for you? How does it enhance your life?

It cuts back on the stress and unhealthy nature of my day job, which is incredibly sedentary and for long periods of time at that. It's no way to live; we were not designed as human beings to spend long hours sitting in cubicles. I also have a family history of cancer, diabetes, and heart disease. I have many "why's" as to my fitness lifestyle, and they contribute to my reasons for being vegan as well. My food intolerances mainly surround animal protein, and I went on a plant-based diet as a result. After reading *Skinny Bitch* and getting a tough love lecture on how dairy cows and chickens are treated, I decided from that point on to go lifestyle vegan. I believe it's best for my health, for the animals, and for the planet. In short, a win-win scenario for us all!

I have so much more energy now and no longer have the horrible digestive issues that plagued me prior to going vegan. I've learned to be more mindful about what I consume and why, and how it affects others and the world around me.

Please share your best nutrition tips for vegans who are interested in healthy diets to support their active lifestyles.

Eat as much food as you possibly can that does not come out of a bag, a can, or a box. Experiment, and learn new ways to appreciate fruits and veggies.

Here are a couple recipes to try:

No-bake chocolate protein bars

Here's what you need:

- ¼ cup chocolate nondairy protein powder (I prefer either *Vega*, chocolate vegan *Shakeology*, or *Sun Warrior*)
- 1 banana
- ¼ cup flax seeds
- ¼ cup nondairy chocolate chips (*Ghirardelli* semi-sweet chocolate chips are dairy-free!)
- ¼ cup slivered almonds
- ¼ cup almond butter

Mix the protein powder with some water to turn it into a sticky paste. Mash the banana into it, and you have a very nice, healthy, and tasty binding agent for your protein bars.

Mix in flax seeds, chocolate chips, slivered almonds, and almond butter.

Stir like crazy! If it's too sticky or stiff, add a bit more water. You want the right consistency: not runny but not something you can't quite stir either.

Spread into a pan and then stick into the freezer. Tasty!

This should make 12–15 bars depending on the size you make them.

Guilt-free ice cream

Peel 2–3 bananas, and freeze overnight. Add them with about ¼ cup unsweetened vanilla almond milk and one tablespoon vanilla extract to either a blender or a food processor (food processor works best), and mix well. Voila, ice cream.

For a chocolate sauce, you can combine either raw cacao or regular cocoa with some water and a nonfrozen banana, and blend. I've made "banana milk" using water; for an ice cream topping you have to get just enough water in there for the right consistency.

As a plant-based athlete, what sorts of foods do you prepare or pack when you travel?

Vega One bars, chocolate vegan and tropical strawberry *Shakeology* packets, and whatever fresh fruit and veggies I can get my hands on. I have a travel blender I take with me for hotel rooms if I know in advance I won't have a kitchen in there, or anything like that. I recently acquired a blender cup and plan to see how much better that works!

How do you think your life would have been different, had you not decided to become vegan?

I would be a lot less healthy and I would frankly be miserable. My weight probably would've shot up even more like it did back when I was in college, and who knows what I would do from there. It's also pretty likely that my life expectancy would not be good; the odds would be against me. I also would not have met and connected with so many people and experiences, which have transformed my life and forced me to rethink so much of what I have taken for granted. Is ignorance truly bliss? I really don't know. But I don't think so.

Do you have any active living tips to share with vegans or vegetarians who are just beginning to exercise or those who want to be more active?

Take it slow, one day at a time. As Tony Horton of P90X fame says, "Rome was not built in a day, and neither was your body." Be patient with yourself and know that small changes pile up and snowball over time. Find an activity you love and enjoy, something that motivates you to get up and moving. Experiment with different forms of exercise until you find your "soulmate workout." Engage in a good blend of cardio, resistance training, and any activity involving stretching and flexibility, such as yoga. Learn the difference between muscle soreness from adapting to a new activity and genuine pain caused by an injury. Get plenty of sleep and take rest days. Find people who have been at it for longer than you, who are experts in the field of fitness, and listen to what they have to say. Also, length does not make strength; spending more than an hour a day working out on a regular basis can increase your risk of overtraining, which can lead to injury and illness.

Fuel your body with tasty, healthy whole foods at least 90 percent of the time, and don't turn food and calories into your enemy. It is sometimes said that "abs are made in the kitchen" but this is only partially true. Abs are made in the gym and *revealed* in the kitchen. Same goes with the rest of your muscles. You cannot out-exercise a bad diet.

What has been the greatest diet- or nutrition-related challenge for you as a plant-based athlete?

Eating healthy, clean, and quick on a tight and incredibly busy schedule, I've had to prepare food in bulk by cooking quinoa, chopping veggies in advance, etc. Sometimes I just turn to quick veggie wraps and fruit protein smoothies. I've come home late from work in some jobs in the past, like 11 p.m. or even midnight. I wind up eating dinner at work and coming home and still getting in a workout before bedtime. Often enough it's the only way to unwind so I don't wake up in a tight, twisted knot from tension and stress. Being flexible and creative with my diet on such a schedule can get interesting! I take advantage of my weekends to make sure I'm prepared for the week ahead, so I'm not tempted to grab or make something that isn't conducive to my healthy lifestyle.

How do you promote muscle recovery?

I get plenty of rest, drink lots of water, stretch, do yoga and foam rolling, etc. All of these things are incredibly useful. I also am patient with myself and my body, and I don't stop exercising just because I am sore. Instead, I monitor myself carefully and watch my form to make sure that I don't exercise to the point of injury. Soreness in the beginning is inevitable, but there are ways to make it better and more manageable. I highly recommend that active people go for massages every six to eight weeks. Consider it maintenance!

What are some athletic achievements you'd like to highlight?

I've done the full sixty-day program of INSANITY, ran my first 5K last summer (2012), and have walked 39 miles over the course of two days every year for the past four years in order to help fight breast cancer. I even now have the ability to do push-ups on my toes for the first time! I honestly never thought I'd get this far, that I'd ever enjoy running or could be strong enough to do "real push-ups." I remember the days back when I could barely even do them on my knees, and never thought I'd be strong enough to do them on my toes. Now I crank them out like they're nothing! I also keep having to buy heavier weights; I'm now on 30-pound dumbbells for squats and deadlifts.

But nothing beats my favorite achievement of all: I'm still here, still going strong, and I'm still having fun on my fitness journey to be happy and healthy.

VICTOR RIVERA

Victor Rivera is a California-based personal trainer who works with a wide range of clients. He says, "I really enjoy being able to help people change their lives for the better through something I am passionate about: physical fitness! Exercise is something that has improved my life in so many ways, so being able to share that with others is truly a fulfilling job for me."

What are some ways in which your active, vegan lifestyle contributes to your quality of life? What does it do for you? How does it enhance your life?

For starters, I enjoy the fact that the food I eat gives me energy. I remember eating double cheeseburgers and feeling so disgusting for hours on end that I wouldn't want to go to the gym because I felt so awful and guilty for cheating.

Now I know that the better your workout is, the more results you're going to get. So it follows that you should eat food that will fuel and enhance your workout, rather than consuming things that will make you operate from a deficit.

Eating a healthy vegan diet also decreases my recovery time and allows me to do more on less sleep. I needed nine to ten hours of sleep in my pre-vegan days to feel like I was at full strength. I can now function quite well in the five to seven hour range (which is key when you have kids).

Being vegan also enhances my life, as it has raised my awareness to a whole new level. I now think about the food on my plate and the impact it has on my body, as well as others' bodies, the animals who suffer, and the environment that is getting destroyed for the sake of factory farming.

Essentially, I now truly understand how my own actions can affect the world at large; so to quote Gandhi, I try to "be the change I wish to see in the world." I believe that becoming vegan is a great way to take a step in that direction.

Please share your best nutrition tips for vegans who are interested in healthy diets to support their active lifestyles.

I remember reading an interview by Coach Dos, 2006 NSCA strength coach of the year (and vegan). He said that he doesn't just eat some green beans; he eats a pound of them! His point is that for vegans training to gain and maintain a good amount of muscle mass, you have to be eating enough healthy food. (So fill your plate with lots of vegetables instead of pasta.)

The next tip is to stick to whole foods. It's very tempting to consume lots of Tofurky sausages, tofu dogs, veggie burgers, and put Daiya cheese on everything; but all of that stuff is clearly processed and unhealthy. I get my protein from tempeh, tofu, legumes, vegetables, and grains.

As a plant-based athlete, what sorts of foods do you prepare or pack when you travel?

I'll bring with me some *Vega* bars or *Clif* bars, bananas, carrots, and other easy-to-pack fruits and veggies for long drives or flights. Rice cakes and peanut butter (the not-so-great kind if I can't get to a fridge) are also hearty and easy for when I'm on the road or camping.

It also helps to use a good app that can show you where the vegan restaurants are! I use Yelp, happycow.net, and Google maps to figure out where I can stop when I'm in places I haven't visited before. The main thing I want to express here is it's really not too difficult to travel as a vegan if you prepare enough for it and have the resources to find places to eat. Even basic grocery stores have plenty we can eat.

How do you think your life would have been different, had you not decided to become vegan?

For one, I would be on my way to a quick death. I was 210 pounds at five foot five. I was extremely obese and gaining weight by the day; I went from 200 to 210 in a week. I knew then it was time for a change.

I would also not be working out. Since I had become so heavy and disgusted with myself, I stopped exercising. I thought life was "over" for me; I'd never look or feel like I did in high school. But after deciding to go vegetarian, and then vegan, the pounds began to shed off me so quickly that I became motivated to exercise again.

This instilled in me the belief that I could reach all of my goals as long as I was determined and maintained my now strong willpower. So if I hadn't become vegan, I wouldn't have chosen the personal training career path, and I would not have this ability to help others improve their own lives.

Do you have any active living tips to share with vegans and vegetarians who are just beginning to exercise or those who want to be more active?

For those who are just beginning to exercise, just focus on being consistent. Results come when you are regularly showing up. It's so tempting to see people's online posts and say, "I want to do that burpee challenge!" That can be a future goal, but for now, build the habit of exercising daily in some fashion (a long walk, a jog, bike ride, etc.).

Plenty of people who are out of shape have asked me for workout routines. When I send them one, they quickly fail more often than not. That's because they haven't made exercise a second-nature presence in their mind. So it's self-defeating to begin an intense routine when you don't even want to walk around your block yet.

From there, weights need to be your foundation. Begin a weight-training program as soon as you feel comfortable. Keep the weights light and focus on your form. Hire a trainer or exercise with a really knowledgeable friend who can show you how to use everything and do the moves properly.

And work your whole body! Push as often as you pull (push-ups and rows, for example); work your glutes as often as your hamstrings (think squats and good mornings). Many of my clients have imbalances due to ignoring many of their muscle regions.

What has been the greatest diet- or nutrition-related challenge for you as a plant-based athlete?

My biggest challenge was getting used to always thinking about what I was going to eat. The focus of my meal decision used to be, "Chicken or turkey tonight?" So I've had to retrain my palate to enjoy green vegetables, tempeh, almond milk, etc.

I also found myself filling up on carbs to take the place of meat when I first adopted a plant-based diet. I quickly learned that two plates of pasta was not conducive to getting a six-pack. I then learned to eat more broccoli, since it's obviously healthier, but quite filling! And I also eat more potatoes now for this reason. Just one potato and I'm satisfied for many hours.

On the athletic performance side of being vegan, I have had no trouble adding muscle, gaining strength, becoming more conditioned, etc. I really enjoy thwarting the stereotype that vegans are pipsqueaks.

How do you promote muscle recovery?

Before recovery can take place, I promote being properly warmed up. I start almost every workout session with quick foam rolling to get the knots out of my muscles. Although the process can be somewhat painful, I feel great afterward! I also do some light cardio, light complexes with a barbell, and some dynamic stretches before my typical session. This ensures less chance of an injury during my workout, and less soreness afterward.

After a workout, I foam roll more extensively, stretch quite a bit, then head home and immediately consume my post-workout meal (protein shake/smoothie or a well-balanced meal). I also use vegan creatine and Vega recovery to aid in my healing.

I really try to be intuitive when it comes to my body. If I'm feeling a little banged up, then I take a day off from the weights, and do some light cardio or interval cardio training. I'll also do some yoga so that I still challenge myself but feel good afterward, since I didn't destroy myself just because my training schedule said I was supposed to.

What are some athletic achievements you'd like to highlight?

I completed Tough Mudder Vegas in March 2013. Tough Mudder Vegas was a 12-mile obstacle course that tested me physically *and* psychologically. Who *wants* to jump into a tub of ice water, then proceed to get electrocuted later on not once, but twice?

Most people run the Tough Mudder in teams, but I had to do it by myself. Though it would have been more fun with friends, I really learned how to keep pushing myself and not give up. Tough Mudder also really taught me that you can't always break records, but you can make sure you cross the finish line. So just give it 100 percent and let the chips fall where they may.

And when this book is published, I'll have done Tough Mudder San Diego!

DRU BROZOVICH

Dru Brozovich is a Seattle native and marathon runner/endurance athlete who's been a self-proclaimed gym rat for most of his life. A man of many talents, Dru has toured with bands, released electronic music tracks, had his art shown at local events, helped to run an electronic event production company, and helped to call play-by-play for women's flat track roller derby.

What are some ways in which your active, vegan lifestyle contributes to your quality of life? What does it do for you? How does it enhance your life?

Being vegan has turned the clock back for me. The nutritional element keeps my body in the best shape it can be at all times, which is important for recovery, repair, and performance. The fact that I know I am not purchasing animal products also gives me peace, even though I know animals are still suffering because of the food industry. On a personal level, I feel that my commitment to my sobriety and my plant-based diet gives me power over my life and shows others that it is *you* in control of what you do, not someone or something else. That commitment has made me stronger.

Please share your best nutrition tips for vegans who are interested in healthy diets to support their active lifestyles.

Don't under-eat when training. I know there are a lot of people out there that claim a million different things. But if you are eating the right foods and are still not performing at your best, you need to make sure you are eating enough for what you do. Everyone is different. A marathon runner is going to eat very differently than a bodybuilder. Make sure your diet works for what *you* do.

As a plant-based athlete, what sorts of foods do you prepare or pack when you travel?

Oh dear, everything possible! I plan my trips and hotels to be within blocks of places to eat, grocery stores, etc. I also make sure I always have a cooler bag with me whenever I leave the house so I can have food when I need it, in case it isn't available nearby.

How do you think your life would have been different, had you not decided to become vegan?

I'd be sick, and probably have a million health issues like the ones my friends have. I wouldn't be as good as an athlete or look as young as I do for my age.

Do you have any active living tips to share with vegans who are just beginning to exercise or those who want to be more active?

Rest! You can kick your butt in training—and you should!—but always make sure you rest. Even if your diet isn't perfect, rest is how you repair yourself. Getting at least seven hours of sleep per night will allow you to perform at your best and recover faster.

What has been the greatest diet- or nutrition-related challenge for you as a plant-based athlete?

Just making sure I have enough protein. When I first started running, I thought I should not eat a lot of protein, as many runners just carb up. I made that mistake thinking I was built like everyone else (which I'm not). My body is very dense muscle-wise, so I have to make sure I feed those muscles. Since I realized this, I've seen improvements just by kicking up my protein intake by 20 grams a day.

How do you promote muscle recovery?

Vega Recovery Accelerator, turmeric, sleep. Water. Yoga. A lot of green veggies. Sleep. More sleep! I also live and die by my foam roller. That thing has saved my legs on many days I thought I would not be able to run for a whole week.

What are some athletic achievements you'd like to highlight?

Being a marathon runner isn't about winning, because being elite is like being one in a million. So you race against yourself. I've had a few top three finishes in 5K and 10K races, and always finished in the top 5 percent of my division (sex/age). I like to put together training plans so I can know I will go into a race prepared. When I used to box I was taught "win the fight in the gym, come fight day, it's easy." I apply this to my running also. Kick your own ass during the training, and you will succeed when the starting gun goes off.

SALLY ANDERSEN

Sally Andersen describes herself as an "adrenaline junkie, personal trainer, group fitness instructor, competitive running nerd, avid bike lover, fitness writer, CrossFitter, Zen yogi and most of all—a healthy, strong, active, compassionate vegan woman!" A woman of many sports, Sally is now getting into cyclocross racing and physique competitions.

What are some ways in which your active, vegan lifestyle contributes to your quality of life? What does it do for you? How does it enhance your life?

Growing up I was the kid that had every desire to be an athlete but no natural skill at any one sport. I was the first to come to practice and the last to leave, but still I was never going to be an elite athlete. I had a competitive drive, heart, and dedication, but thought that scoring for the team, winning the race, or being the best, was all that mattered.

When I headed to college, unable to compete for any sport at the collegiate level, I stopped all activity all together. Between an all-you-can-eat cafeteria, a sudden lack of exercise, and weekly frat parties, my health declined greatly and my weight increased.

Soon, I was on eight medications, wheezing from asthma symptoms when walking up stairs. I wasted almost seven years of my life living this way. Until I woke up.

I became vegan and I started working out again.

Now I know that—in the game of health and wellness—drive, heart, and dedication greatly outweigh natural-born skill. Now I am off all of my medications, free of asthma symptoms, and in the best shape of my life. And now I want to help other people do the same!

Since going vegan and becoming an athlete, my life has improved—probably in more ways than I have even noticed. Physically: I can breathe better, have more energy, and feel lighter overall. Mentally: I am more focused and driven. Committing to a vegan life tested, trained, and strengthened my will power. Having such a fine-tuned ability to self motivate and stay dedicated to a goal has made me more productive in my workouts and has made avoiding late nights and alcohol easy. And, of course, emotionally: I am tuned into global pain and suffering but have learned how to manage the impact it has on me by going out and doing something about it, while maintaining a stable understanding that I can't fix everything.

Please share your best nutrition tips for vegans who are interested in healthy diets to support their active lifestyles.

Be ready and willing to learn more about nutrition and try new foods. Listen to the advice of others but stay true to your instincts and your body's reactions. My specific advice: avoid processed and premade foods; don't become reliant on pasta; drink green smoothies; use nutritional yeast and hemp seeds; eat a wide variety of foods and include tempeh and broccoli; and most of all, don't be afraid to eat a lot of food.

As a plant-based athlete, what sorts of foods do you prepare or pack when you travel?

I keep a tub of Vega Sport Performance and a shaker cup in my car at all times. It helps for making sure I get my post-workout protein and recovery and also saves me when I get stuck somewhere, hungry, and with zero healthy vegan options. When I'm in higher cardio training with lots of running, I take homemade trail mix everywhere. And as weird as it sounds, I snack on plain, right-out-of-the-package tempeh! I'll grab protein bars like Clif Bars only if I'm desperate to find something decent at a gas station.

How do you think your life would have been different, had you not decided to become vegan?

I don't think not becoming vegan was ever a possible path for my life to have taken. Timing was the only variable. I was raised on a healthy, vegetable-centric diet and, although I liked the taste of meat, I always connected it to being an animal. I would never eat anything that came on a bone. I had to have all the fat cut off, skin pulled off, etc. I basically tried to make it as un-animal-like as possible. Finally one day I questioned the meat itself.

Do you have any active living tips to share with vegans who are just beginning to exercise or those who want to be more active?

Pick activities that are enjoyable for you and specific to your goals and fitness level. If you've never lifted weights, don't worry about having a "back day," "chest day," etc., or about increasing weight/reps right from the start. Focus on learning the classic moves and developing good form. If you've never run, don't try to train for a marathon. Play around with seeing how far or how fast you can run. Try treadmills, hills, walk/run, track workouts, etc. If you need to lose weight, constantly change up your workouts, making sure your heart rate is high. And regardless of any goals . . . get sweaty, have fun, and don't take it too seriously!

What has been the greatest diet- or nutrition-related challenge for you as a plant-based athlete?

I hate to sound like a braggart, but nutrition has always been easy and fun for me. My parents set me up for becoming a healthy-eating adult. Becoming vegan was a learning curve, but it was fun and easy as long as I kept reading, asking questions, and trying things out.

The Paleo diet trend has caused people following its plan to feel open to teasing, harassing, and questioning vegans and our food choices. But I am confident in my choices and have learned to remain calm, not get defensive or preachy, and provide just the right amount of educated responses.

How do you promote muscle recovery?

Recovery is crucial for everyone, but it's especially important when you plan on training every twelve hours or so. I stay hydrated, stretch constantly, take yoga classes, and use the modality that I know I most need in the moment. For example, after hard efforts for running, I know that my glutes and IT bands will tighten, so I use myofascial release techniques to roll and massage those areas with the Stick, a foam roller, a lacrosse ball, and my hands. After heavy leg training, I need to ice my knees, because they have a tendency to swell and be achy otherwise.

A healthy vegan diet is a huge aid in recovery. Your body can easily digest fresh, whole, plant-based foods and quickly get the nutrition it needs with minimal effort. That way, your body can focus on repair and recovery instead of digestion.

Post workout, I have recently started making sure to have glutamine and BCAAs (branched chain amino acids), which also aid in recovery, especially for heavy weight training. I spend more money on Vega Sport Performance Protein than I would for other protein powders because it has both of these supplements in it.

A new addition to my recovery—or rather, injury rehab and prevention—has been visiting a sports doctor regularly. He does heat/ice/electrical stimulation treatments; chiropractic adjustments; joint stabilization physical therapy; myofascial and active release techniques; PNF stretching, and trigger point massage. He also keeps me in check with the realities of what I can ask my body to handle and reminds me to take rest days.

What are some athletic achievements you'd like to highlight?

Finding myself as an athlete has been a journey. I started out running for fun, teaching Pilates, and cycling for transportation. Then I became a sponsored USATF athlete competing as a post-collegiate athlete on a college team, only to be run over by a car while biking home from practice. My injuries made running difficult, so I dove into weight training and body building. Now that I am able to run again, I'm trying to find balance between my fitness goals and desires. I want to win a 5K (the closest I came pre-injury was to win my age division); I want to race cyclocross on my bike; and I am contemplating figure competitions. I want to do it all!

Specific achievements worth bragging about:

- Recognized by *Philadelphia* magazine and *Be Well Philly* as one of the top health and fitness heroes in the city, September 2012
- ACSM certified personal trainer also certified in kickboxing, Pilates, group weightlifting and much more
- M.Ed. in Therapeutic Recreation
- I've written for *Philly Fit* magazine (as their vegan nutrition expert!) and *Liberty Sports* magazine (and was their cover model one month!)
- I've been sponsored by or an ambassador for JACO Clothing, Ragnar Relays, SONY, and Scott Running shoes.
- And, most brag-worthy, Brendan Brazier follows me on Instagram and likes my pics! Yup, I'm a little starstruck over kick-butt vegan athletes that know their stuff about nutrition.

CHRISTY MORGAN

Austin, Texas-based Christy Morgan is a vegan chef, educator, and cookbook author known as "The Blissful Chef." Christy loves cooking and teaching others how to cook delicious, healthy meals with private cooking instruction, her blog (see blissfulandfit.com), and through cooking videos and cooking demos at events across the US.

She became obsessed with fitness post-thirty, doing a sprint triathlon in 2011, and a bikini competition and another sprint triathlon in 2013. Christy says, "Showing others that you can be healthy, fit, strong, and sexy on a vegan diet brings me so much joy!" She loves cooking, watching movies, doing yoga, swimming, kickboxing, pumping iron, and traveling to new cities.

What are some ways in which your active, vegan lifestyle contributes to your quality of life? What does it do for you? How does it enhance your life?

I was already vegan when I started getting serious about fitness and training, and I am shocked at what my body can do. Faster recovery, longer and harder workouts, I've put on more muscle than I thought I would be able to as a woman, and have dropped my body fat without any starvation or deprivation. Eating a plant-based diet is a not-so-well-kept secret to enjoying the best performance ever. Being healthy and strong just feels good, and no one has to get hurt in the process. I feel blessed that I can do the least harm possible while having the best life possible. I don't understand why anyone wouldn't want to be vegan!

Please share your best nutrition tips for vegans who are interested in healthy diets to support their active lifestyles.

I encourage people to take baby steps if they can't go 100 percent plant-based overnight. It's better to do something than to do nothing at all. If you crowd out the "bad" stuff while adding in all the delicious plant foods you can get your hands on, then the not-so-great foods will fall away. Focus on the abundance of foods you can eat rather than what you can't eat. My diet is more exciting and varied than it ever was before I went vegan. You'll discover new and exciting foods once you start paying attention to the fuel you feed yourself. Try to focus your diet on whole, unprocessed foods and eat all the colors of the rainbow—especially green. I have a rule that I eat a green vegetable at every single meal, even breakfast. And get in the kitchen and cook! That is the way to true health and the best performance as an athlete. Packaged and processed foods will just slow you down. Also, don't get enticed by wacky or restricted diets. Eat a balanced diet of cooked and raw foods, move your body every day, and be gentle with yourself and others.

As a plant-based athlete, what sorts of foods do you prepare or pack when you travel?

If I'm traveling by car I fill up a cooler with chopped veggies, hummus, almond milk, frozen bananas, fruit, and other staples along with my blender to make smoothies! If traveling by plane I always take protein powder with me and other snack foods like rice crackers and hummus, homemade granola, rice cakes and nut butter, bars, and fruit. Sometimes you can't get a good meal in airports, so snacks are super important to have on hand.

Before I get to a destination I always check HappyCow.net to see what veg-friendly restaurants are nearby, and I try to stay with friends so I have access to a kitchen. That's the best way to ensure you'll eat healthy while traveling.

How do you think your life would have been different, had you not decided to become vegan?

Wow, it's hard to think about it since I've been vegan for so long and it now encompasses my whole being. I imagine I would have been sucked into the superficiality of the fashion and movie industry, which was my path before discovering my love of cooking and going to culinary school. I would have continued to live with blinders on, like so many in our population. My health would have declined. I probably wouldn't have found my love for fitness.

Do you have any active living tips to share with vegans and vegetarians who are just beginning to exercise or those who want to be more active?

You don't need fancy clothes, expensive equipment, or even a gym membership to start an exercise program. My favorite type of workout for myself and for beginners is HIIT (high-intensity interval training). This is a short twenty-to-thirty-minute workout where you alternate intervals of high-intensity, all-out moves with short rests. The internet has many great resources for workouts you can do at home with no special equipment required, so there are really no excuses! Everyone can carve out 30 minutes in their day to devote to their health.

What has been the greatest diet- or nutrition-related challenge for you as a plant-based athlete?

When I first got into fitness I was eating a pretty restricted diet. I had stopped eating oil and was eating a lot of raw foods. Coupled with intense exercise, this eventually left me completely drained and fatigued. It was the worst three weeks of my life. I didn't even have the energy to leave the house! Turns out I wasn't eating enough fat. Once I added coconut oil back into my diet and had more cooked meals, my energy came back. Now I have found the balance that works for my body, which is a varied diet of whole, unprocessed vegan food—both cooked and raw—with small amounts of healthy fats and coconut oil.

Also, supplementing with protein powder is a big discussion in the fitness field. For me, supplementing with plant-based protein has helped greatly in building and maintaining muscle mass.

How do you promote muscle recovery?

I think my super healthy diet does wonders for my recovery. I'm pretty active every day with usually one active rest day when I do a power yoga class. I do love some foam rolling, though! It hurts so good! For joint health I take a vegan glucosamine with MSM supplement as well as B12.

What are some athletic achievements you'd like to highlight?

Sprint Triathlon 2011
Tough Mudder 2012
Bikini Competition 2013
Sprint Triathlon 2013

DR. ANASTASIA ZINCHENKO

Anastasia earned a PhD in Biochemistry from the University of Cambridge, after which she conducted research in the field of sports nutrition and exercise science.

She is an online strength and nutrition coach, as well as a competitive bodybuilder and powerlifter who represented Great Britain at the bench press world championships in South Africa.

Anastasia is the co-founder of and chief scientist at Science Bakes. She combined her scientific knowledge, coaching experience, and athletic background to create nutritious, quick-to-prepare, protein-packed meals for the modern consumer.

What are some ways in which your active, vegan lifestyle contributes to your quality of life? What does it do for you? How does it enhance your life?

The answer is very simple: it makes me feel great. Feeling great and comfortable in your skin is the best motivation to keep going. Who wants to feel sluggish like an unhealthy couch potato? Most people don't.

In addition to this, there is the identity point: What is the "ideal person" I want to be? People mostly want to see themselves as good people who do things that are right. Here, veganism comes in. The more I learned about the negative impacts of factory farming, the more I felt that living a vegan lifestyle is morally the right thing to do for me. I don't want to support something and contribute to something I consider to be wrong or unnecessary. For me, veganism is about doing the least harm possible, and respecting all living beings, the environment, and ourselves.

Please share your best nutrition tips for vegans who are interested in healthy diets to support their active lifestyles.

- Educate yourself. Learn what you should eat and what supplements you should take (e.g., Vitamin B12) to support your body, your health, and your athletic performance.
- Eat enough protein, while balancing your calories. If you are a big guy or a very active person (e.g., an endurance athlete), you can use more whole foods that contain not only protein, but also lots of carbs or fat (e.g., legumes or nuts, respectively) to cover your protein needs. However, if you are a petite female or want to lose weight or don't move very much, then you need to choose your protein sources smartly to keep your calories

in check. For the latter case, great protein sources are tofu, seitan, homemade protein bread, protein powder, or fat-reduced nut or seed flours for cooking or baking.

- Eat enough nutrient-rich foods like fruits and veggies, but don't overdo it. Too much fiber can cause digestive problems like bloating or constipation.

As a plant-based athlete, what sorts of foods do you prepare or pack when you travel?

When I travel, I have vegan protein sources with me and get fruits, veggies, and nuts in supermarkets.

Here's what I pack:
- Protein powder portioned in small bags or containers. You can just put it into a glass and add water to it.
- Protein bars.
- Space bars or similar vegan faux meats that are high in protein and don't have too much fat. I pay attention to ensure that the products are vacuum-packed, and you can store at room temperature.
- Small portion sizes of dry roasted chickpeas.
- Homemade protein pancakes or doughnuts.

How do you think your life would have been different, had you not decided to become vegan?

This is difficult to say, as you can't turn back time. However, one thing I can say for sure is that I wouldn't have met many amazing vegan athletes who've become my very good friends.

Do you have any active living tips to share with vegans who are just beginning to exercise, or those who want to be more active?

Just do it. It's hard to start and it will get easier as you keep going. Choose a training program, stick to it, learn from more experienced people, and educate yourself. If you get discouraged and lose motivation, look back to see how far you have come.

What has been the greatest diet- or nutrition-related challenge for you as a plant-based athlete?

Not to overeat on peanut butter!

But seriously, when I had just started, it was not letting myself be influenced by things other people/athletes do, and finding what the right thing is for me. Just because a top vegan athlete drinks a green smoothie every morning, doesn't mean that you need to do the same. Just because someone you admire eats eight meals a day, doesn't mean that you can't eat less often and still get great results.

I don't mean that you shouldn't get inspiration from other athletes. I just mean that you need to adjust everything individually to you and your lifestyle. Also, consider the option that sometimes athletes do stupid stuff when it comes to nutrition because they aren't scientists or nutritionists.

It's not necessarily a certain diet that makes a talented athlete exceptional, it's the exceptional genetics that make the athlete perform well, despite a sub-optimal diet.

How do you promote muscle recovery?

To be honest, I don't do anything special to promote muscle recovery. My body recovers well from training. I just make sure not to do anything stupid in training that can make me sore. Many people think that soreness is a sign of efficient training. However, the opposite is the case. Soreness is a sign that you have exceeded the recovery capacity of your body.

What are some athletic achievements you'd like to highlight?

My top achievements as a vegan athlete were becoming the British Bench Press Vice-Champion in 2016 and representing Great Britain at the World Championships in the same year.

DANIEL AUSTIN

Daniel Austin is a punk musician turned animal rights activist turned competitive powerlifter from Texas. Daniel went vegan in 2005, but he didn't begin to compete in powerlifting until 2015, at the age of 32. He has since gone on to compete in national and international championships in raw powerlifting's most reputable federations. His debut book, *The Way of The Vegan Meathead: Eating for Strength*, is a manifesto of Vegan Power for aspiring strength athletes.

What are some ways in which your active, vegan lifestyle contributes to your quality of life? What does it do for you? How does it enhance your life?

My powerlifting regimen has helped me develop self-discipline in many aspects of my life beyond just lifting. It keeps me oriented to stay organized and prepared to deal with life's curve balls while maintaining my sight on my immediate and long-term goals. Since I compete in a weight class specific sport, the powerlifting lifestyle has made me dial in my nutrition strictly as needed, and it has made me hyper-aware of how I need to fix my schedule each week for making appropriate time for the gym. I wasn't always so good at planning or regimenting my life in general.

Psychologically, I have reaped many benefits from regular heavy lifting, and I've taken it to a higher level still through being competitive in my sport. Regular physical activity is proven to give your brain a boost and enhance productivity in other aspects of your life, and my experience completely aligns with those findings. I think lifting has helped me become a better writer, reader, thinker, communicator, and so on. Even if I am deadlifting super heavy, it's still a form of meditation, and I'd even say it's a form of yoga, because you are listening to your body's signals about what weaknesses need to be addressed within you, what your current limitations are, and it makes you more in touch with the presence of being in your own body.

Please share your best nutrition tips for vegans who are interested in healthy diets to support their active lifestyles.

This is a slightly weird one for me to answer, because as we discussed together on your podcast (nobullshitvegan.com/016), health has never really been my concern. I am an ethical vegan, so health was always a secondary concern for me when it came to my vegan lifestyle. I also train for max strength, and I have found that strength diets and health diets are not the same thing. Strength diets tend to be higher in fat and protein, and more moderate on carbohydrates, which seems to be a controversial stance on diet to take if you're talking to the "Whole Foods Plant-Based" crowd. They think high fat and high protein means an instant heart attack, which is silly, of course. However, the caveat there is that I do think a vegan strength diet, as put forth in my book *The Way of The Vegan Meathead*, is far less likely to increase health risks than a non-vegan strength diet, just for the absence of dietary cholesterol alone.

But to answer your question properly, I think anyone who wants to train for strength as a vegan should not be afraid of *fat*. Fat intake affects natural cholesterol levels, which happens to be a primary component of testosterone production, which is absolutely essential for strength and recovery. High carb vegans tend to have a harder time developing elite levels of strength, at least in part due to lower fat intake leading to less testosterone production. If you're trying to build muscle or increase your one-rep maxes, definitely experiment with eating over 20 percent of your calories from fat. As for me, I usually eat in the ballpark of 30 to 35 percent fat per day, or even slightly more.

After six years of eating a high fat and high protein vegan diet, my cholesterol is still at healthy and safe levels, and at my last employer I even got kickback money for my excellent bloodwork, which was among the best in the company. I don't recommend high fat diets for people not pursuing serious strength, but it does seem to be that higher fat intake is essential if strength is your focus, so don't be afraid to experiment with higher fat intake. The ten percent or less approach offered by the WFPB crowd and Forks Over Knives doctors simply does not cut it for getting strong.

As a plant-based athlete, what sorts of foods do you prepare or pack when you travel?

I always bring protein powder with me, and protein bars as well. I notoriously get stopped at the TSA checkpoint when I fly, because the agents there always want to swab my protein and creatine. Traveling is no excuse to eat less protein or forego proper supplementation, so you must prepare to have your required goods by your side at all times. Other than basic protein sources, I usually have almonds or cashews for healthy sources of fat (and a fair amount of protein) to consume while in transit. It's easy to get carb-heavy foods wherever you go, but wholesome fats and proteins are not as easy to find in airports or gas stations, especially vegan sources, so I make sure I always have options with me. If I'm just making a day drive for an event or a show, I will prep my usual meals of fake meats and green vegetables in Tupperware to eat in the car, but of course, if I have to fly somewhere it is more limiting, and that is when I rely more on supplemental foods like protein powder, bars, and nuts. Other than that, I just do my best to prep properly or stock a fridge as needed whenever I get to my destination.

How do you think your life would have been different had you not decided to become vegan?

I think I would feel worse about my body and performance, be less motivated to act for change in the world, and I also think I would enjoy eating less. If I could eat treat foods like donuts or pizza everywhere, all the time, I'd—for one—be in much worse shape than I am now, and two, I'd be so glutted by those kinds of foods I'd likely take them for granted because it wouldn't be a big deal or special occasion to eat them. There is also the paradox that the dietary limitations I placed on myself by becoming an ethical vegan actually made me experiment with more kinds of foods. Before I went vegetarian (seven years before going vegan), I didn't know what falafel was. Then, even when I became vegan, I didn't know the joys of eating an Ethiopian veggie platter, or chana masala. All the years in which I had a million other generic food options in America, I never thought to try those cuisines, or many others. They seemed intimidatingly exotic and weird to my spoiled and sheltered mind. After going vegan I became more open to trying anything and everything that didn't have animal parts in it, and I found whole new worlds of flavor. I think eating has only become more interesting because of veganism. Convenience really does dull us more often than not.

Do you have any active living tips to share with vegans who are just beginning to exercise, or those who want to be more active?

Aim at a version of you that you want to be, and stay focused on that version of you, especially in the beginning because that ultimate focus might be the only thing to get you through at first. You really have to give your body and nervous system time to adapt to the new movements you're teaching them, especially if you've been unconditioned most of your life. Being strong or in shape is a lifestyle, not just something you do from time to time. The adjustment to getting into better shape than you were before is almost always going to be most uncomfortable at first, but if you eat well (according to your goals), sleep well, and maintain some consistency with your training, you'll see major differences in the long term that you weren't able to discern in the day to day along the way. Also, in a matter of time you'll notice that you're handling more volume and intensity than you were at first and you'll delight in the fact that you feel unphased by the very same weight or intensity that used make you hobble around and groan for a week afterward. Conditioning simply takes time.

As a competitive powerlifter, I can say this: it took me about four years of inconsistent powerlifting training and developing my skills with compound lifts before I decided to get totally consistent and get the guts to start competing. Once I started competing, it took me almost another year to start placing in the top three or winning meets, and from there it took another year or so to start qualifying for national competitions. When I look back on it all, it was actually a really long process, but when I approached my goals day by day, workout by workout, programming cycle by programming cycle—all with my long-term *aim* in mind—it never felt like a monumental task at all. We must always proceed from where we are. Do not be ashamed to start wherever you are at. All that matters is that you do your best to move forward from there.

What has been the greatest diet- or nutrition-related challenge for you as a plant-based athlete?

Back to talking about fat . . . The years it took me to discover the hormonal benefits of eating a higher fat intake were certainly filled with challenges. When I first started doing some form of weight training as a vegan, which would have been late 2010, I definitely started gaining a lot of weight, but I certainly didn't look great with my shirt off doing it. Granted, I am not in a sport where aesthetics matter, but still, no one wants to look flabby, especially when you do a lot of work in the gym and train hard. Yes, I made some gains while hyper-bulking and eating every bit of vegan food in sight, but I realize now that I could have been more responsible with my diet and gotten just as strong, if not stronger, just as fast. Back then I was aiming for high protein target numbers each day, but I never evaluated how many carbs were attached to my protein sources. Once I started to experiment with the fat-carb-protein balance of my diet and began eating more fat overall, I found I was maintaining (or even gaining) strength while I was losing bodyweight and body fat percentage. That was a balance I had to find through experimentation, and it took time, but as of now I have my high-fat diet approach on lock, and I have been maintaining competition bodyweight while gradually improving my max strength ever since.

How do you promote muscle recovery?

I've got a four-pronged approach to recovery:

- Meet caloric and macronutrient targets with your diet. Every day.
- Supplement accordingly. (I find creatine and glutamine particularly helpful for managing soreness and fatigue, and other vitamins and minerals are essential as well, but I can get long-winded about all that . . .)
- On average, sleep enough or slightly more than enough. Life happens, and sometimes sleeping well consistently can be really hard to achieve, especially if you're super busy. Research has shown that we can often get away with two or three days of poor sleep before it really catches up with us in performance quality, but to chronically sleep poorly can shut down your ability to make gains quickly, even if you train, eat, and supplement properly. So do whatever you can to prioritize and defend your time to sleep as often

as possible. Resting is actually when our bodies do the most repair work and replenish growth hormones.

- Utilize recovery days in the gym to elongate tight or sore muscle groups and get more blood flow to them. More blood flow to affected muscles means more mineral and antioxidant delivery to relieve the soreness in stressed muscles.

What are some athletic achievements you'd like to highlight?

Last year I placed second in the 82.5kg (182-pound) weight class at the IPL Drug Tested World Powerlifting Championships in Ireland. It was my first time traveling abroad to compete, and I think the stress of the long travel and extreme time zone change caused me to sleep poorly and come down with a cold, so I ended up missing my target weight class of 75kg (165 pounds) by about one pound. Had I made my intended weight I would have placed first in the 75kg weight class. Either way, I consider that trip a success, and I learned a lot about managing my health when traveling to compete. Also, to be at the absolute bottom of a weight class in terms of bodyweight and place near the top is something worth noting.

The year before, I was the only vegan male to compete in the USAPL Raw Nationals in Washington. USAPL qualification standards are considerably tougher to meet than USPA/IPL standards, and the USAPL two-hour weigh-in rule is a real killer. Though I didn't do as well as I hoped, I'm proud that I've been able to put up numbers that have qualified me for the highest levels of competition in both major powerlifting organizations in the world, and likewise rank in the top quartile of lifters for each. Aside from that, I have won first or placed in the top three at most of my local or qualifying meets.

MATT TERRY

After struggling with obesity most of his life, Matt turned his pain into a passion for all things sports and nutrition. He completed his degrees in exercise science and has spent the last nineteen years as a trainer and nutrition coach helping change minds and transform lives.

Matt played college football, has competed in all strength sports from powerlifting to Olympic lifting and natural bodybuilding. He was a member of the men's US national team for Olympic weightlifting, winning three national championships, he took part in the 2000 Olympic trials (missed qualifying for the Olympics by only one spot!), and lifted in world championships and the Pan Am games.

What are some ways in which your active, vegan lifestyle contributes to your quality of life? What does it do for you? How does it enhance your life?

Being vegan has helped revitalize my joy of eating. Previously, as a meat eater, I felt bored by my food, often not really wanting to eat. I find being plant-based and the many colors on my plate make me want to eat, feel better about what I am eating, and feel better and more vital overall.

Please share your best nutrition tips for vegans who are interested in healthy diets to support their active lifestyles.

Food prep is key. Having lots of ready-to-eat foods prepped ahead of time, having all the veggies and fruits washed, chopped, and ready to go really makes a difference. I also default to eating most things raw as it's just easier. One thing I would say especially as you transition is cook harder-to-digest foods very well. When I first transitioned, my fiber intake was too high and caused a few stomach issues.

As a plant-based athlete, what sorts of foods do you prepare or pack when you travel?

Usually fruit, nuts, seeds, plant-based protein bars, tofu, beans, etc.

How do you think your life would have been different, had you not decided to become vegan?

Given the health condition I switched to vegan for, I probably would have been dead, or at least dying.

Do you have any active living tips to share with vegans who are just beginning to exercise, or those who want to be more active?

Start slow, find things you enjoy, and build over time. Do not try to win the CrossFit games your first workout!

What has been the greatest diet- or nutrition-related challenge for you as a plant-based athlete?

At first it was just learning how to structure things and which foods could help balance out my meals better so I wasn't just eating fruits and veggies.

How do you promote muscle recovery?

Eating enough, sleeping, and active recovery days.

What are some athletic achievements you'd like to highlight?

Right now, training seven days a week with little to no soreness, increased recovery, and really pushing my limits in terms of endurance and strength that I don't think I could have done even in my twenties when I was a world-class athlete.

While in my twenties I was an elite Olympic Lifter for the US in the 94 kilo (207-pound) class. I won three National titles, competed in the World Championships and won several Pan-American game medals. My best lifts at that time was a 341 snatch, 440 clean & jerk, 640 back squat, and a 305 standing military press. I was a huge meat and dairy eater, in chronic pain, and always bloated. I lived on anti-inflammatories and pain meds. My joints constantly ached, and my digestion was a mess. I thought it was normal. As the cliché goes, I wish I knew then what I know now. I still train very hard, daily in fact, with little to no joint pain and even though my recovery has always been great, now it feels the best it's ever been.

TOBIAS SJÖSTEN

Tobias has been a vegan since 2014. A jack of all sports and master of none, he's competed in CrossFit, Brazilian jiu-jitsu, and powerlifting. His most memorable competition was placing first at Arnold Fighters, but between a day job as a software architect, a family of three (soon to be four!), and running Athlegan.com, there's never enough time to do all the training and have all the fun he'd want to.

What are some ways in which your active, vegan lifestyle contributes to your quality of life? What does it do for you? How does it enhance your life?

Being vegan is a huge relief for my conscience. I've always had this nagging feeling that something didn't add up and however confident I used to feel about eating meat, I never really wanted to dig into it because I somehow knew I couldn't explain how my values justified my actions. They didn't. And now that I am living my values, it's like a stone has been lifted from my shoulders.

Please share your best nutrition tips for vegans who are interested in healthy diets to support their active lifestyles.

Finish your plate, then have another! So many new vegans run into problems because they're simply not eating enough. Get your energy intake under control before thinking about micro-optimizations in your diet.

Also, explore other cuisines. My current favorites are Ethiopian, Mozambican, Vietnamese, and Mexican. Lots of "accidental vegan" meals there and others that can easily be veganized.

As a plant-based athlete, what sorts of foods do you prepare or pack when you travel?

Nuts and bananas! Occasionally I stock up on Clif bars as well. If I'm flying, I opt for cashew, hazel, and walnuts (just in case someone has a peanut allergy), but otherwise peanuts are my go-to.

How do you think your life would have been different, had you not decided to become vegan?

I would never have started Athlegan, that's for sure! And that's had a huge impact on my life. Other than that, I believe I might not have been as empathetic to others, regardless of their species. It's really a system of abuse and one end feeds another.

Do you have any active living tips to share with vegans who are just beginning to exercise, or those who want to be more active?

Get on a structured program and follow it for at least three months. In fact, pick one quality to improve at a time and focus on that for at least three months, while maintaining your past progress. Serving two masters and all that.

Also, be patient. Anyone can make huge changes and see big results in just a few months, but it takes a long time and lots of patience and grinding to create long-term lasting results.

What has been the greatest diet- or nutrition-related challenge for you as a plant-based athlete?

It was actually surprisingly easy to transition for me. I was expecting it to be confusing and hard but then the weeks passed and nothing really came up. It was just food, albeit with some minor tweaks, and I've been eating food since I was a kid.

The biggest challenges about veganism have nothing to do with diet and everything to do with non-vegans.

Though, if I had to say something, it'd probably be learning to pick and combine foods to nail all the micronutrients. But that's tricky even as an omnivore, so nothing really unique for vegans.

How do you promote muscle recovery?

I lift heavy and consistently and I eat plenty of carbs and protein. I also try to sleep as much as I can—I'm a firm believer that alarm clocks are our worst enemies, waking us up before we're done sleeping for the night. If you have to get up early, simply go to bed early.

What are some athletic achievements you'd like to highlight?

I hate to rest on old laurels but I haven't done a whole lot since I won gold at Arnold Fighters in Barcelona—Brazilian jiu-jitsu—back in 2016. Some second and third places in tournaments after that.

I also managed to hit a new all-time squat personal best of 150 kg (330.7 pounds) last year, nine months after a knee surgery, which I'm proud of because it shows I took rehabilitation and training seriously and worked consistently for a long time.

SCOTT SHETLER

Scott Shetler is the owner of Extreme Performance Training Systems and a personal trainer living in Atlanta, Georgia. He has a degree in Health and Physical Education, is certified by the National Strength and Conditioning Association, a certified Taijiquan instructor under Master Jesse Tsao of Tai Chi Healthways, a certified Westside Barbell Special Strengths Coach, and a World Kettlebell Club Kettlebell Lifting Coach. Through his training center and online coaching program, he works with clients on their health and fitness programs, and athletes from strength, combative, and Olympic sports on their strength and conditioning programs. Scott has competed in powerlifting and kettlebell sport

and is currently studying Brazilian Jiu Jitsu and Taijiquan. As an advocate for animal welfare and vegetarian for ten years, vegan for the last seven, he fuels his training with a plant-based diet. To learn more about Scott, visit his website at eptsgym.com.

What are some ways in which your active, vegan lifestyle contributes to your quality of life? What does it do for you? How does it enhance your life?

I try to keep balance in my training. I used to compete in kettlebell sport and powerlifting, but still follow a very intense strength training and conditioning program. In addition I train Brazilian Jiu Jitsu and am a student and teacher of Taijiquan and qigong. I practice meditation and try to spend as much time as possible with my feet on a skateboard, whether it's hitting the local skatepark or carving downhill on my longboard. On top of my active lifestyle I own a sports performance and training center where I train motivated fitness enthusiasts and athletes from many different sports at all levels of competition. My business includes online coaching and consulting, writing and self-publishing books as well as blog articles, social media content, video content, and podcasting. At forty-five years of age, between my busy workload and activity I need to stay fueled with high quality nutrition. I have found that a healthy vegan diet delivers everything I need for health and performance. After switching to a vegan diet the biggest thing I noticed was my recovery from hard training sessions had improved dramatically. In fact after following a healthy whole food plant-based diet for only four months I had reduced my bodyweight from 230 to 178 pounds and at my annual physical, my doctor was completely blown away at how much my lab work had improved. It was the first time all my numbers were in the excellent range and while skeptical of my vegan diet, he encouraged me to keep doing what I was doing.

Please share your best nutrition tips for vegans who are interested in healthy diets to support their active lifestyles.

I feel it is important to keep the emphasis on health. It is very easy to jump on the processed and junk food bandwagon since there are so many options for vegans nowadays. While I certainly think an occasional indulgence is fine (vegan donuts and chocolate chip cookies are usually my favorite), the bulk of a healthy vegan diet should be made up of fruits, vegetables, beans and legumes, nuts and seeds, and whole grains. Hydration is incredibly important as well. For people who are training hard adequate protein intake is important but generally overrated. For the most part, provided an individual is eating an appropriate number of calories from a wide variety of whole plant foods, protein needs should be met easily. Many vegan athletes I know usually consume a protein and carbohydrate recovery drink around training to make sure their bases are covered. There are a few supplements that should be considered. Vitamin B12 is important to supplement with, and I know many health professionals recommend supplementing with Vitamin D3 and a vegan EPA/DHA supplement as well.

As a plant-based athlete, what sorts of foods do you prepare or pack when you travel?

Honestly I don't travel much but when I do I always make sure to have water and some vegan protein bars or trail mix on hand as a backup in case I can't find food. A simple combo of mixed nuts (almonds, walnuts, and Brazil nuts are my personal favorites) and some dried fruit can really help in a pinch. On the road, I usually look for Mexican or Asian restaurants as it is very easy to load up on rice, beans, and vegetables. It is getting easier to find vegan specialty restaurants, particularly in larger cities, and the Happy Cow app has been very helpful in that regard. When I get to where I'm staying, I always look for vegan-friendly restaurants in the area and usually hit a grocery store to stock up on food to keep at my Airbnb or hotel. I know traveling and food will be a bigger concern with bodybuilders and physique athletes, but for me it requires little planning.

How do you think your life would have been different, had you not decided to become vegan?

Honestly I don't know how to respond to this. I have always been compassionate towards animals so becoming vegan was a very natural part of my personal growth. I definitely feel that my health would not be anywhere near as good as it is currently. While appearance is something I am not concerned with, I am often told that I look much younger than I am and I feel a lot of that has to do with the emphasis I've placed on eating a healthy diet and maintaining an active lifestyle.

Do you have any active living tips to share with vegans who are just beginning to exercise, or those who want to be more active?

If someone is just beginning an exercise program, building consistency is more important than intensity. It actually takes very little training to stimulate muscular development and improve cardiovascular function. I think people new to exercise may look at bodybuilders or competitive athletes for inspiration and become overwhelmed with everything they are doing to be competitive. For people looking to lose weight and improve their body composition, two to three strength training sessions and three to four cardiovascular training sessions per week would be plenty. That literally works out to be five to seven days of low to moderately intense exercise per week and thirty to sixty minutes per session. This is more than enough for someone looking to improve health and fitness. When it comes to losing body-fat, nutrition is more important than training as training is just a stimulus for muscle growth and fat loss. Making sure your caloric intake is appropriate for your activity level and goal is crucial. For those that fall into the general fitness category nutrition should simply be focused on healthy whole foods. Aside from Vitamin B12 and the supplements mentioned earlier, there is no need to worry about consuming anything other than healthy whole plant foods and staying properly hydrated.

What has been the greatest diet- or nutrition-related challenge for you as a plant-based athlete?

The biggest challenge has been getting enough calories through healthy foods. The downside to eating a whole food plant-based diet is that it can be calorically sparse, particularly if you don't have a huge appetite like I do. I tend to drink a lot of green smoothies and eat pretty high fiber foods so I get full easily. On days where I am training Brazilian Jiu Jitsu plus heavy weightlifting and conditioning I can feel pretty wiped out and it can be tough to keep my body weight stable, let alone try to put weight on. This is why I don't sweat it when I eat the occasional donut or cookies! Getting more fat in my diet through nuts, nut butters, and avocado has helped push my calories up as well.

How do you promote muscle recovery?

There are a few things I do to enhance recovery. One is nutrition. I eat a lot of fresh fruits and vegetables daily. I think berries and greens are very important in particular. I use a protein and carbohydrate drink around training that consists of 1 gram of protein to about 2-4 grams of carbohydrates. I drink a little before training and the rest immediately after and I do feel this helps facilitate recovery from training. I average around 0.8-1 gram of protein per kilogram of body weight and pretty much eat whatever I want, whenever I want with about 85 to 90 percent of my diet being healthy whole foods. I have been experimenting with time restricted eating and have found that I feel really good when I stop eating about three hours prior to going to bed and wait a minimum of one hour after waking to begin eating. I also find that I feel much better eating the bulk of my calories mid-morning to early afternoon. Hydration is essential for recovery as well and I drink plenty of water throughout the day. I am not a big supplement guy and try to focus on whole foods, but I find creatine to be beneficial for recovery. I also take a supplement that provides a daily dose of B12, D3 and EPA/DHA. I use quite a bit of turmeric daily, a minimum of ¼-½ teaspoon daily usually mixed into a smoothie or salad. I've also experimented with a systemic enzyme supplement called Restorazyme from Mike Mahler that I feel is very beneficial as well. Outside of nutrition and supplements I strive to get seven to eight hours of sleep a night and a twenty-minute power nap most afternoons. I have a joint mobility and flexibility exercise series I do daily, and practice qigong and Taijiquan four to five times a week which, along with low intensity aerobic activity (heart rate 130-150bpm) serve as great active recovery modalities. On occasion I use various types of salt baths, contrast showers, ice, massage, and other therapeutic modalities as well. As I've gotten older I've found that monitoring the intensity of my training is important for recovery. I use a heart rate variability (HRV) recovery app called Morpheus to help monitor my daily physical readiness and can adjust my training as needed.

What are some athletic achievements you'd like to highlight?

Most things I've done have not been at a high level so I hesitate to call them "athletic." Like in powerlifting, while I have set state and national records in a couple different federations, there are something like twenty-seven sanctioned powerlifting federations, so unless the records that lifters claim are on the all-time lists I take them with a grain of salt. I mean literally every lifter on Instagram is a powerlifting record holder, it's absolutely absurd. That being said some of my favorite personal achievements were in kettlebell sport. Placing third at the first ever kettlebell sport competition at the Arnold Sports Festival in 2009 was a big accomplishment. I had always wanted to compete at the Arnold and to be part of the first ever kettlebell sport event which had over 110 lifters was awesome. In addition I got to play a small part in the growth of kettlebell sport in the US. I started the first organized kettlebell sport organization in the state of Georgia and hosted meets for a decade from 2004 to 2014 before passing the reins to a friend and colleague. Winning the 2013 and 2014 Florida State Kettlebell Sport Championships in the long cycle event, both my weight class and best lifter overall, were pretty big accomplishments as well. Outside of that staying competitive in powerlifting from 2004–2008 then making a comeback in 2014 and 2015 to compete with Team Plantbuilt on their powerlifting squad was awesome. My focus now is on health and longevity and exploring my martial arts training and practice at a deeper level. As a coach, my focus is on my athletes and their competitive careers. I find helping others succeed to be incredibly rewarding and in many ways more fulfilling than my own competitive endeavors were.

CHAPTER 10: RECIPES

These recipes are intended to be easy to make, absolutely delicious, and ridiculously healthy. They've been created with active people in mind. We need nutritious food that will fuel our workouts and support muscle recovery between workouts, and we need to be able to make our food fairly quickly.

I must admit that I have a love/hate relationship with cooking. Sometimes I could putter around in the kitchen all day, but many days it feels more like a chore cutting into time I'd rather spend doing other things. It's days like those that have inspired the recipes in this book—they're meant to appeal to those of us who, at least during the workweek, are too busy working, exercising, taking care of family, and generally being awesome to have much time to spend in the kitchen.

I've tried to keep the preparation time for each of the recipes as short as possible, while still giving you great "bang for your buck" when it comes to taste. Some recipes will take a bit longer to cook (e.g., Crunchy Roasted Chickpeas on page 159, Scalloped Potatoes on page 174, or Caramelized Onions and Fennel on page 175), but in these cases all you're doing is waiting for your food to cook. By all means leave the kitchen and do something else while you wait!

Behold: my collection of more than 100 obsessively tested, athlete-endorsed, top-secret recipes.

BREAKFAST AND BRUNCH

We all need healthful, energizing starts to our days. The recipes in this section will help you to choose nutrient-packed breakfasts and brunches. Many of the recipes you can make ahead (like granola or baked oatmeal), and others are quick enough to make on a hurried workday morning (like the Open-Face Smoky Melt).

TOFU SCRAMBLE

This protein-packed meal is sure to kickstart your day (and your muscles)! Feel free to add in some greens—like spinach—during the last few minutes of cooking to up the nutritional ante.

2 tablespoons olive oil or coconut oil
1 small onion, diced
3 cups vegetables of choice (e.g., mushrooms, asparagus, kale, red pepper, tomato)
1 (350-gram) package extra firm tofu
1 teaspoon turmeric
1 tablespoon nutritional yeast
Salt & ground black pepper to taste
Ketchup to taste (optional)

Heat oil in a large saucepan or skillet over medium heat, and cook onion for 4 to 5 minutes.

Add vegetables and cook about 5 minutes, until they're almost done to your liking. If ingredients start to stick to the pan, add a few tablespoons of water.

Crumble tofu into saucepan or skillet. Add turmeric, nutritional yeast, salt, and pepper, and mix well. Cook for 2 to 3 minutes to heat through, then serve. Try it with ketchup!

Serves 4

GRANOLA

I love eating cereal as a midday snack, and this is one of my favorites. Below is a basic granola recipe to which you can add your favorite ingredients after baking. Suggestions: cranberries, shredded coconut, goji berries, diced sugar-free dried fruit (e.g., mangoes, papaya, apricots, apples, raisins, or nuts.). This recipe makes a large batch so you can store it for later use. Enjoy it with plant-based milk or soy yogurt, or snack on it dry while at work or out and about.

- -

4 cups rolled oats
¼ cup olive oil or melted coconut oil
¼ cup agave nectar
½ teaspoon cinnamon

- -

Preheat oven to 300°F and line 2 rimmed baking sheets with parchment paper.

In a medium mixing bowl, mix all ingredients until well combined, then spread in a single layer onto baking sheets.

Bake for 50 to 60 minutes, stirring every 15 minutes, until granola is lightly browned and crunchy.

Makes about 4 cups, or 4 servings

CRUNCHY QUINOA GRANOLA

Similar to oat-based granola but far higher in protein, turn a typical dinner superfood into breakfast! This recipe can be customized with whatever add-ins you like. Add spices like cloves or nutmeg before baking. Serve with fresh berries and your choice of plant-based milk.

1 cup dry quinoa
2 cups pure apple juice
1 tablespoon coconut oil, melted
1 tablespoon chia seeds
1½ teaspoons ground cinnamon
¼ cup agave nectar or maple syrup

Rinse quinoa in a fine mesh sieve under running water. In a medium saucepan, bring apple juice to a boil. Add quinoa, cover, reduce heat to low, and cook for 15 to 20 minutes, until all juice is absorbed. Let cool completely.

Preheat oven to 350°F and line rimmed baking sheet with parchment paper.

In a mixing bowl, stir together quinoa and coconut oil, chia seeds, cinnamon, and agave nectar or maple syrup.

Spread evenly on baking sheets and bake for 20 to 30 minutes, until lightly browned. Stir the mixture every 10 minutes to help it bake evenly.

Makes 2 large or 3 medium servings

APPLE SPICE BAKED OATMEAL

Baked oatmeal is like eating a delicious oatmeal cookie for breakfast—without the nutritionally empty sugar and fat calories! You can double the recipe and use an 8 by 8-inch baking dish if you'd like to make enough for a few breakfasts. You can also try making individual ramekins (reduce baking time to 15 to 20 minutes). This is one of the quickest recipes in this book to throw together—try 5 minutes on for size—but one of my all-time favorites.

. . . .

1½ cups rolled oats
1 teaspoon baking powder
2 tablespoons brown sugar or agave nectar (optional)
1 teaspoon cinnamon
¼ teaspoon ground nutmeg
¼ teaspoon ground ginger
1 apple, cored and diced into small pieces
1¼ cups plant-based milk
½ cup unsweetened applesauce

. . . .

Preheat oven to 350°F and lightly coat a 5 by 9-inch loaf pan (or other oven-safe dish of similar size) with cooking spray.

Combine all ingredients in a mixing bowl, then transfer to loaf pan.

Bake for 30 to 40 minutes, until toothpick inserted in the center comes out clean.

Makes 2 large servings or 4 small servings

TROPICAL BAKED OATMEAL

Less rustic than the traditional apples-and-spice combo, this version of baked oatmeal is a deliciously tropical way to start your day. Who knew oatmeal could be so exciting?

1½ cups rolled oats
1 teaspoon baking powder
¼ cup unsweetened shredded coconut
2 tablespoons brown sugar or agave nectar (optional)
½ cup apricots, diced into small pieces (or ¼ cup dried apricots, sliced thinly)
½ cup mango, diced into small pieces
½ cup plant-based milk
¾ cup coconut milk
½ cup unsweetened applesauce

Preheat oven to 350°F and lightly spray a 5 by 9-inch loaf pan (or other oven-safe dish of similar size) with cooking spray.

Combine all ingredients in a mixing bowl, then transfer to loaf pan.

Bake for 30 to 40 minutes, until toothpick inserted in the center comes out clean.

Makes 2 large servings or 4 small servings

OPEN-FACE SMOKY MELT

2½ cups grated or finely cubed smoked tofu
½ cup plain or vanilla soy or almond yogurt
½ cup carrots, diced
½ cup apple, cored and diced
½ cup green onion, finely chopped
1 teaspoon ground black pepper
8 thick slices whole grain bread
1 cup *Daiya* shredded nondairy cheese

In medium bowl, mix together the smoked tofu, soy yogurt, carrots, apple, green onion, and black pepper.

Divide between bread slices, top with 2 tablespoons Daiya cheese each, and bake in toaster oven (or broil on low in oven) for 5 to 10 minutes, or until cheese is melted and lightly browned.

Serves 4

SMOKED PAPRIKA HASH BROWNS

Smoked paprika is one of my favorite seasonings. You can use regular paprika if you don't have the smoked variety on hand, but I highly recommend you buy smoked paprika ASAP!

1 onion, diced
3 tablespoons olive oil or coconut oil
2 Russet potatoes, peeled and cut into ½-inch cubes
1 teaspoon smoked paprika
Salt and pepper to taste
2 green onions, finely chopped

In a nonstick saucepan over medium heat, cook onion in oil for 3 to 5 minutes, until translucent.

Add potatoes, smoked paprika, salt, and pepper. Stir to evenly distribute seasonings. Cover saucepan and sauté for 10 minutes, stirring often. Uncover saucepan and continue cooking, stirring often, until potatoes are well browned (an additional 10 minutes or so).

Top with green onions right before serving.

Serves 3–4

SNACKS, SIDES & SAUCES

These snack and side dish recipes give you plenty of options for smaller-scale fare. Whether you need a quick pick-me-up between meals, a pre- or post-workout energy source, or side dish ideas for your next dinner party, this section fits the bill. Here you'll find recipes for snacks, dips, spreads, and side dishes, as well as sauces and dressings.

HOMEMADE ENERGY BARS

Much more nutritious than store-bought versions (which are usually loaded with sugar), these energy bars take almost no time to make. Wrap bars in plastic wrap to pack for work or the gym. Prepared bars will last in the fridge for up to a week.

1½ cup rolled oats
⅓ cup dried fruit of your choice, cut into small pieces
½ cup natural nut butter of your choice (e.g., almond, peanut, hazelnut)
1 teaspoon vanilla extract
3 tablespoons agave nectar

In a mixing bowl, combine all ingredients until well mixed. Press mixture into the bottom of an 8 by 8-inch baking dish and refrigerate for 2 to 3 hours, until set. Cut into bars.

Makes 8 bars

SAVORY EDAMAME

Created by Holly Burton

Chili oil is red in color and is made from dried chili peppers infused in vegetable oil. Holly suggests taking out your contact lenses if you wear them and using the exhaust fan of your stove when using this seriously spicy oil!

. . . .

4 garlic cloves, chopped
4 teaspoons vegetable oil
2 teaspoons chili oil
4 cups cooked edamame (in pods)
¼ cup Chinese-style soy sauce

. . . .

In a saucepan over medium heat, sauté garlic in vegetable and chili oils for one minute.

Add edamame and coat with soy sauce. Mix well and cook for one minute to heat through.

Serves 3–4

HOMEMADE SEASONED TORTILLA CHIPS

Here's a quick 'n' easy snack recipe that contains much less fat than store-bought tortilla chips and lets you customize your own flavoring. Feel free to experiment! If plain salt and pepper are too boring for you, why not try any of the following: garlic powder, nutritional yeast, smoked paprika, chili powder, or Italian seasoning. Try these with Tomato Mint Salsa (recipe on page 169) or Hummus (recipe on page 164).

6 corn, wheat, or gluten-free tortillas
¼ cup olive oil or melted coconut oil
Salt and pepper to taste
2 teaspoons your choice of additional seasoning (optional)

Preheat oven to 350°F and line 2 baking sheets with parchment paper.

Stack tortillas on top of each other. Using a sharp knife, slice the stack into eighths. Place tortilla wedges in a single layer on baking sheets. Brush lightly with oil, then sprinkle with salt, pepper, and additional seasoning (optional).

Bake for 6 to 10 minutes, until edges are lightly browned. They can burn quickly, so check every minute or so starting at 5 minutes. Tortilla chips will continue to crisp as they cool.

Serves 4

CRUNCHY ROASTED CHICKPEAS

This is a delicious snack that provides lots of protein to build muscle and keep you full. Make large batches, then take smaller portions to work and the gym, and make sure to keep a stash for movie nights! Salt, ground black pepper, and chili powder make a deliciously simple seasoning combination. If you want to kick it up a notch, one of my favorite flavoring combinations is ¾ tablespoon nutritional yeast, ¼ tablespoon garlic powder, and a sprinkling of salt and ground black pepper.

2 (15-ounce) cans chickpeas
1½ tablespoons olive oil or melted coconut oil
1 tablespoon seasoning of your choice

Preheat oven to 375°F.

Rinse chickpeas in cold water, then blot dry with paper towel.

Place chickpeas in a rimmed baking dish in a single layer. Drizzle with oil and seasoning, and mix to distribute.

Bake for 45 to 60 minutes, stirring every 20 minutes or so, until chickpeas are crunchy all the way through and have turned medium brown. Each oven varies, so make sure you test your chickpeas starting at about 40 minutes. You'll want your chickpeas to end up similar to corn nuts in texture—nice 'n' crunchy!

Serves 4

ON-THE-GO SNACK MIX

My personal training and nutrition clients are often surprised by how simple healthy eating can be. I often suggest taking a few minutes each week to prepare a healthy snack mix. Divide it into individual-serving containers or Ziploc bags, and keep them handy so you can grab and go.

. . . .

2 cups mixed nuts (e.g., almonds, cashews, walnuts, Brazil nuts)
½ cup pumpkin seeds
¾ cup dried fruit (e.g., apricots, apples, banana chips, cranberries, goji berries)
¼ cup nondairy dark chocolate chips

. . . .

Mix all ingredients together in a bowl.

Makes approximately 3½ cups.

STOVETOP POPCORN

A recipe for popcorn?! You bet. We're not talking microwave bag popcorn chock-full of trans fats and artificial flavorings here. We're talkin' wholesome, preferably organic popcorn made from plain kernels and coconut oil (plus my secret popcorn-making method, of course). If you like your popcorn with a bit of added flavor, experiment with toppings like nutritional yeast, cracked black pepper, smoked paprika, chili powder, or garlic powder.

¼ cup coconut oil
¾ cup popcorn kernels
½ teaspoon salt

In a large saucepan or Dutch oven, heat coconut oil over medium heat for 2 minutes. Drop in 3 popcorn kernels, cover, and wait 'til you hear at least one pop. That's your cue that the oil has reached the correct temperature.

Add salt and the rest of the popcorn kernels, cover, and gently shake the pot (wearing oven mitts!) every 20 seconds or so to prevent burning the kernels.

Once popping has slowed to about once every 3 seconds, remove saucepan from heat and uncover immediately to let steam escape.

Serves 4

RAW CASHEW DILL DIP

Created by Jeff Golfman

Like hummus, this dip can be used in countless ways. Just rely on your imagination! For liquid sweeteners, Jeff suggests agave nectar, coconut nectar, or maple syrup.

- -

2 cups cashews, soaked in water for a few hours
1 clove garlic, minced
½ cup fresh dill
1 tablespoon liquid sweetener
¼ cup fresh lemon juice

- -

Place all ingredients in food processor and blend 'til smooth.

Serves 4

HUMMUS

A classic multipurpose spread to enjoy on pita, in sandwiches, or in wraps. Also try it as a dip for fresh veggies.

- -

1 (15-ounce) can chickpeas
1 tablespoon tahini
Juice of ½ lemon
1–2 cloves garlic, sliced
Ground black pepper to taste
2 tablespoons olive oil

- -

Place all ingredients in food processor and process until smooth. If the mixture is too thick, add a bit more lemon juice and/or olive oil.

Serves 4

MASHED POTATOES

A common favorite among comfort foods, it's easy to make entirely plant-based mashed potatoes. If you leave the potato skins on for "smashed" potatoes, the dish will have a higher nutrient content. Try adding fresh herbs or roasted garlic for an extra fancy touch.

4 large Russet potatoes, peeled and cubed
1 tablespoon olive oil or coconut oil
¼ cup–½ cup creamy plant-based milk

Place potatoes in a large saucepan and cover with water. Bring to a boil, then reduce heat to medium. Cook for about 15 minutes, until potatoes are easily pierced with a fork. Drain well, and return potatoes to saucepan.

Add oil and plant-based milk. Using a potato masher, mash until smooth. If the mixture is too dry, add a few tablespoons of plant-based milk and mix well.

Serves 4

AVOCADO MAYO

Created by Jeff Golfman

This versatile spread can be used for anything from sandwiches to wraps to a dip for crackers or tortilla chips. It's featured in Jeff's Asian-inspired Lettuce Wraps (see page 171 for the recipe).

Flesh of 4 avocados
2 cloves garlic
Juice of 2 limes
4 fresh basil leaves, chopped
2 tablespoons fresh cilantro, chopped

Blend all ingredients in food processor until smooth.

Serves 4

MAPLE-GLAZED SWEET POTATOES WITH ROSEMARY AND CINNAMON

Maple syrup brings out the sweet potatoes' natural sweetness, and rosemary adds interest. This side dish is great for a fancier holiday meal, or for a more simple weeknight dinner.

- -

4 medium sweet potatoes, cubed (1-inch pieces; no need to peel)
¼ cup maple syrup
2 tablespoons olive oil or melted coconut oil
1 teaspoon ground cinnamon
Salt and pepper to taste
2 tablespoons fresh rosemary, chopped

- -

Preheat oven to 400°F and line 2 baking sheets with parchment paper.

In a large bowl, stir together all ingredients until well mixed. Place onto baking sheets and roast in the oven for 30 to 40 minutes, until sweet potatoes are soft and lightly browned.

Serves 4

TOMATO MINT SALSA

This refreshing salsa is delicious in wraps, sandwiches, and burritos. Why not try it with Homemade Seasoned Tortilla Chips (page 157)?

2 medium tomatoes, diced very small
1 teaspoon olive oil
1 tablespoon fresh lime juice
¼ cup green onion, chopped
2 tablespoons fresh mint, chopped
Salt and ground black pepper to taste

In a medium bowl, stir together all ingredients. Let stand 5 minutes.

Serves 4

ROSEMARY, FENNEL, AND GARLIC INFUSED FINGERLING POTATOES

I created this recipe during a birthday getaway in Gibsons, BC. My husband and I paired this dish with grilled corn on the cob, grilled tofu in barbeque sauce, portobello mushrooms, and steamed carrots and broccoli. This recipe works incredibly well on a barbeque!

1 pound fingerling (or other small nugget) potatoes
3 sprigs fresh rosemary
1 fennel bulb, diced
6 cloves garlic, peeled and chopped
1 small red onion, diced
2 tablespoons olive oil

Preheat oven to 375°F.

Prick each potato with a fork a few times. On a large sheet of tinfoil, place potatoes, rosemary, fennel, garlic, and red onion. Drizzle with olive oil and wrap foil to enclose ingredients.

Roast for 30 to 40 minutes, until potatoes are soft when pricked with a fork. Discard rosemary sprigs.

Serves 4

LETTUCE WRAPS

Created by Jeff Golfman

This recipe is 100 percent raw, and 100 percent awesome—just like Jeff! Feel free to add in or substitute any of your favorite veggies.

. . . .

8 large lettuce leaves (e.g., butter lettuce)
2 cups Avocado Mayo (recipe on page 167)
3 cups sprouts (e.g., alfalfa, mung bean)
2 cups sliced tomato
1 cup sliced cucumber
Pinch ground black pepper
Fresh mint and/or basil to taste, finely chopped

. . . .

Spoon ¼ cup Avocado Mayo onto the bottom half of each lettuce leaf. Top with all other ingredients, equally divided among lettuce leaves.

Roll each lettuce leaf to seal in the filling, serving with the seam facing down.

Serves 4

BASIC ROASTED VEGGIES

This dish makes a nutritious and colorful side dish. Experiment with adding seasonings—rosemary, sage, and thyme, for example. A lower oven temperature and longer cooking time than most roasted vegetable recipes means the vegetables become thoroughly infused with the flavors of the garlic, oil, and any seasonings you might add. Create a well-balanced meal by adding a protein source (e.g., grilled or baked and marinated tofu) and side salad.

1 medium onion, diced
3 carrots, peeled and thickly sliced
2 parsnips, thickly sliced
2 beets, peeled and diced
2 cups cubed potatoes (peeled Russet potatoes or unpeeled nugget potatoes)
3 cloves garlic, chopped
2 tablespoons low sodium soy sauce
3 tablespoons olive oil
Ground black pepper to taste

Preheat oven to 375°F. Line two 8 by 8-inch dishes or one 9 by 13-inch baking dish with parchment paper. Place vegetables into baking dish(es) and add soy sauce, olive oil, and ground black pepper. Stir gently to evenly coat vegetables with seasonings.

Bake for 45 to 60 minutes, rotating baking sheet and stirring vegetables halfway through, until vegetables are soft and lightly browned.

Serves 4

VEGAN SCALLOPED POTATOES

Conventional scalloped potatoes are a stockpile of empty calories and animal-based fats from milk, cream, and cheese. This equally delicious plant-based version is much better for your health (and, of course, for animals).

. . . .

5 medium yellow potatoes, cut into thin round slices
¾ cup coconut milk
¾ cup soy milk
2 cloves garlic, minced
1 tablespoon nutritional yeast
Pinch salt
½ teaspoon ground black pepper
5 tablespoons spelt flour
3 tablespoons olive oil
½ medium onion, thinly sliced

. . . .

Preheat oven to 375°F. Lightly oil an 8 by 8-inch baking dish with cooking spray or olive oil.

In a large pot of boiling water, cook potato slices for 3 minutes. Drain and let cool for 5 minutes.

In a medium bowl, combine coconut milk, soy milk, garlic, nutritional yeast, salt, pepper, spelt flour, and olive oil. Whisk to mix well.

Layer one-third of the potato slices onto the bottom of the dish, followed by half of the onion. Pour about one-third of the coconut milk mixture evenly onto potato slices. Layer another third of the potato slices, and half of the onion, followed by another third of the coconut milk mixture. Layer the final third of potato slices over the top, and pour remaining coconut milk mixture evenly on top.

Cover with tinfoil and bake for 60 minutes. Remove foil and bake a further 15 minutes, until potatoes are lightly browned and soft when pierced with a fork.

Serves 4

CARAMELIZED ONIONS & FENNEL

A delicious and flavorful addition to sandwiches, roasted veggies, scalloped potatoes, or anything you can think of. This recipe requires very little preparation work but takes a while to cook. Depending on how caramelized you'd like your onions and fennel, leave up to 2½ hours for cooking. Start taste-testing after about an hour, and cook to your liking.

Fennel has a distinct licorice flavor when raw, but this flavor becomes subdued with cooking. If you like, add a few tablespoons of finely chopped fresh fennel to the finished dish for interest.

. . . .

5 tablespoons olive oil or coconut oil
2 large onions, sliced in half lengthwise, then thinly sliced into half rings
1 bulb fennel, thinly sliced with green parts removed

. . . .

In a large, shallow pan, heat oil over medium-high heat.

Add onions and fennel, stir to coat in oil, and cook for 5 minutes.

Turn heat to low, and cook for 1 to 2½ hours. Stir every 20 minutes or so, scraping any browned bits from the bottom of the pan (those are the tastiest parts!)

Makes about 1 cup

CRISPY BAKED TOFU WITH SESAME ORANGE DIPPING SAUCE

Baking tofu gives it a lightly browned, crunchy outside, while keeping it soft on the inside. This dish works well as an appetizer when you have guests over. (Provide toothpicks for guests to use for dipping the tofu.)

. . . .

1 (350-gram) package extra firm tofu, cut into ¾-inch cubes or triangles
Juice of 1 orange
1 teaspoon chili powder
½ teaspoon ground black pepper
1 tablespoon agave nectar
1 tablespoon toasted sesame oil
¼ cup low sodium soy sauce
2 tablespoons rice vinegar
3 cloves garlic
2 tablespoons fresh ginger, finely chopped

. . . .

Preheat oven to 400°F and line a baking sheet with parchment paper.

Place tofu on baking sheet in a single layer. Bake for about 25 minutes, flipping tofu halfway through, until evenly browned and slightly crispy on the outside.

To make the dipping sauce, place all remaining ingredients in a blender and process until smooth.

Serves 3 to 4

PERFECT ROAST POTATOES

This dish is inspired by my grandma's famous roast potatoes. She made them only for special occasion dinners such as Christmas or Thanksgiving, so they've become a somewhat coveted dish in my family. As a former high school home economics teacher, you can bet my grandma knew what she was doing.

. . . .

4 medium Russet potatoes, peeled and quartered
¼ cup olive oil
½ teaspoon salt

. . . .

Preheat oven to 375°F.

Line two 8 by 8-inch baking dishes or one 9 by 13-inch baking dish with parchment paper. Add potatoes and drizzle with olive oil. Stir to coat potatoes evenly with oil, then sprinkle with salt.

Bake for about an hour, rotating baking dish(es) and stirring potatoes halfway through. Potatoes are done when well-browned and crispy on the outside.

Serves 4

CRANBERRY DILL RICE 'N BEANS

This easy-to-make side dish can be prepared in a saucepan or rice cooker. If you're using a rice cooker (which often results in more evenly cooked and fluffy rice), cook everything except the beans in there, then transfer the rice mixture to a saucepan, add beans, and heat through over medium-low heat.

2 cups dry brown rice
4½ cups vegetable stock
1 teaspoon dried dill
1 cup dried cranberries
1 can (15 ounces) beans of your choice (e.g., pinto, navy, cannellini), drained and rinsed

In a large covered saucepan, bring rice, vegetable stock, dill, and cranberries to a slow boil, then reduce heat to low and cook until rice is tender (30 to 45 minutes).

Add beans and stir to mix, heating through for 3 to 5 minutes.

Serves 4

BITTER GREENS & POTATOES

Created by Holly Burton

Here's a delicious way to increase your intake of super healthy greens. As a variation, Holly suggests using kale instead of arugula or dandelion greens, reducing the amount of lemon juice, and adding chickpeas instead of potatoes.

. . . .

3 cups new potatoes, cut in half (to create bite-size pieces)
2 tablespoons olive oil
6 cloves garlic, minced
½ cup lemon juice
1 tablespoon dried rosemary
2 teaspoons low-sodium vegetable stock powder
12 cups packed greens (e.g., arugula or dandelion greens)
2 teaspoons sugar
Ground black pepper to taste

. . . .

In a saucepan filled with water, boil potatoes until just tender, then drain. Do not overcook—ensure skin is still intact.

In a saucepan over medium heat, sauté garlic in olive oil until fragrant.

Add lemon juice, rosemary, and stock powder, and mix to distribute.

Add greens and sugar, and sauté until wilted.

Add drained potatoes and season to taste with pepper.

Serves 4

CREAMY SPINACH

Created by Holly Burton

Holly was inspired to create this recipe by a dish my mom used to make for us when we were in high school. Imagine that—teenagers willingly gobbling up large servings of spinach!

1 tablespoon olive oil or coconut oil
1 onion, diced very small
2–3 cloves garlic, sliced
2 (283-gram) packages frozen spinach, defrosted on countertop for 30 minutes or in microwave for 3 minutes
¼ teaspoon nutmeg
3 tablespoons nutritional yeast
Salt and pepper to taste
¾ cup soy milk (divided)
1 teaspoon cornstarch

In a saucepan or skillet over medium heat, sauté onions and garlic in the oil until onions are translucent (3 to 5 minutes).

Add frozen spinach. Stir for about a minute to make sure spinach heats evenly.

Add nutmeg, nutritional yeast, salt, and pepper. Stir well.

In a small bowl or mug, combine ¼ cup soy milk with cornstarch until well mixed. Add this and the additional ½ cup soy milk to the spinach mixture. Cook about 5 minutes more, until sauce thickens and all ingredients are heated through.

Serves 3–4

THEY-WON'T-BELIEVE-IT'S-PLANT-BASED GRAVY

You won't believe how easy this delicious gravy is to make. I like it on Shepherd's Pie (recipe on page 217), but you can also try it on veggie or portobello burgers or roasted veggies.

. . . .

½ small onion, diced
2 tablespoons olive oil or coconut oil
3 cups vegetable stock
3 tablespoons low sodium soy sauce
½ teaspoon smoked paprika (optional,but highly recommended)
2 tablespoons nutritional yeast
¼ teaspoon ground black pepper
¼ cup all-purpose flour

. . . .

In a medium saucepan over medium heat, sauté onion in oil for 3 to 5 minutes, until it turns translucent.

Add vegetable stock, soy sauce, smoked paprika (if using), nutritional yeast, and black pepper. Bring to a low boil, then reduce heat to low and simmer for 10 minutes.

In a small bowl, whisk flour with about 6 tablespoons of water, until smooth. Bring heat back up to medium, add flour and water mixture to the saucepan, and stir. Cook for 2 minutes, stirring constantly, until gravy thickens.

Makes about 3 cups

HONEY MUSTARD DIP/DRESSING

This versatile recipe can be used as a salad dressing or dip. I like using it on kale salad and as a dip for fresh veggies.

½ cup olive oil
1 tablespoon apple cider vinegar
2 tablespoons agave nectar
2 tablespoons Dijon mustard

Whisk all ingredients together in a bowl. Easy as that!

Makes about 1⅓ cups

LEMONGRASS-SPIKED ORANGE SAUCE

Perhaps not surprisingly, citrus flavors pair well with lemongrass. Use this tangy sauce in stir fries, on steamed greens, or as a dipping sauce.

. . . .

1 tablespoon olive oil or coconut oil
¼ cup onion, finely chopped
1 tablespoon fresh lemongrass, outer peel removed and finely chopped
1 tablespoon fresh ginger, grated
3 cloves garlic, minced
½ cup vegetable stock
2 tablespoons low-sodium soy sauce
1 cup orange juice
1 tablespoon toasted sesame oil

. . . .

In a medium saucepan, heat oil over medium heat. Add onion, lemongrass, ginger, and garlic. Cook 3 minutes.

Add vegetable stock, soy sauce, and orange juice, and mix well. Reduce heat to medium-low and simmer for 5 to 8 minutes, until sauce has slightly thickened. Add sesame oil and mix well to incorporate.

Makes about 1½ cups

PEANUT LIME SAUCE

This mouth-watering sauce can be used as vinaigrette on salad (try kale or mixed baby greens) or as a dipping sauce (e.g., for roasted veggies). You can also use this sauce to flavor Asian-inspired stir fries.

Juice of 2 limes
1 teaspoon low sodium soy sauce
2 tablespoons creamy natural peanut butter
¼ cup light-flavored olive oil
2 tablespoons toasted sesame oil

In a small bowl, whisk together all ingredients until well blended.

Makes about ¾ cup

BERRY SAUCE

I enjoy this delicious sauce on pancakes and waffles. Use whatever combination of berries you like. If you use strawberries, cut them into quarters.

. . . .

1 cup berries of your choice (e.g., blueberries, strawberries, blackberries, raspberries)
½ cup water or unsweetened fruit juice
1 tablespoon cornstarch
1 tablespoon agave nectar or maple syrup

. . . .

In a small saucepan over medium-high heat, bring berries, water or fruit juice, and cornstarch to a boil, then reduce heat to medium-low.

Stir continuously until sauce begins to thicken (3 to 5 minutes). Stir in agave nectar or maple syrup. Serve warm.

Makes about 1½ cups

THE MOST DELICIOUS PASTA SAUCE ON EARTH

This is my go-to pasta sauce with my top secret add-ins. Another secret: This recipe yields about 6 cups' worth of sauce, so freeze a few portions of about 2 cups each in airtight containers. When you need a quick meal, place a container of frozen sauce in a bowl of hot water for about 5 minutes. Then pop out the sauce into a small saucepan and heat 'til bubbling. Mix in your pasta, and enjoy!

8 medium tomatoes
8 cloves garlic, peeled
2 tablespoons olive oil
¼ cup fresh basil, shredded
½ teaspoon dried oregano
Salt and ground black pepper to taste
1½ cups vegetable stock
¾ (340-gram) package *Yves Cuisine* veggie ground round
2 tablespoons green onion, chopped

Preheat oven to 400°F and lightly spray two 8-inch rimmed baking dishes with cooking spray. Cut tomatoes and garlic cloves into halves. Stuff half a garlic clove into each tomato half, and place face down into baking dishes. Drizzle with olive oil and sprinkle with salt and black pepper.

Roast for 60 minutes, or until tomatoes have shrunk and browned around the edges.

Empty tomatoes and juices into a large pot. Add basil, oregano, salt, pepper, and vegetable stock. Using a handheld immersion blender (or in batches in a food processor), blend mixture until smooth.

Place puréed sauce over low heat. Crumble in veggie ground round and let heat through.

Toss with pasta (or grain of your choice), and garnish with chopped green onions.

Makes 6 cups

ENTRÉES

You can make any of the soup or stew recipes in this section in a slow cooker. Recipe instructions assume you're making the dishes in a saucepan on the stove, but modifying them for the slow cooker is simple. Just throw in all ingredients and cook on low for about six hours, or on high for about four hours. If you have a bit of extra time, sauté onions and garlic in a pan for a few minutes before adding to the slow cooker, to give your dish extra flavor. Add fresh herbs, greens, and pasta (if applicable) during the last thirty minutes of cooking.

THAI BASIL EGGPLANT

Created by Holly Burton

A super-easy and super-tasty recipe that perfectly combines savory, sweet, and spicy flavors. If you'd like to increase the protein content, cut firm tofu into cubes and bake for 20 minutes at 400°F on a parchment-lined baking sheet. Add tofu once eggplant has cooked and allow it to soften slightly.

Sauce

⅓ cup mushroom oyster sauce (ensure it's vegan)
4 teaspoons chili sauce (e.g., *Rooster* brand)
2 tablespoons brown sugar
1 tablespoon lime juice
2 tablespoons water
8 garlic cloves, finely diced
2 tablespoons olive oil or coconut oil
2 large eggplants, or 4–5 Japanese eggplants, cubed
2 red bell peppers, cut into ¼-inch slices
⅔ cup fresh basil leaves, sliced into ribbons

In a small bowl, mix together sauce ingredients (mushroom oyster sauce, chili sauce, brown sugar, lime juice, and water).

In a saucepan over medium heat, sauté garlic in oil for one minute. Add eggplant, increase heat to medium-high, and stir until edges start to soften.

Add sauce and keep stirring. Once eggplant is mostly cooked (softened), add bell pepper and cook for 4 to 5 minutes, until peppers are cooked through.

Remove from heat and stir in basil.

Serves 4

THAI RED CURRY

One of my favorite healthy takeout options is Thai food. Create your own delicious Thai curry, but make sure to check the ingredients of your curry paste to ensure they're vegan—many contain anchovies or shrimp. Lemongrass really makes this dish, but it's not often used in Western cooking. To prepare fresh lemongrass, strip off the outer layers of hard leaves, then cut the stalk into a few pieces. Using a knife placed flat over each piece, crush lightly to release some of the juices.

2 tablespoons olive oil or coconut oil
1 large onion, chopped
½ (350-gram) package extra firm tofu, cubed
3 cups vegetable stock
2 tablespoons red curry paste (ensure it's plant-based)
2 large carrots, sliced
2 cups cauliflower, chopped into 1-inch florets
1½ cups broccoli, chopped into 1-inch florets
2 medium yellow potatoes (e.g., Yukon Gold), cut into 1-inch cubes
1 stalk fresh lemongrass, peeled, cut into quarters, and lightly crushed
2 bay leaves
½ teaspoon ground black pepper
1 (15-ounce) can coconut milk
4 cups cooked jasmine or brown rice

In a large saucepan over medium heat, cook onion in oil for 3 to 5 minutes, until it turns translucent. Add tofu and cook for another 2 to 3 minutes, until it starts to brown. Add vegetable stock and curry paste, and stir to ensure curry paste distributes evenly.

Add carrots, cauliflower, broccoli, potatoes, lemongrass, bay leaves, and black pepper. Cover and cook for 15 minutes, or until potatoes are soft when pierced with a fork.

Remove lemongrass and bay leaves, and stir in coconut milk. Let heat through for a minute or two, then serve over rice (about 1 cup per serving).

Serves 4

THAI COCONUT SOUP WITH MUSHROOMS, WATER CHESTNUTS, BAMBOO SHOOTS, AND MANGO

Created by Melanie Hackett

Melanie lives in North Vancouver, BC. While exploring her neighborhood, she enjoyed a delicious soup at a Thai restaurant, which inspired her to create something similar in her own kitchen.

3 (15-ounce) cans coconut milk

1–2 cups *So Delicious* original coconut beverage

1 medium Russet potato, peeled and cubed

3-inch piece of fresh ginger, grated

1 red bell pepper, sliced

1 Thai yellow hot pepper, sliced

2 cups white mushrooms, sliced

1 (8-ounce) can sliced bamboo shoots, drained

2 (8-ounce) cans water chestnuts, drained

1 (15-ounce) can mango in juice

1 cup fresh basil leaves, sliced

1 cup fresh mint leaves, sliced

1 stalk fresh lemongrass, cut into quarters and lightly crushed

Pinch salt

2 bay leaves

2 tablespoons olive oil or coconut oil

1 (350-gram) package extra firm tofu, cubed

Place all ingredients except olive or coconut oil and tofu into a large pot or Dutch oven. Bring to a slight boil, then simmer on low heat for 30 to 60 minutes.

Heat olive oil or coconut oil in a skillet on medium heat. Add tofu cubes and sauté until lightly browned on all sides. Add to soup and remove bay leaves just before serving.

Serves 6

THAI PEANUT CURRY WITH VEGGIES, TOFU, AND PINEAPPLE

I was inspired to create this peanut curry while in Kona on the Big Island of Hawaii. A Thai restaurant there made this so well, I just had to create my own!

2 tablespoons olive oil or coconut oil
1 large onion, chopped
½ (350-gram) package extra firm tofu, cubed
3 cups vegetable stock
1 tablespoon red curry paste (ensure it's plant-based)
1 tablespoon curry powder
½ cup natural peanut butter
2 large carrots, sliced
1 cup green cabbage, chopped
1½ cups diced pineapple (fresh or canned)
1½ cups broccoli, chopped into 1-inch florets
2 bay leaves
½ teaspoon ground black pepper
1 (15-ounce) can coconut milk
1 cup fresh basil, chopped
4 cups cooked jasmine or brown rice

In a large saucepan over medium heat, cook onion in oil for 3 to 5 minutes, until it turns translucent.

Add tofu and cook for another 2 to 3 minutes.

Add vegetable stock, curry paste, curry powder, and peanut butter. Stir to ensure curry paste and peanut butter distribute evenly.

Add carrots, cabbage, pineapple, broccoli, bay leaves, and black pepper. Cover and cook for 15 minutes, or until veggies are soft when pierced with a fork.

Remove bay leaves, and stir in coconut milk. Let heat through for a minute or two, then serve over rice. Top with fresh basil.

Serves 4

COCONUT LENTIL CURRY

A hearty, protein-rich meal inspired by fragrant Indian spices. Serve with a side salad and/or flatbread such as naan.

3 tablespoons olive oil or coconut oil
1 large onion, diced
1½ cups red lentils
5 cups vegetable stock
2 medium carrots, sliced
1½ cups cauliflower, cut into ½-inch florets
2 medium tomatoes, chopped
2 tablespoons curry powder
1 cup coconut milk
¼ cup green onion, chopped

Heat oil in a medium saucepan over medium heat. Sauté onion 5 minutes, until it turns translucent.

Add lentils, vegetable stock, carrot, cauliflower, tomatoes, and curry powder. Cover and cook for 15 minutes, until lentils and vegetables are well cooked.

Add coconut milk, stir, and let heat through (about 3 minutes). Serve topped with green onion.

Serves 4

BHINDI KI SABJI

Created by Holly Burton

If you haven't already tried okra, this traditional Indian okra curry dish is a great introduction to the vegetable. You can use green beans instead of okra, but they will need to cook an additional 5 minutes, until tender.

. . . .

2 tablespoons canola oil or very light-flavored olive oil
4 teaspoons whole cumin seeds
3–4 teaspoons coriander seeds
1 large onion, diced
3–4 tablespoons grated fresh ginger
2 teaspoons powdered cumin
6 cups okra, diced
4 medium tomatoes, diced
2 (15-ounce) cans navy beans, rinsed and drained (optional)
½ teaspoon salt

. . . .

Heat oil over medium-high heat, and sauté cumin and coriander seeds until they start popping. Add onions and sauté for about 5 minutes, or until almost translucent.

Add ginger and powdered cumin and cook for 1 minute, then add okra and cook for another 2 minutes.

Add tomatoes and cook for about 5 minutes, until cooked but still holding their shape.

If using navy beans, add and cook until heated through. Stir in salt.

Serves 4

CHINESE TOMATO TOFU

Created by Holly Burton

This recipe is based on a well-known Chinese dish, using tofu instead of eggs. Holly recommends adding the ground black pepper liberally—at least two teaspoons— because it's important to the flavor of this dish.

. . . .

1 tablespoon canola oil or very light-flavored olive oil
8 green onions, sliced
3 tablespoons Japanese-style soy sauce (e.g., *Kimlan* brand)
2 (454-gram) packages medium firm tofu, cut into 1-inch cubes
6 medium tomatoes, cut into large dices
Ground black pepper to taste
2 teaspoons sugar

. . . .

Heat oil in a saucepan over medium heat. Add green onion and sauté for 2 minutes. Add soy sauce and let bubble.

Add tofu and stir to coat with sauce. Roughly cut some of the tofu pieces in half with a spoon so that some pieces are lightly mashed. Add tomatoes and stir to combine.

Add black pepper.

Add sugar and let simmer for about 5 minutes, until tomatoes are soft.

Serves 4

NO-CREAM OF CAULIFLOWER SOUP

A popular comfort dish made vegan. Round out your meal by serving this soup with a side salad.

- -

2 tablespoons olive oil or coconut oil
1 medium onion
3 cups vegetable stock
1 medium head cauliflower, cut into florets
1 Russet potato, peeled and cubed
½ teaspoon garlic powder
1 cup coconut milk
1 tablespoon nutritional yeast
½ teaspoon ground black pepper
2 tablespoons fresh parsley, chopped

- -

In a large saucepan over medium heat, cook onion in oil for 3 to 5 minutes, until it turns translucent.

Add vegetable stock, cauliflower, and potato. Cover and cook for 10 minutes, until potato and cauliflower are very soft.

Add garlic powder, coconut milk, nutritional yeast, and ground black pepper, and heat through.

In batches in a food processor, or with an immersion blender, purée soup until completely smooth. Garnish with chopped parsley.

Serves 4

VEGETABLE FRIED RICE

A veganized (and healthier) version of the Chinese restaurant classic! Instead of eggs, this dish features crumbled tofu tinted yellow with turmeric. If you're in a rush, mixed frozen vegetables work well. I usually use frozen veggies created specifically for stir fries. The mix includes mushrooms, red pepper, water chestnuts, and carrot.

. . . .

1 (350-gram) package extra firm tofu
2 teaspoons turmeric
3 tablespoons olive oil or coconut oil
1 large onion, diced
6 cloves garlic, minced
2 tablespoons fresh ginger, grated
4 cups mixed sliced vegetables of your choice
¼ cup low-sodium soy sauce
¼ cup sesame oil
6 cups cooked brown rice

. . . .

Crumble tofu into a bowl. Add turmeric and mix well. Set aside.

In a large wok or saucepan, cook onion in oil for 3 minutes, until it starts to turn translucent. Add garlic and ginger, and cook for 1 minute.

Add vegetables and soy sauce, and cook for 5 minutes.

Add sesame oil, tofu and turmeric mixture, and cooked brown rice. Stir to mix well. Heat through for 2 to 3 minutes.

Serves 4

SHIRATAKI TOFU NOODLE SOUP WITH SUI CHOY

I like this Asian-inspired simple soup for an easy, light dinner on busy work days. Shirataki tofu noodles are made from a type of root vegetable (shirataki, sometimes called "elephant yam"), with tofu added for texture. I like using the thin-style noodles, almost like spaghetti, but you can also try the fettucine type. If you can't find shirataki tofu noodles, you can use plain shirataki noodles, or rice noodles.

. . . .

2 (226-gram) packages shirataki tofu noodles
2 tablespoons miso paste
9 cups vegetable stock
8 white mushrooms, thinly sliced
1 cup carrots, thinly sliced
2 cups sui choy (Chinese cabbage), thinly sliced

. . . .

Prepare shirataki noodles as per package directions (rinse, boil for a few minutes, then drain).

In a large saucepan over medium heat, dissolve miso paste in vegetable stock. Add mushrooms and carrots, and cook for 3 minutes.

Add sui choy and shirataki tofu noodles and cook for 1 minute to heat through.

Serves 4

AFRICAN STEW

This hearty West African–inspired stew features an eclectic mix of flavors. Serve over brown rice or quinoa.

. . . .

2 tablespoons olive oil or coconut oil
1 large onion, chopped
4 cups vegetable stock
Juice of 1 lemon
½ cup natural peanut butter
½ teaspoon ground black pepper
½ teaspoon chili powder
2 tablespoons low-sodium soy sauce
6 small nugget potatoes, quartered
1 medium yam, peeled and cut into 1-inch cubes
2 cups cauliflower, cut into 1-inch florets
1 large carrot, chopped
1 (15-ounce) can chickpeas, drained and rinsed
1 cup kale, coarsely chopped
Chili sauce to taste

. . . .

In a large saucepan over medium heat, cook onion in oil for 3 to 5 minutes, until it turns translucent.

While onion cooks, in a large bowl, stir together vegetable stock, lemon juice, peanut butter, black pepper, chili powder, and soy sauce until smooth.

Add stock mixture, potatoes, yam, cauliflower, carrot, and chickpeas to saucepan. Cover and cook 15 minutes, until yam and potatoes are soft when pierced with a fork.

Add kale and cook for 3 minutes, then add chili sauce to taste.

Serves 4

CARROT, DATE, AND CHICKPEA TAGINE

Originating in North Africa, tagines are named after the clay pots used to cook the dish. Like my version here, they often combine sweet and savory flavors. This dish has an intricate flavor profile but is extremely easy to make. Definitely a win-win, if you ask me! Serve over brown rice, quinoa, or other whole grain.

2 tablespoons olive oil or coconut oil
1 large onion, diced
5 (yes, you read that right!) cloves garlic, minced
2 large carrots, diced
2 cups low-sodium vegetable stock
1 (15-ounce) can crushed tomatoes
2 (15-ounce) cans chickpeas, drained and rinsed
1 teaspoon ground ginger
1 teaspoon ground cumin
1 teaspoon ground coriander
1 teaspoon ground cinnamon
½ teaspoon ground black pepper
1 cup pitted dates, quartered
½ cup raisins
Juice of 1 lemon
¼ cup green onion, finely chopped

Heat oil over medium heat. Sauté onion for 5 minutes. Add garlic and cook for another minute.

Add carrots, vegetable stock, tomatoes, chickpeas, ginger, cumin, coriander, cinnamon, and black pepper. Stir to mix well, then cover and cook on medium for 10 minutes, until carrots soften.

Add dates, raisins, and lemon juice, and cook on low for 5 minutes.

Garnish with green onion.

Serves 4

MINESTRONE SOUP

There is no set recipe for this traditional Italian soup. Recipes vary by region and family, and are often based on which vegetables are in season. Feel free to experiment with the thickness of this soup. For a more brothy soup, add an extra cup of vegetable stock. For a more stewlike texture, use 7 cups instead of 8 cups of vegetable stock.

2 tablespoons olive oil or coconut oil
1 large onion, diced
2 cloves garlic, minced
8 cups vegetable stock
1 (15-ounce) can diced tomatoes
2 tablespoons tomato paste
1 (15-ounce) can white beans (e.g., navy or cannellini), drained and rinsed
2 carrots, sliced
2 cups additional vegetables of your choice (e.g., broccoli, cauliflower, zucchini, celery)
2 bay leaves
½ teaspoon dried thyme
1 teaspoon dried oregano
½ teaspoon ground black pepper
2 tablespoons fresh parsley, chopped
¾ cup dry small pasta (e.g., ditalini or mini shells)
1 cup chopped spinach or kale

Heat oil in a large saucepan over medium heat. Add onion and cook for 3 to 5 minutes, until it turns translucent. Add garlic and cook for one minute.

Add vegetable stock, tomatoes, tomato paste, beans, carrots and other veggies, bay leaves, thyme, oregano, black pepper, and parsley. Cover and bring to a boil, then cook over medium-low heat for 15 minutes, until carrots are soft.

Increase heat to high, and add pasta as soup comes to a boil. Continue cooking on a low boil until pasta is cooked (about 10 minutes).

Remove bay leaves, remove from heat, and stir in spinach or kale.

Serves 6

FLATBREAD PIZZA: THE MARGHERITA

Use 6-inch multigrain pita or naan and you'll have a delicious and healthy pizza dinner in no time. You can even find gluten-free and wheat-free pizza crusts, such as those made by Glutino, Ener-G, Kinnikinnick Foods, and Udi's. In 1889 during a visit to Naples, Queen Margherita was served a pizza with Italian flag-colored toppings: tomato, mozzarella cheese, and basil. This now-classic pizza features a simple but flavorful combination of toppings (veganized, of course).

. . . .

4 (6-inch) flatbreads
8 tablespoons tomato paste
½ cup cherry or grape tomatoes, halved
1 cup fresh basil, shredded
¾ cup shredded or grated nondairy cheese (e.g., *Daiya* brand)
Ground black pepper to taste

. . . .

Preheat oven to 375°F.

Spread 2 tablespoons tomato paste on each flatbread.

Add tomato halves, basil, nondairy cheese, and black pepper.

Place pizzas on ungreased baking sheets and bake for 10 to 15 minutes, until nondairy cheese is bubbling.

Makes 4 small pizzas

FLATBREAD PIZZA: THE CLEAN 'N GREEN

This pizza features my two favorite pizza toppings: spinach and artichokes.
I sometimes like to use spinach naan for the pizza base.

4 (6-inch) flatbreads
8 tablespoons tomato paste
2 large handfuls spinach, washed and coarsely chopped
   (or use whole baby spinach leaves)
1 cup fresh basil, whole leaves
½ medium onion, finely chopped
1 cup jarred artichoke hearts
¾ cup shredded or grated nondairy cheese (e.g., *Daiya* brand)
Ground black pepper to taste

Preheat oven to 375°F. Spread 2 tablespoons tomato paste on each flatbread.

Place spinach leaves and basil leaves evenly on flatbread, followed by onion, artichoke hearts, and cheese. Add black pepper.

Place pizzas on ungreased baking sheets and bake for 10 to 15 minutes, until nondairy cheese is bubbling and veggies are cooked.

Makes 4 small pizzas

FLATBREAD PIZZA: THE VEGGIE FEAST

The addition of smoked tofu gives this pizza a delicious (almost meaty) flavor. Grate it the same way you'd grate cheese.

. . . .

4 (6-inch) flatbreads
8 tablespoons tomato paste
½ cup smoked tofu, grated
½ medium onion, finely chopped
2 white mushrooms, thinly sliced
½ bell pepper (any color), diced
2 Roma tomatoes, sliced
¾ cup shredded or grated nondairy cheese (e.g., *Daiya* brand)
Ground black pepper to taste

. . . .

Preheat oven to 375°F.

Spread 2 tablespoons tomato paste on each flatbread. Add smoked tofu evenly across each flatbread.

Distribute onion, mushrooms, bell pepper, tomatoes, and nondairy cheese evenly across the four flatbreads. Add black pepper.

Place pizzas on ungreased baking sheets and bake for 10 to 15 minutes, until nondairy cheese is bubbling and veggies are cooked.

Makes 4 small pizzas

PASTA SALAD

Great hot or cold, this is a nutritious dish that transports well. Enjoy it for a picnic or pack some for lunch at work.

. . . .

2 tablespoons olive oil
Juice of 2 limes
Zest of 1 lime
¼ teaspoon ground cumin
¼ teaspoon ground black pepper
2 large tomatoes, diced
1 (15-ounce) can of beans of your choice, drained and rinsed
½ cup fresh basil, chopped
6 cups cooked pasta; small shape of your choice

. . . .

In a large bowl, whisk together olive oil, lime juice, lime zest, cumin, and black pepper. Add tomatoes, beans, and basil. Toss to coat.

Once pasta is cooked, add it to the bowl and mix well.

Serves 4

HERBED RICE AND LENTIL STUFFED SPAGHETTI SQUASH

I created this dish as part of a Thanksgiving feast while my husband and I were in Hawaii for our honeymoon. I served it with roast potatoes and carrots, and Hawaiian local greens.

. . . .

6 tablespoons olive oil, divided
1 medium onion, diced
2 cloves garlic, minced
4 cups vegetable stock
1½ cups brown rice (dry)
½ cup red lentils
1 medium carrot, diced
1 teaspoon dried dill
1 teaspoon dried thyme (or oregano)
¼ cup chopped green onion
2 small spaghetti squashes
Ground black pepper to taste

. . . .

In a large saucepan over medium heat, cook onion in 2 tablespoons of olive oil for 5 minutes, until beginning to turn translucent. Add garlic and cook for an additional minute.

Add vegetable stock, brown rice, lentils, carrot, dill, and thyme or oregano. Cover and bring to a boil, then reduce heat to low and simmer for 45 to 50 minutes, until rice is cooked. Add green onions and stir to mix well.

While rice mixture cooks, preheat oven to 375°F and line a baking sheet with parchment paper. Cut each squash in half lengthwise, and scoop out seeds with a spoon.

Brush the cut side of each half with 1 tablespoon olive oil, and place cut-side up on baking sheet. Bake 15 minutes to give the squashes a head start before adding stuffing.

When rice stuffing is cooked, divide evenly among squash halves. Top with ground black pepper to taste. Bake for 20 to 25 minutes, until squashes are browned in places, and soft when pricked with a fork.

Serves 4

SHEPHERD'S PIE

Serious comfort food made seriously healthy. Try it with They-Won't-Believe-It's-Plant-Based Gravy (recipe on page 183) and a side salad.

. . . .

Mashed Potato recipe on page 165
3 tablespoons olive oil or coconut oil
1 large onion, diced
2 cups vegetable stock
½ cup red lentils
2 medium carrots, diced
1 cup asparagus, chopped
1 cup cauliflower, chopped
1 cup broccoli, cut into small florets
1 cup grated smoked tofu
1 teaspoon dried oregano
1 teaspoon dried dill
2 tablespoons nutritional yeast
½ teaspoon ground black pepper
¼ cup spelt flour
½ (340-gram) package *Yves Cuisine* veggie ground round

. . . .

Lightly spray your baking dishes with cooking spray and preheat oven to 400°F.

In a large saucepan, heat oil over medium heat. Add onion and cook for 5 minutes.

Add vegetable stock, lentils, and carrots. Cover and cook for 5 minutes.

Add asparagus, cauliflower, broccoli, smoked tofu, oregano, dill, nutritional yeast, black pepper, and spelt flour. Mix to ensure seasonings and flour are evenly distributed. Cover and cook for another 5 minutes.

Add veggie ground round and mix to incorporate.

Spoon filling evenly into baking dish(es), filling about ¾ full. Top with mashed potatoes, using the back of a spoon to spread them evenly. Use a fork to fluff up potatoes a bit, creating small peaks that will brown nicely.

Bake for 20 to 30 minutes, until mashed potatoes are well browned.

Serves 4

SPICY BLACK BEANS 'N GREENS

Created by Holly Burton

Combining the high vitamin C content in hot peppers with the protein in beans and nutrients in dark leafy greens, this dish makes for an excellent dinner after an active day.

. . . .

2 teaspoons olive oil or coconut oil
1 large onion, diced
2 teaspoons whole cumin seeds
2 jalapeño peppers, chopped
2 tablespoons chili sauce (e.g., *Rooster* brand)
1 tablespoon ground cumin
1 tablespoon dried oregano
2 tablespoons lime juice
2 tablespoons low sodium Chinese style soy sauce
2 (15-ounce) cans black beans, drained and rinsed
4 medium tomatoes
2 bunches Swiss chard, chopped
2 green bell peppers, diced
½ cup fresh cilantro, chopped

. . . .

Heat oil in frying pan over medium-high heat. Add onion and cumin seeds, and sauté until onions are translucent (about 5 to 8 minutes).

Add jalapeños, chili sauce, ground cumin, oregano, lime juice, and soy sauce. Stir to mix well and sauté for 30 seconds.

Add black beans and tomatoes, and cook for 5 minutes. Add Swiss chard and green pepper and cook until just tender (about 3 minutes).

Remove pan from heat, stir in cilantro, and serve immediately.

Serves 4

FAJITAS

These well-spiced fajitas pack in a lot of protein and a lot of flavor. I heat the black beans and kidney beans in the microwave for about 45 seconds right before serving. If you're serving these to guests, fajitas make a great build-your-own meal, where each person chooses filling and toppings to his or her liking.

8 whole-grain or gluten-free tortillas

Fajita filling

3 tablespoons olive oil or coconut oil
1 large onion, chopped
2 carrots, peeled and diced
1½ cups white mushrooms, sliced
1 bell pepper (any color), cut into thin strips
1 (350-gram) package extra firm tofu
½ teaspoon each salt and ground black pepper
½ teaspoon smoked paprika (or regular paprika)
½ teaspoon chili powder
½ teaspoon ground cumin
½ teaspoon garlic powder
½ cup fresh cilantro, chopped

Fajita Fixins

1 (15-ounce) can black beans, drained, rinsed, and heated
1 (15-ounce) can kidney beans, drained, rinsed, and heated
2 cups salsa
4 cups mixed baby greens or shredded lettuce

In a large skillet, heat oil over medium heat. Add onion and cook 3 to 5 minutes, until it turns translucent. Add carrots and mushrooms, and cook 5 minutes.

Add bell pepper and crumble in tofu. Add salt and pepper, smoked paprika, chili powder, ground cumin, and garlic powder. Stirring often, cook 5 minutes to ensure all ingredients are heated through. Add a few tablespoons of water if you notice anything sticking to the skillet. Stir in cilantro.

To assemble fajitas, place about ½ cup fajita filling in the center of a tortilla. Add about ¼ cup each of black beans and kidney beans. Top with salsa and mixed greens or lettuce. Fold up the bottom edge of the tortilla, then each side.

Serves 4 (2 fajitas per person)

PASTA WITH SLOW-ROASTED TOMATO AND GARLIC SAUCE

This simple pasta sauce is delicious on its own, or as a base for additional ingredients. Go nuts with experimenting if you like. Fresh herbs? Diced carrots? Artichokes? A splash of balsamic vinegar? Choose whole wheat pasta, and don't be afraid to experiment with a variety of pastas beyond wheat, such as spelt, kamut, or brown rice.

- -

8 medium tomatoes
16 cloves garlic, peeled
3 tablespoons olive oil
Salt and ground black pepper to taste
1 cup vegetable stock
8 cups cooked pasta
¼ cup fresh parsley, chopped

- -

Preheat oven to 400°F and lightly spray a large rimmed baking dish with cooking spray. Cut tomatoes into halves. Stuff a garlic clove into each tomato half, and place facedown into baking dish. Drizzle with olive oil and sprinkle with salt and black pepper.

Roast for 60 minutes, or until tomatoes have shrunken and slightly browned.

Empty tomatoes and juices into a medium saucepan. Add vegetable stock. Using a handheld immersion blender (or in batches in a food processor), blend mixture until smooth.

Toss with pasta and garnish with chopped parsley.

Serves 4

CARAMELIZED ONION AND PESTO-STUFFED PASTA SHELLS IN SLOW-ROASTED TOMATO AND GARLIC SAUCE

Perfect for having guests over for dinner, or for a no-particular-reason fancy meal. Serve with a simple side salad (and crusty French bread as a special treat!).

- -

3 tablespoons olive oil plus 2 tablespoons olive oil or coconut oil

1 large onion, diced

1 (12-ounce) box jumbo pasta shells

2 medium carrots, finely chopped

1½ cups low-sodium vegetable stock

1 cup kale, finely chopped

2 cups spinach, finely chopped

¼ cup parsley, finely chopped

¼ cup fresh basil, finely chopped

2 tablespoons nutritional yeast

3–4 tablespoons spelt flour (or other flour)

Ground black pepper to taste

One recipe Slow-Roasted Tomato and Garlic Sauce (recipe on page 221)

- -

Caramelized onions:

In medium skillet, heat oil over medium heat. Cook onion for 5 minutes. Reduce heat to low and cook (uncovered) for at least 1 hour, stirring every 15 to 20 minutes. Onions should be thoroughly browned and fragrant when ready.

In a large saucepan, boil water and cook pasta per package directions. Drain, rinse with cold water, and set aside.

Pesto stuffing:

While onions are cooking, heat olive oil in saucepan over medium heat. Sauté carrots for 3 to 4 minutes.

Add vegetable stock and kale, and cook for 5 minutes. Add spinach, parsley, basil, and nutritional yeast and cook for another few minutes, until spinach is wilted.

Add spelt flour to thicken the stuffing and mix thoroughly. Add black pepper to taste, and let the stuffing cool for a few minutes. Once caramelized onions are done cooking, add them to the stuffing mixture.

Preheat oven to 350°F. Spoon a layer of tomato and garlic sauce into a large rimmed baking dish. Stuff each pasta shell with a scant tablespoon of stuffing, and place into the sauce in a single layer. Spoon the remaining sauce over the pasta shells, and bake for 25 minutes.

Serves 4

QUICK VEGGIE CHILI

Created by Philip C. Breakenridge

This chili is perfect for busy days when you need a nutritious, filling, and protein-rich meal but you're short on time.

- -

1 large (28-ounce) can diced tomatoes
1 (340-gram) package veggie ground round (e.g., *Yves Cuisine* brand)
½ cup chopped cilantro
2 tablespoons chili powder
½ cup frozen corn
1 (15-ounce) can black beans
1 (15-ounce) can red pinto beans
1 (15-ounce) can chickpeas

- -

Combine all ingredients in large saucepan on medium-high until heated through.

Serves 4

MURRAY'S CHILI

If you can spare the time, let this chili simmer for an hour or more to let the flavors develop. Just remember to add the veggie ground round last, right before serving.

2 tablespoons olive oil
1 large onion, diced
1 clove garlic, minced
6 cups veggie stock
1 (5.5-ounce) can tomato paste
1 (14-ounce) can refried beans
1 (28-ounce) can diced tomatoes
1 (14-ounce) can black beans
2 (14-ounce) cans kidney beans
2–3 large carrots, chopped
1 jalapeño pepper, minced
½ tablespoon chili powder
½ tablespoon cumin
½ tablespoon oregano
½ teaspoon ground black pepper
1 (340-gram) package Mexican flavor *Yves Cuisine* Veggie Ground Round

In a large saucepan over medium heat, cook onion in oil for 2 to 3 minutes. Add garlic and cook for another minute.

Add vegetable stock, tomato paste, and refried beans. As these contents heat up, stir until refried beans are dissolved. Add diced tomatoes, both beans, carrots, and jalapeño pepper. Add chili powder, cumin, oregano, and black pepper and cover. Cook for 25 minutes, until carrots are softened, stirring occasionally.

Add Veggie Ground Round. Stir to incorporate, and heat through (about 5 minutes).

Serves 4

CARROT COCONUT GINGER SOUP

I once went to a restaurant with friends where the only vegan option was a carrot ginger soup. It was so delicious—a far cry from many other restaurants' only vegan options—that I had to create my own.

2 tablespoons olive oil or coconut oil
1 large onion, chopped
3 cloves garlic, chopped
5 large carrots, chopped
1 medium Russet potato, peeled and chopped
1 orange or yellow bell pepper
1 tablespoon grated fresh ginger
½ teaspoon ground black pepper
¾ teaspoon curry powder
5 cups vegetable stock
1 (14-ounce) can coconut milk
¼ cup fresh mint, chopped (optional)
¼ cup green onion, chopped (optional)

In a large saucepan over medium heat, cook onion in oil for 3 to 5 minutes, until it turns translucent. Add garlic and cook for one minute.

Add carrots, potato, bell pepper, ginger, black pepper, curry powder, and vegetable stock. Bring to a boil, then reduce heat and simmer for 20 minutes, or until carrots are very soft.

Add coconut milk and let heat through for a minute or two. Purée soup until smooth using a handheld immersion blender, or in batches in a food processor.

Top with 1 tablespoon fresh mint and 1 tablespoon green onion directly before serving (optional).

Serves 4

HERBED FAUX MEATBALLS

Inspired by Tosca Reno's The Eat Clean Diet Vegetarian Cookbook

These protein-rich, flavorful bean balls can be used just like meatballs. Enjoy them in tomato sauce with pasta, or make submarine sandwiches using whole wheat baguette, lettuce, and tomato sauce. See recipe for The Most Delicious Pasta Sauce on Earth on page 189

1 (15-ounce) can white beans (e.g., cannellini, white kidney, great northern)
½ medium onion
3 cloves garlic, peeled
½ cup fresh parsley
½ cup fresh basil leaves
1 cup cooked quinoa or brown rice
2 tablespoons low-sodium soy sauce
¼ cup nutritional yeast
½ teaspoon smoked paprika
½ cup whole wheat bread crumbs
½ cup wheat germ
2 tablespoons olive oil or melted coconut oil
¼ teaspoon each salt and ground black pepper

Line a baking sheet with parchment paper and preheat oven to 350°F.

Place beans, onion, garlic, parsley, and basil in a food processor. Process until smooth. Scrape out into a large bowl. Add all other ingredients and stir to mix thoroughly.

Check the mixture's consistency. If the mixture doesn't hold its shape when rolled into a ball, add a few more tablespoons of wheat germ and bread crumbs.

Roll into 1-inch balls and place on baking sheet. Bake for 40 to 45 minutes, until firm and lightly browned.

Makes about 20

HEARTY SPLIT PEA SOUP

This is one of my favorite dinners to make. The smoked paprika is absolutely essential, giving the dish a smoky, "meaty" flavor. It's also an easy way to increase your intake of dark leafy greens. Prep time is minimal—you just need to wait for the peas to cook. This recipe works very well in a slow cooker, or pressure cooker like an Instant Pot, if you're short on time.

2 tablespoons olive oil or coconut oil
1 large onion, chopped
3 cloves garlic, chopped
6 cups vegetable stock
3 carrots, peeled and chopped
1½ cups green split peas, rinsed
½ teaspoon to 1 teaspoon smoked paprika
1 bay leaf
½ teaspoon ground black pepper
1 cup dark leafy greens of your choice (e.g., spinach, kale)

Heat oil over medium heat in a large soup pot or Dutch oven. Add onion and sauté for 5 minutes. Add garlic and cook for another minute.

Add stock, carrots, split peas, smoked paprika, bay leaf, and black pepper. Bring to a boil, then reduce heat and simmer on medium-low for about 1 hour, until peas are soft, stirring occasionally.

Add dark leafy greens and cook for 3 minutes. Then remove bay leaf and purée with a handheld immersion blender (or in batches in a blender or food processor) until smooth.

Serves 4

SALADS

Many of these salads make complete meals—either for lunch or for dinner. With a variety of ingredient and flavor combinations, you're sure to find something new and exciting to try.

QUINOA SALAD PRIMAVERA

Quinoa is an excellent plant-based source of complete protein. Paired here with a variety of fresh veggies, this salad packs well as a healthy work lunch or picnic dish.

1 cup dry quinoa
2 cups vegetable stock
¼ cup olive oil
2 tablespoons red wine vinegar
2 tablespoons Dijon mustard
½ cup green onion, chopped
½–¾ cup cucumber, sliced
1½ cups cherry tomatoes, sliced
½ cup carrots, peeled and chopped
½ cup bell pepper (any color), chopped

Using a fine mesh sieve, rinse quinoa under running water. Bring quinoa and vegetable stock to a boil in a medium saucepan (covered). Reduce heat to medium-low, and simmer for about 15 minutes, until liquid has been absorbed. You can also cook quinoa in a rice cooker.

In a small bowl, whisk together olive oil, red wine vinegar, and Dijon mustard until smooth.

In a large bowl, stir together cooked quinoa, green onion, cucumber, cherry tomatoes, carrots, and bell pepper. Stir in olive oil mixture. Chill before serving.

Serves 4

RICE NOODLE SALAD WITH TOFU, WATER CHESTNUTS, AND HERBS

This salad could easily be a meal in itself. It tastes like fresh spring rolls, but without the preparation work! If you can't find smoked or flavored tofu, marinate regular firm tofu in the dressing for 30 minutes before serving.

4-ounce package dried rice noodles

Dressing
Juice of 2 limes
¼ cup low-sodium soy sauce
2 tablespoons agave nectar
1 clove garlic, minced
½ teaspoon chili powder
¼ teaspoon ground black pepper

Salad
1 (8-ounce) package smoked or flavored tofu, cut into small cubes
1 (8-ounce) can sliced water chestnuts, drained
1½ cups purple cabbage, thinly sliced
1 cup cucumber, thinly sliced
½ cup white mushrooms, thinly sliced
¾ cup fresh mint, chopped
¾ cup fresh cilantro, chopped
½ cup fresh basil, chopped
½ cup roasted peanuts

Place noodles into medium saucepan and cover with boiling water. Let stand 3 to 5 minutes (until soft), then drain. Rinse with cold water.

In a small bowl, whisk together all dressing ingredients. In a large bowl, toss together all salad ingredients except peanuts. Add rice noodles and toss to separate and evenly distribute.

To serve, divide noodle and vegetable mixture among 4 bowls. Pour dressing over top and garnish with chopped peanuts.

Serves 4

HOLLY'S KALE SALAD

Created by Holly Burton

If you're new to kale and are wondering what to do with it, start here. The dressing is a delicious combination of savory and tart, pairing perfectly with crisp kale. Kneading your kale for a few minutes transforms it from slightly bitter and tough into a softer, sweeter green.

About 10 cups kale (large mixing bowl full, or one bunch), shredded into bite-size pieces.

Dressing:
½ teaspoon chili oil
Pinch garlic powder
2 teaspoons miso paste
¼ cup tahini
Juice of ½ lemon
¼ cup plus 1 tablespoon water

In a small bowl, whisk together dressing ingredients until well combined.

Place kale into a large mixing bowl. Knead kale for a minute or two to soften it slightly, then add dressing. Knead for another few minutes to evenly coat each kale leaf with dressing, and to allow the lemon juice in the dressing to soften the kale leaves.

Serves 4

RED LEAF LETTUCE AND PERSIMMON SALAD

Created by Holly Burton

Holly suggests pairing this salad with some whole grain bread and spicy tofu, such as tandoori tofu or jerk tofu.

. . . .

Salad:
1 head butter lettuce, torn
2 cups red leaf lettuce, cut into strips
2 persimmons, cubed (or ½ ripe papaya, cubed)
Dressing:
1 tablespoon olive oil
3 tablespoons white wine vinegar
2 teaspoons agave nectar
1 teaspoon Dijon mustard (without grains)
Salt to taste

. . . .

In a large bowl, toss together lettuces, and persimmons.

In a small bowl, use a fork to mix together all dressing ingredients until smooth.

Drizzle dressing onto salad, and toss to mix.

Serves 4

MEDITERRANEAN MEDLEY SALAD

Created by Jeff Golfman

This recipe can be adapted to various volumes of salad. Start by dicing your tomatoes, which should constitute about ⅔ of the total volume of salad. Add seasoning ingredients to taste.

Main ingredients:
Tomato (⅔ of total volume)
Cucumber
Avocado
Green onion

Seasoning:
Dulse
Dill
Italian seasoning
Apple cider vinegar
Fresh lemon juice

Chop, cube, or dice all 4 main ingredients. Add seasoning to taste, and toss until well mixed.

TOMATO CUCUMBER SALAD

Created by Holly Burton

A refreshing salad ideal for outdoor picnics and summer barbeques.

. . . .

1 English cucumber, quartered lengthwise, then sliced
4 medium tomatoes, diced into ¼-inch pieces
2 teaspoons olive oil
1–2 tablespoons lemon juice
Few dashes *Club House* brand Garlic Plus seasoning
Salt and pepper to taste

. . . .

Mix all ingredients together in a bowl. Let stand for 5 to 10 minutes, then enjoy!

Serves 4

RAINBOW CAESAR SALAD

Created by Jeff Golfman

This recipe allows you to make any quantity of salad. Start with lettuce, which will be half of the total volume of your salad, and add the remaining ingredients to taste.

. . . .

Salad:

Lettuce (50 percent of total salad volume)
Tomatoes, diced
Cucumbers, sliced
Green onion, finely chopped
Leeks, finely chopped
Peppers, any color, roughly chopped
Raw sauerkraut (e.g., *Karthein's* brand)
Avocados, sliced
Hemp seeds or hemp hearts to garnish

Dressing (for 2 servings):

¼ cup hemp, flax, or olive oil
1 tablespoon tahini
1 tablespoon fresh lemon juice
1 teaspoon apple cider vinegar

. . . .

In a large bowl, toss together lettuce, tomatoes, cucumbers, green onion, leeks, peppers, sauerkraut, and avocados.

To make the dressing, place all dressing ingredients in a food processor and process until smooth.

Drizzle dressing onto salad, toss to distribute, and top with hemp seeds or hemp hearts.

KARINA'S GO-TO SALAD

This is the salad I most often make for myself. I usually make an extra 2 or 3 portions and keep them in the fridge for the next few days.

. . . .

4 kale leaves, shredded into bite-size pieces (or approx. 2 cups baby kale)
4 cups mixed greens
1 cup red cabbage, chopped
1 cup cucumber slices
4 white mushrooms, sliced
¼ cup olive oil
¼ cup balsamic vinegar
2 tablespoons hemp hearts
2 teaspoons chia seeds

. . . .

Toss together kale, mixed greens, red cabbage, cucumber, and mushrooms.

In a small bowl, combine olive oil and balsamic vinegar, and whisk or stir with a fork.

Place salad into 2 bowls (or 1 if you're really hungry!), drizzle with dressing, and sprinkle with hemp hearts and chia seeds. Store leftovers in the refrigerator.

Serves 4

BEVERAGES

This section includes recipes for both hot and cold beverages. You'll find smoothies—a staple in many active people's healthy diets—teas, lattes, and more. The method for making smoothies is (not surprisingly) the same for all recipes. Throw everything into a food processor or blender, and smoothify to your liking. You can also use an immersion blender, which is my favorite smoothifying appliance. All smoothie recipes yield one serving.

PEANUT BUTTER & CHOCOLATE ENERGY SMOOTHIE

Delicious as an afternoon pick-me-up. Also great as a post-workout recovery drink.

. . . .

1½ cups plant-based milk
¼ cup berries of your choice
1 banana
1 tablespoon peanut butter
1 tablespoon unsweetened cocoa powder

HEALTH NUT SMOOTHIE

This smoothie packs in essential fatty acid sources, antioxidants, fruits, protein, and greens.

. . . .

2 cups plant-based milk
1 tablespoon ground flax seeds
1 tablespoon hemp hearts
2 tablespoons plant-based protein powder
1 banana
½ cup berries of your choice
¼ cup fresh or frozen spinach

BERRY-FEST SMOOTHIE

Get your antioxidants! Feel free to substitute other types of berries, such as blackberries.

1½ cups plant-based milk
½ avocado
½ cup fresh or frozen strawberries
½ cup fresh or frozen blueberries
½ cup fresh or frozen raspberries

TROPICAL SMOOTHIE

This smoothie combines the fruity and coconutty flavors of the tropics for a refreshing and nutritious treat. Great for beach vacations—or at least, pretending you're on one.

1 cup plant-based milk
1 cup coconut milk
Flesh of 1 small mango
1 banana
¼ cup blueberries or strawberries
2 tablespoons unsweetened shredded coconut

CHOCOLATE-DIPPED STRAWBERRY SMOOTHIE

One of the simplest—but most delicious—desserts ever invented, in smoothie form. Yum!

. . . .

2 cups plant-based milk
1 banana or ½ avocado
4 medium strawberries
1½ tablespoons unsweetened cocoa powder

MOJITO SMOOTHIE

A classic flavor combination, this smoothie is perfect for a hot, sunny day.

. . . .

2 cups plant-based milk
1 banana
Juice of 1 lime
1 teaspoon lime zest
1 teaspoon agave nectar
8–10 fresh mint leaves

ORANGE, CARROT, AND GINGER SMOOTHIE

A refreshing combination of flavors that works well as a breakfast treat or afternoon snack.

. . . .

2 cups plant-based milk (or 1 cup plant-based milk and 1 cup orange juice)
1 orange, peeled and segmented
1 medium carrot, chopped
½-inch piece fresh ginger
½ banana or ½ avocado

KEY LIME PIE SMOOTHIE

Try this recipe if you need a refreshing change from your usual fruit-and-plant-based-milk combination.

. . . .

2 cups plant-based milk
1 teaspoon agave nectar
½ teaspoon vanilla extract
Juice of 1 lime
1 teaspoon lime zest
1 banana
½ avocado
2 tablespoons unsweetened shredded coconut

FUZZY PEACH SMOOTHIE

Here's a healthy version of the Fuzzy Peach candies some of us used to enjoy as kids (and maybe still do?!).

. . . .

2 cups plant-based milk
2 small- to medium-size peaches, sliced
½ avocado
1 teaspoon vanilla extract
1 teaspoon agave nectar

GREEN MACHINE SMOOTHIE

We all know leafy greens are important to our health. To easily ramp up your leafy green intake, try drinking them!

2 cups plant-based milk
½ cup fresh or frozen spinach
½ apple, sliced
1 kiwi, peeled
½ cup cucumber, sliced
½ avocado

OMEGA EXTRAVAGANZA SMOOTHIE

This smoothie features three of the world's best plant-based sources of essential fatty acids (omega-3 and omega-6), which are vital to our health in many ways. Essential fatty acids boost brain and nervous system function; contain natural anti-inflammatory properties; reduce the risk of cardiovascular disease; improve joint, skin, and bone health; and can help to prevent cancer.

2 cups plant-based milk
2 tablespoons hemp hearts
1 tablespoon ground flax seeds
1 tablespoon chia seeds
1 banana or ½ avocado
½ cup fruit and/or berries of your choice

MATCHA LATTE

A fresh, earthy pick-me-up loaded with antioxidants. Choose a creamy plant-based milk such as soy, which lends itself well to frothing. In some studies, regular consumption of green tea has been linked to lower cancer rates.

1½ teaspoons matcha green tea powder
3 tablespoons water
½ teaspoon liquid sweetener (optional)
1½ cups plant-based milk

In a latte mug, whisk together matcha powder and water until smooth. Add sweetener if desired.

In a small saucepan, heat milk over medium heat until steaming, but be careful not to boil it.

A handheld milk frother is the best choice for frothing your milk, but you can also use a whisk. With a frother, let it spin for about 20 seconds, until a thick foam forms. With a whisk, whisk vigorously for about 30 seconds.

Slowly pour frothed milk into mug with matcha.

Makes 1 serving

SLOW COOKER CHAI CONCENTRATE

This is my all-time favorite warm beverage. I'll bet once you've tried making your own chai concentrate, you'll be hooked! I make twice this recipe every week in the slow cooker (you can use a large pot or Dutch oven if you don't have a slow cooker). Feel free to adjust spice levels to your liking.

6 cups water
2 cinnamon sticks
10 fresh ginger slices, 3mm thick
½ teaspoon black peppercorns
1½ teaspoons whole cloves
1 teaspoon allspice berries
1½ teaspoons green cardamom pods
2 star anise pods (optional)
6 teaspoons loose leaf black tea (my favorite is Indian Assam)
1 tablespoon agave nectar

Place all ingredients except the tea and agave nectar into a slow cooker or large saucepan. Cover and cook on low for 4 hours if using a slow cooker, or 2 hours if using a saucepan on the stove.

Add the loose-leaf tea and steep for 5 minutes. Using a fine sieve or mesh strainer, strain the mixture into a large pot.

Add agave nectar and stir to dissolve. Once cooled, you can store the concentrate in a pitcher in the fridge for up to 2 weeks.

To make a chai latte, combine half a cup of plant-based milk (soy is my favorite) with 1 cup of the concentrate. Enjoy it chilled or hot.

Makes 6 cups of concentrate (about 6 servings of chai latte)

GINGER, PEPPERMINT, AND LIME TEA

This is one of those accidental recipes that started as an experiment and became an instant hit. I started making plain ginger tea but had a few extra ingredients lying around that I thought would round it out. Each ingredient complements the others very nicely to create a delicious minty-spicy-tangy tea. Ginger and peppermint are some of the best natural digestive aids known to humankind, and this tea is just as delicious served hot as it is iced.

8 cups water
3-inch piece ginger, sliced thinly
2 cups fresh peppermint leaves
Juice of 2 limes

Place all ingredients into medium saucepan over medium-high heat. Bring to low boil, then reduce heat to low and simmer for 20 minutes.

Strain into mugs, and enjoy!

Makes 4 servings

JAMAICAN GINGER BEER

Ginger beer is one of my favorite summertime beverages. Too bad the store-bought versions contain a ridiculous amount of sugar! My version here is a delicious and healthy alternative that won't spike your blood sugar levels but will still satisfy your sweet tooth. Traditional ginger beer is made with yeast and is fermented over a number of days, but this version is much simpler. Double the recipe to share at a summer beach party, or to store in a pitcher in the fridge.

1 cup fresh ginger, grated or chopped in food processor
1 lemon
2 cups pure apple juice
¼ cup agave nectar
Chilled sparkling water to taste (4–6 cups)

Scrub ginger under running water (you don't need to peel it). If using a grater, grate ginger. If using a food processor (much faster!), first cut ginger into one-inch pieces, then pulse in food processor.

Cut lemon into quarters. Squeeze juice into medium saucepan and place squeezed quarters into saucepan.

Add grated or chopped ginger, apple juice, and agave nectar, and bring to a boil. Reduce heat to low and simmer for 30 minutes. Remove from heat and let cool.

Using a fine sieve or mesh tea strainer, strain concentrate mixture into a pitcher or punch bowl and allow to cool. Add between 4 and 6 cups chilled sparkling water, depending on your flavor intensity preference.

Alternatively, serve ginger concentrate and sparkling water separately and mix to taste.

Makes 3–4 servings

DESSERTS & TREATS

Delicious desserts don't have to be loaded with empty calories! From fruit-based desserts to a chocoholic's dreams come true, here you'll find many ways to create indulgent—but healthy—desserts.

Recipes in the Treats section are still healthier than conventional nonvegan fare, but they're labeled "treats" because they contain one or more ingredients that are more processed than whole foods. There are always ways to "healthify" recipes that contain treat ingredients, but sometimes you just gotta go all out and indulge!

We should all enjoy treat foods once in a while. What "once in a while" means to each of us is different and based on our goals. Professional figure and bodybuilding competitors may eat 100 percent whole foods and treat themselves to one small treat food per week or less (especially when preparing for the stage). Other athletes have a small treat a few times per week, and still others more generally aim to consume 80 to 90 percent whole foods. Some of my clients like using a treat (or two) as something to look forward to after a week of healthy eating. If you eat healthy foods most of the time and work out regularly, go ahead and enjoy an indulgence once in a while—guilt free.

SPICED APPLE CRUMBLE

This is one of my favorite desserts to serve to dinner guests. I often enjoy leftovers for breakfast (if there are any)! When using apples in crumble recipes, there's no need to peel them. The skin has a high concentration of nutrients, which you don't want to waste. I make large batches and fill individual ramekin dishes, which I then freeze. These take only 2½ minutes in the microwave to thaw and heat, and are great to take to work. You can also use an 8 by 8-inch baking dish to make one larger crumble.

. . . .

Topping

1¼ cups rolled oats
1 cup whole grain wheat or spelt flour
1 teaspoon ground cinnamon
½ teaspoon ground ginger
¼ teaspoon ground cloves
¼ cup agave nectar
¼ cup light-flavored olive oil or melted coconut oil

Filling

4 cups apple, cored and diced
2 tablespoons agave nectar
¼ cup whole grain wheat or spelt flour
½ teaspoon ground cinnamon

. . . .

Preheat oven to 375°F and grease baking dish(es) with cooking spray.

In a small bowl, mix together topping ingredients.

In a separate bowl, mix together filling ingredients.

Place filling in baking dish(es), topping evenly with topping mixture.

Bake for 25 minutes, until topping is crisp and lightly browned, and filling is bubbling.

Makes 8 individual servings (in ramekins), or one 8 by 8-inch crumble

STRAWBERRY RASPBERRY CRUMBLE

This antioxidant-rich crumble can be made with other berries, too. Just keep in mind that blueberries and blackberries tend to release more juices than strawberries and raspberries, so you may need to add one or two extra tablespoons of flour to the filling. You can use frozen berries if fresh ones aren't in season. As with the Spiced Apple Crumble, you can make one 8 by 8-inch crumble, or about 8 small individual ramekins.

Topping
1 cup whole wheat or spelt flour
1 cup rolled oats
½ teaspoon ground cinnamon
¼ cup light-flavored olive oil or melted coconut oil
¼ cup agave nectar or maple syrup

Filling
2 cups raspberries
2 cups strawberries, sliced
¼ cup whole grain wheat or spelt flour
1 tablespoon agave nectar or maple syrup

Preheat oven to 375°F and grease baking dish(es) with cooking spray.

In a small bowl, mix together all topping ingredients.

In a separate bowl, mix together filling ingredients.

Place filling in baking dish(es), topping evenly with topping mixture.

Bake for 25 minutes, until topping is crisp and lightly browned, and filling is bubbling.

Makes 8 individual servings (in ramekins), or one 8 by 8-inch crumble

CHOCOLATE PEANUT BUTTER ROCKET FUEL

Created by Melanie Hackett and Taras Chouinard

If you're very active and need to think about taking in enough calories to power your workouts, this is the energy storehouse for you. Perfect as a pre-workout snack for endurance events or a directly post-workout recovery food after intense weight training, these bites should be eaten in moderation if your activity levels are low to moderate!

Melanie and Taras made large batches of this recipe and kept it on hand during their many wilderness and endurance adventures. They raced in the 2011 Grand Columbian Half Iron Aquabike event, completed a three-month cycle tour of the Hawaiian Islands (including many multiday hikes and gruelling bike treks), and enjoyed countless wilderness trips between Alaska and California.

- -

1 cup (approx. 150 grams) dark chocolate chips (or dark chocolate bar broken into small pieces)
1 cup natural peanut butter
1 tablespoon agave nectar or maple syrup
½ cup shredded coconut
½ cup rolled oats
¼ cup raisins, cranberries, goji berries, or other dried fruit
¼ cup nuts of your choice (e.g., cashews, almonds, hazelnuts)

- -

Line a baking sheet with parchment paper and set aside.

Fill a large saucepan with a few inches of water and place on medium heat. Place chocolate and peanut butter into slightly smaller saucepan and melt over the steam, stirring regularly. You can also use a double boiler for this step if you have one. Be sure not to let any water splash into the chocolate mixture—this will cause it to seize up and become impossible to work with.

Once chocolate and peanut butter have melted, add agave nectar or maple syrup, coconut, oats, dried fruit, and nuts. Mix well.

Let cool 10 minutes, then drop tablespoonfuls onto baking sheet. Cool in the refrigerator for at least 1 hour.

Makes about 2 dozen

CHOCOLATE CHIA PUDDING

Chia seeds produce a gel when added to liquid, and here they work their magic to create a delicious pudding. Chia seeds are very filling, given their ridiculously high fiber and protein content, so this recipe makes a great between-meal snack or post workout energy source.

. . . .

2 cups plant-based milk
½ cup chia seeds
¼ cup unsweetened cocoa powder
2 tablespoons agave nectar or maple syrup
2 tablespoons dark chocolate shavings (optional)

. . . .

Combine plant-based milk, chia seeds, cocoa powder, and agave nectar or maple syrup in a bowl, and whisk until well mixed. Place in fridge 2 hours or more (best if left overnight).

Stir well before serving, and add a few tablespoons of plant-based milk to alter thickness, if desired. Garnish with dark chocolate shavings (optional).

Makes just over 2 cups of pudding (or 4 servings)

PEANUT BUTTER CHOCOLATE PROTEIN BALLS

Looking for a scrumptious treat that also packs in some muscle-building protein? Try these. Great as a pre- or post-workout energizing treat.

¾ cup natural peanut butter
1 cup puffed cereal (e.g., kamut puffs, puffed rice, 7-grain puffed cereal)
¼ cup natural- or vanilla-flavored protein powder (e.g., *Sunwarrior* brand)
1–3 tablespoons plant-based milk (if needed)
¾ cup nondairy chocolate chips or chocolate bar broken into small pieces

Line a baking sheet with parchment paper.

Place peanut butter into a medium mixing bowl and heat in the microwave for about 30 seconds to soften. Add puffed cereal and protein powder, and mix well. If mixture is too dry to stick together, add a few tablespoons of plant-based milk. If it's too moist, add a few teaspoons of protein powder. Use your hands to roll mixture into 16 1-inch balls and place them on the baking sheet.

In a separate bowl, melt chocolate in the microwave in 30-second increments, stirring each time. You can also melt the chocolate in a double boiler or in a small saucepan held within a larger saucepan containing a few inches of steaming water.

Dip each ball into the melted chocolate, turning to coat. Use a fork to remove each ball from the chocolate. Place on baking sheet to cool.

Place in the fridge for 1 to 2 hours to set.

Makes 16 1-inch balls

APPLESAUCE

A classic comfort dessert or snack, made without the refined sugar found in many store-bought versions. This recipe makes a big batch, so you can freeze leftovers in small containers. As with the fruit crumble recipes, there's no need to peel your apples. Keep the skins on for higher nutritional value (and you won't notice them once the applesauce is puréed). This recipe results in a fairly thick applesauce, so feel free to add a bit of water while blending to adjust the consistency.

You can make applesauce using any type of apple, but these work particularly well: Gala, Spartan, Fuji, Braeburn, Ambrosia, Pink Lady, Golden Delicious, McIntosh, Jonathan, Jonagold and Granny Smith (very tart). Try blending apple types, such as a sweet Gala with a few tart Granny Smiths thrown in for balance.

I usually use Pink Lady apples, which gives the finished product a pink tint.

10 medium apples
1½ cups water
1 teaspoon cinnamon
2 tablespoons agave nectar or maple syrup (optional)

Core apples and slice into 6 to 8 slices each. An apple coring/slicing gadget would be handy here.

Place apple slices and water into large pot over high heat, cover, and bring to a boil. Reduce heat to medium and cook 15 to 20 minutes, stirring occasionally, until apples are soft.

Mash with a potato masher, add cinnamon and agave nectar or maple syrup (if using), then use a handheld immersion blender (or a food processor in batches) to create a smooth applesauce. If you like it chunky, by all means skip the blending! For a thinner consistency, add water ¼ cup at a time and blend again.

Makes 5–6 cups

DARK CHOCOLATE–DIPPED STRAWBERRIES

This is a simple but elegant dessert that boasts high levels of antioxidants—both in the strawberries and in the dark chocolate. These work well as finger food for parties, or paired with another dessert like chocolate cake. If you've never made these before, you might be surprised how simple it is!

. . . .

12 large strawberries
1 cup nondairy dark chocolate chips, or chopped dark chocolate bar (70 percent cocoa or more)
½ cup unsweetened shredded coconut
½ cup nuts of your choice, chopped

. . . .

Line a baking sheet with parchment paper. Wash strawberries and pat dry. Ensure strawberries are thoroughly dry, or chocolate won't bind to them.

In a bowl or small saucepan set over a small pot of simmering water, melt the chocolate. Alternatively, heat the chocolate in 30-second increments in the microwave, stirring after each heating. If using the steaming water and pot method, ensure the chocolate doesn't come into contact with any water—this will cause the chocolate to seize up and be impossible to work with. If microwaving, ensure the chocolate doesn't burn.

Holding a strawberry by its stem, dip it in the chocolate. Twirl it around a few times to evenly cover about ¾ of the berry. Once you've let any excess chocolate drip back into the bowl, lightly dip the strawberry in either coconut or chopped nuts. Place on prepared baking sheet and repeat with the remaining berries.

Refrigerate chocolate-dipped strawberries for about 30 minutes to set. Best enjoyed the day they're made.

Makes 1 dozen

ABSURDLY HEALTHY SUPERCOOKIES

I often make a large batch of these and freeze for an easy on-the-go snack. Packed full of nutrition, try these as a simple breakfast (perhaps with a piece of fresh fruit) or a pre-workout energy source. Of course they also work as a healthy dessert!

1 large banana, well mashed
2 tablespoons ground flax seeds
¼ cup plant-based milk
⅓ cup melted coconut oil
⅓ cup agave nectar
1 teaspoon vanilla extract
2 cups spelt flour
2 teaspoons cinnamon
1 teaspoon ground ginger
½ teaspoon nutmeg
1½ teaspoons baking soda
Pinch salt
2 cups rolled oats
3 tablespoons chia seeds
1 cup raisins

Preheat oven to 350°F and line 2 baking sheets with parchment paper.

In large mixing bowl, mix together banana, flax seeds, plant-based milk, coconut oil, agave nectar, and vanilla extract until smooth.

Add spelt flour, cinnamon, ginger, nutmeg, baking soda, and salt until moistened. Fold in oats, chia seeds, and raisins.

Drop tablespoonfuls of dough onto baking sheets, about 2 inches apart.

Bake for 12 to 14 minutes, until tops and edges turn golden brown. After a few minutes of cooling on the baking sheets, transfer to cooling racks to cool completely. These cookies freeze very well, if they stick around long enough!

Makes about 3 dozen cookies

FRUIT SALAD WITH GINGER AND MINT

A delicious fruit salad that makes a refreshing finish to any meal. Cooling mint and zesty ginger add interest to succulent watermelon, grapefruit, and orange.

2 cups watermelon, peeled and cubed
2 pink or red grapefruit, peeled, segmented, and cut into bite-size pieces
2 oranges, peeled, segmented, and cut into bite-size pieces
2 tablespoons crystallized ginger, cut into very small pieces
2 tablespoons finely chopped fresh mint leaves
¼ cup slivered almonds (optional)

Toss together watermelon, grapefruit, and orange pieces. Right before serving, top with ginger and mint, as well as slivered almonds (if using).

Serves 4–6

APPLE SPICE MUFFINS

Enjoy these muffins for breakfast or as a quick snack. They also freeze very well.
The classic apple-spice flavor combination gives these healthy muffins an extra kick.
You can also make this recipe in the form of a bread by using one 9-inch loaf pan
(increase baking time to about 30–35 minutes).

2¼ cups whole grain spelt flour
1½ teaspoons baking soda
Pinch salt
½ cup granulated sugar
2 teaspoons ground cinnamon
½ teaspoon ground nutmeg
1 teaspoon ground ginger
1 cup plant-based milk
⅓ cup coconut oil, melted
1 tablespoon vinegar
1 tablespoon vanilla extract
1 apple, cored and diced into very small pieces

Preheat oven to 400°F and line muffin pan with paper liners.

In a medium bowl, sift together the flour, baking soda, salt, sugar, cinnamon, nutmeg, and ginger.

In a large mixing bowl, combine milk, coconut oil, vinegar, and vanilla extract. Mix well. Add the flour mixture and stir until ingredients are just blended. Without over-mixing, fold in the apple pieces using a rubber spatula.

Fill muffin cups about ¾ full. Bake for 18 to 20 minutes, until muffins are lightly browned and a toothpick or skewer inserted into the center comes out clean. Cool on a wire rack.

Makes 1 dozen muffins

ORANGE MUFFINS WITH GINGER
AND HEMP HEARTS

A nourishing breakfast or snack packed with vitamin C, fiber, and omega-3s. I use Demerara sugar, which is light brown, large grained, raw, and much less refined than regular white sugar. It has a slight caramel flavor and crunchy texture that works well in these muffins.

2¼ cups whole grain spelt flour
1½ teaspoon baking soda
Pinch salt
½ cup Demerara sugar (or regular granulated sugar)
½ cup hemp hearts
Zest of one orange
1 cup orange juice/plant-based milk
   (juice of 1 orange, topped up with milk to create 1 cup total)
¼ cup grated fresh ginger
⅓ cup coconut oil, melted
1 tablespoon vinegar
1 tablespoon vanilla extract
Flesh of one orange, cut into small pieces

Preheat oven to 400°F and line muffin pan with paper liners.

In a medium bowl, mix together the flour, baking soda, salt, sugar, and hemp hearts.

Zest and juice the orange into a measuring cup. Add plant-based milk to bring the total liquid to 1 cup. Add the freshly grated ginger. In a large mixing bowl, combine orange juice and milk mixture, coconut oil, vinegar, and vanilla extract. Mix well. Add the flour mixture and stir until ingredients are just blended. Without over mixing, fold in the orange pieces using a rubber spatula.

Fill muffin cups about ¾ full. Bake for 18 to 20 minutes, until muffins are lightly browned and a toothpick or skewer inserted into the center comes out clean. Cool on a wire rack.

Makes 1 dozen muffins

COCONUT MILK DARK CHOCOLATE MOUSSE

This rich, thick mousse is every chocolate lover's dream. It's also extremely simple to make! I was inspired to create this recipe after enjoying a similar mousse at Wild Rice restaurant in Vancouver, BC. I like to be able to stand a fork in my mousse, but if you like yours less thick, use a bit less chocolate. Once fully chilled, top with fresh berries, shredded coconut, or serve as is for a decadent finish to any meal. Feel free to add flavorings of your choice, like peppermint or almond extract, along with the vanilla extract.

1 (14-ounce) can coconut milk
1 tablespoon vanilla extract
7 ounces (200 grams, or about 1¼ cups) 70 percent or more dark chocolate chips or chocolate bar pieces

In a medium saucepan over medium-low heat, bring coconut milk to steaming. Make sure the coconut milk doesn't boil—you want to get it steaming with small bubbles appearing around the rim of the pot.

Remove from heat and stir in vanilla extract. Add chocolate chips or pieces. Without stirring, let coconut milk and chocolate mixture stand for 5 minutes to allow chocolate to soften. Gently stir until mixture is smooth.

Pour into 4 dessert glasses or glass tumblers and chill in the fridge for 3 hours (or overnight).

Serves 4

APPLE STRUDEL WITH BRANDY AND SPELT PHYLLO PASTRY

First you'll need to find yourself some dairy-free phyllo pastry. I use packages from The Fillo Factor. You can get both wheat and spelt varieties. Defrost the box of phyllo by placing it in the fridge overnight or for 7 to 8 hours, then let the box sit at room temperature for 2 hours. The trick to working with phyllo is to work fast: prepare all your ingredients first before opening the package. Phyllo dries out very quickly!

8 sheets vegan phyllo pastry
¼ cup plus 2 tablespoons melted vegan margarine

Filling:
½ cup granulated sugar
2 teaspoons ground cinnamon
5 tablespoons spelt flour

5 Gala apples, peeled and sliced
Juice of 1 small lemon
2 teaspoons lemon zest
2 tablespoons brandy

Topping:
3 tablespoons granulated sugar
1 teaspoon ground cinnamon

Preheat oven to 400°F and line a large baking sheet or rimmed baking dish with parchment paper. In a medium bowl, mix together all filling ingredients.

On a large piece of parchment paper, brush one phyllo sheet with melted margarine. Cover the phyllo you're not using with a damp towel to prevent it from drying out. Add another phyllo sheet, brush it with margarine, and continue until you've got a stack of 8 sheets.

Place filling along the long edge of your phyllo rectangle, leaving about 2 inches at the bottom, left, and right. Start rolling up the phyllo to create a log, using the parchment paper to help you roll. Tuck in the sides as you roll.

Place seam down on your baking sheet or dish (you can use the parchment paper to help you lift the log). Brush with melted margarine and sprinkle with topping.

Bake for 25 minutes, or until golden brown. Cut into slices and enjoy!

Serves 4

BROWNIE-IN-A-MUG

There are many things I like about this recipe (like how simple it is, how little time it takes, and its deliciousness), but what I like most is that you make individual serving sizes. I'm the type to eat a lot of treats if they're available. Instead of making a regular-size batch of brownies in a baking pan—with the risk of eating them all!—make yourself a single serving. For extra indulgence, sprinkle nondairy chocolate chips on top of your brownie as soon as it comes out of the microwave.

. . . .

¼ cup flour (I often use spelt flour)
2½ tablespoons granulated sugar
2 tablespoons unsweetened cocoa powder
Pinch salt
2 tablespoons melted coconut oil (or very light-flavored olive oil)
2 tablespoons plant-based milk

. . . .

In a mug, use a fork to whisk together flour, sugar, cocoa powder, and salt until well combined. Add oil and plant-based milk, and mix well. Ensure all the flour has been moistened.

Microwave on high for 1 minute if you like your brownies more moist and gooey, or 1 minute and 15 seconds if you like them more cakey.

Makes 1 serving

CHOCOLATE CUPCAKES WITH GANACHE TOPPING

Adapted from Sarah Kramer's La Dolce Vegan!

This is one of my favorite dessert recipes, and it's incredibly easy to make. There's lots of room for creativity here. You can add flavorful extracts like orange or peppermint, and create many different types of decoration. Try topping with chocolate-dipped strawberries, dark chocolate curls (take a vegetable peeler to a bar of chocolate), sliced fruit, shredded coconut, or dark chocolate squares. Try substituting ⅓ of the water in this recipe with orange juice or rum.

Cupcakes:

1½ cups all-purpose flour or 1¾ cups
   spelt flour
⅓ cup cocoa powder
1 cup granulated sugar
1½ teaspoons baking soda
Pinch salt
1 cup cold water

⅓ cup light-flavored olive oil or melted
   coconut oil
1 tablespoon vinegar
1 tablespoon vanilla extract

Ganache:

⅓ cup coconut milk
1½ cups nondairy dark chocolate chips,
   or chocolate bar pieces

Preheat oven to 350°F and line muffin pan with paper liners.

In a large mixing bowl, sift together flour, cocoa powder, sugar, baking soda, and salt. Add water, oil, vinegar, and vanilla extract. Mix, using as few strokes as possible. A few lumps are OK, as long as all the flour has been moistened.

Using a soup ladle, fill each cupcake liner ⅔ full. Bake for 17 to 20 minutes, until skewer or knife inserted in the middle comes out clean. Place on cooling rack and let cool completely.

To make the ganache, place chocolate in a medium bowl. In a small saucepan over medium heat, heat the coconut milk until lightly steaming and small bubbles form around the saucepan's rim. Don't let the coconut milk get too hot or start boiling. Pour the coconut milk over the chocolate and let sit for 5 minutes without stirring.

Gently stir the coconut milk and chocolate mixture until smooth. Spoon over cooled cupcakes, then let set for 30 to 60 minutes.

Makes 1 dozen cupcakes

FRUIT WITH SPICED WINE SYRUP

This refreshing dessert can be made with almost any type of fruit. Why not try it with mango, strawberries, or apples (or all three at once)? The sweet, tangy, and cinnamon flavors of this syrup complement each other very well, reminding me of Christmas aromas.

1 cup red wine
½ cup granulated sugar
1 cinnamon stick
4 whole cloves
2 lemon slices
1 teaspoon vanilla extract
4 cups fresh fruit, diced

In a medium saucepan, bring wine, sugar, cinnamon stick, cloves, and lemon slices to a boil. Reduce heat to medium-low and simmer for 15 minutes.

Strain using a mesh sieve, then stir in vanilla extract.

Divide fruit among 4 bowls, and drizzle with syrup.

Serves 4

NOTES

Introduction

[1] Michael Tjepkema, "Adult obesity in Canada: Measured height and weight," *Nutrition: Findings from the Canadian Community Health Survey*, Statistics Canada, accessed September 10, 2013, http://www.aboutmen.ca/application/www.aboutmen.ca/asset/upload/tiny_mce/page/link/Adult-Obesity-in-Canada.pdf.

[2] A. Pan et al., "Red meat consumption and mortality: results from 2 prospective cohort studies," *Archives of Internal Medicine* 172, no. 7 (2012): 555–563.

[3] "Harvard launches 'Healthy Eating Plate' in response to USDA's MyPlate," http://www.health.harvard.edu/healthbeat/harvard-launches-healthy-eating-plate-in-response-to-usda-myplate.

[4] T. Colin Campbell and Thomas M. Campbell II, *The China Study: Startling Implications for Diet, Weight Loss and Long-term Health* (Dallas: BenBella Books, 2006).

[5] Food and Agriculture Organization of the United Nations, *Livestock's long shadow: Environmental issues and options*, accessed October 3, 2013, http://www.fao.org/docrep/010/a0701e/a0701e00.HTM.

[6] Joanne Stepaniak, *The Vegan Sourcebook,* 2nd ed. (Lincolnwood, IL: Lowell House, 2000).

Chapter 1

[1] Steven C. Moore et al., "Leisure Time Physical Activity of Moderate to Vigorous Intensity and Mortality: A Large Pooled Cohort Analysis," *PloS Medicine,* Nov. 6, 2012, doi: 10.1371/journal.pmed.1001335

[2] Robert Simons and Ross Andel, "The Effects of Resistance Training and Walking on Functional Fitness in Advanced Old Age," *Journal of Aging and Health* 18, no. 1 (2006): 91–105.

[3] A. H. Taylor et al., "Physical activity and older adults: a review of health benefits and the effectiveness of interventions," *Journal of Sports Sciences* 22 (2004): 703–725.

[4] Taylor, "Physical activity and older adults," 703–725.

[5] Shawn M. Arent, Daniel M. Landers, and Jennifer L. Etnier, "The effects of exercise on mood in older adults: A meta-analytic review," *Journal of Physical Activity and Aging* 8, no. 4 (2000): 407–430.

Chapter 2

[1] "Guidelines for Adults," Canadian Society for Exercise Physiology, accessed September 10, 2013, http://www.csep.ca/english/view.asp?x=949.

[2] "2008 Physical Activity Guidelines for Americans," US Department of Health and Human Services, accessed September 10, 2013, http://www.health.gov/paguidelines/pdf/paguide.pdf.

[3] "Heart damage risk from excess endurance training," CBC News, accessed September 30, 2013, http://www.cbc.ca/news/health/story/2012/06/01/marathon-endurance-heart.html.

[4] Jonathan Goodman, "Why is the Fitness Industry Failing so Badly?" http://www.theptdc.com/2013/05/what-the-fitness-industry-really-needs-to-be-providing/.

Chapter 3

[1] D. P. Micklewright et al., "Blood lactate removal using combined massage and active recovery," *Medicine & Science in Sports & Exercise* 35, no. 5 (2003): S317.

[2] C. A. Boyle et al., "The effects of yoga training and a single bout of yoga on delayed onset muscle soreness in the lower extremity," *Journal of Strength and Conditioning Research* 18, no. 4 (2004): 723–729.

[3] Becky Miller, "Sleep & Muscle Recovery," last modified December 18, 2013, http://www.livestrong.com/article/155363-sleep-muscle-recovery.

[4] M. Datillo et al., "Sleep and muscle recovery: Endocrinological and molecular basis for a new and promising hypothesis," *Medical Hypotheses* 77, no. 2 (2011): 220–222.

[5] "Brain basics: understanding sleep," National Institute of Neurological Disorders and Stroke: National Institutes of Health, last modified December 5, 2013, http://www.ninds.nih.gov/disorders/brain_basics/understanding_sleep.htm#for_us.

Chapter 5
[1] Sadie Whitelocks, "Calorie counts on food labels could be inaccurate by up to 50 percent as they rely on 100-year-old calculation method," last modified February 4, 2013, http://www.dailymail.co.uk/femail/article-2273331/Calorie-counts-food-labels-inaccurate-50per-cent-rely-100-year-old-calculation-method.html.

[2] Brian Wansink and Pierre Chandon, "Can 'Low-Fat' Nutrition Labels Lead to Obesity?" *Journal of Marketing Research* 43, no. 1 (2006): 605–617.

[3] "Sodium in Canada," Health Canada, last modified June 8, 2012, http://www.hc-sc.gc.ca/fn-an/nutrition/sodium/index-eng.php.

[4] "Iron: Dietary Supplement Fact Sheet," Office of Dietary Supplements: National Institutes of Health, last modified August 24, 2007, http://ods.od.nih.gov/fact sheets/Iron-HealthProfessional.

Chapter 7
[1] Robyn L. Kievit, "Health Benefits of Tea," Advance Healthcare Network, posted on September 27, 2011, http://nurse-practitioners-and-physician-assistants.advanceweb.com/Columns/Nutrition-Now/Health-Benefits-of-Tea.aspx.

[2] Ryan Andrews, "What you should know about tea," Precision Nutrition, accessed October 26, 2013, http://www.precisionnutrition.com/what-you-should-know-about-tea.

METRIC AND IMPERIAL CONVERSIONS

(These conversions are rounded for convenience)

Ingredient	Cups/Tablespoons/ Teaspoons	Ounces	Grams/Milliliters
Coconut Oil	1 cup=16 tablespoons=2 sticks	7.5 ounces	209 grams
Non-dairy cheese, shredded	1 cup	4 ounces	110 grams
Flour, all-purpose	1 cup/1 tablespoon	4.5 ounces/0.3 ounces	125 grams/8 grams
Fruit, dried	1 cup	4 ounces	120 grams
Fruits or veggies, chopped	1 cup	5 to 7 ounces	145 to 200 grams
Fruits or veggies, puréed	1 cup	8.5 ounces	245 grams
Agave or maple syrup	1 tablespoon	.75 ounces	20 grams
Liquids: non-dairy milk, water, or juice	1 cup	8 fluid ounces	240 milliliters
Oats	1 cup	5.5 ounces	150 grams
Quinoa, uncooked	1 cup	6 ounces	170 grams
Salt	1 teaspoon	0.2 ounces	6 grams
Spices: cinnamon, cloves, ginger, or nutmeg (ground)	1 teaspoon	0.2 ounces	5 milliliters
Sugar, brown, firmly packed	1 cup	7 ounces	200 grams
Sugar, white	1 cup/1 tablespoon	7 ounces/0.5 ounces	200 grams/12.5 grams
Vanilla extract	1 teaspoon	0.2 ounces	4 grams

OVEN TEMP CONVERSIONS

Fahrenheit	Celsius	Gas Mark
225°	110°	¼
250°	120°	½
275°	140°	1
300°	150°	2
325°	160°	3
350°	180°	4
375°	190°	5
400°	200°	6
425°	220°	7
450°	230°	8

ACKNOWLEDGMENTS

Many people have been instrumental in creating this book during the two-and-a-half years I took to write it, and to them I'm very grateful. My sincere thanks to John Watson of Image Maker Photographic Studio for his exquisite photography, artistic sense, and extremely hard work over the course of four demanding, full-day food photo shoots in the tiny apartment I was living in at the time. His work and artistic vision brought my recipes to life and are vital to the success of this book. I couldn't have asked for a better photographer and collaborator. I'm also very thankful for the incredible and energetic assistance of my mom, Angelika Hackett, during our photo shoots (including an emergency avocado-purchasing and kitchen knife-sharpening mission), as well as her incredibly detailed manuscript editing. I thank her and my dad, Robert Hackett, for being so supportive of this project, lending an ear, and giving advice.

I would like to acknowledge the contributions of the twenty vegan athletes interviewed for this book: Robert Cheeke, Melody Schoenfeld, Jeff Golfman, Manny Escalante, Matthew Woodman, Megan Storms, Michelle Risley, Mike Mahler, David O'Meara, Austin Barbisch, Andrea Berman, Victor Rivera, Dru Brozovich, Sally Andersen, Christy Morgan, Anastasia Zinchenko, Tobias Sjösten, Matt Terry, Scott Shetler, and Daniel Austin. I appreciate their insight into active, plant-based living and am grateful for their informative and candid responses. An additional thank you to Robert Cheeke for providing the foreword to this book.

My thanks to Susan Levin of the Physicians Committee for Responsible Medicine and my sister Melanie Hackett for their excellent contributions to the nutrition section of this book. Their expertise deepened the scope of information I could present to readers.

I'd like to acknowledge the recipe contributors who provided inspired, delicious, and healthy creations: Joyce Hackett, Jeff Golfman, Philip Breakenridge, Melanie Hackett, Taras Chouinard, and especially Holly Burton for her many and varied contributions.

I gratefully acknowledge the work of my literary agent, Jill Marsal, and the great people at Skyhorse Publishing, including my excellent editor, Leah Zarra, for believing in this project and bringing it to fruition.

A select group of fantastic people have been rooting for me since Day 1 of this project: my amazing clients all over the world; my "G's" (Heidi Braacx, Holly Burton, and Kevin Lee); my oldest friend and workout buddy Setareh Bateni; my friend and thrice-a-week training partner Vanessa Sparrow; and my wonderful husband Murray for enduring my long writing days (and resulting brain fog) as well as being the official taste tester for the recipes, including his excellent cooking while testing them. And Murray also contributed the chili recipe!

GENERAL INDEX

*Recipe Index follows Main Index

A

Abs Deck of Cards workout, 30

abs exercises
bicycle crunch, 31
crunch, 32
hip raise, 32
jackknife, 33
Russian twist, 35
v-up, 39
accountability, 94–95
added sugar, 47
advanced exercise list, 30–39
bear crawl, 30–31
burpee, 31
close push-up, 32
front kick, 32
high knees, 32
hip raise, 32
jump lunge, 33
jump squat, 33
jumping jack, 33
mountain climber, 33–34
in-and-out jump squat, 32–33
pike push-up, 34
plank, 35
plank with alternating arm and leg raise, 35
push-up, 35
side kick, 35–36
side plank with leg lift, 36
single leg squat, 36
Superman plank walk-out, 38
triceps dip, 38
v-up, 39
walking push-up, 39

advanced workouts
Abs Deck of Cards, 30
Cardio Deck of Cards, 29
Evil Twin Deck of Cards, 29
It's a Bird, It's a Plane, 26
Strength Deck of Cards, 30
Strength Superpowers, 26–27
Superhero Abs, 25
aerobic exercise, 16, 17
agave nectar, 58
aging, 11–12, 13–14, 17, 90, 99, 108, 109, 118
algae, 68
allergies, 11–12, 40
almond butter, 86
almond flour, 86
almond milk, 54
almonds, 86
amaranth, 86
American Journal of Clinical Nutrition, 89
amino acids, 59, 87, 90, 91, 97
anaphylaxis, 11
Andersen, Sally, 119–122
animal agriculture, 8–9, 10, 110, 112, 115, 125
animal welfare, 8–9
antioxidants, 6, 7, 59, 63, 84
apps
Cronometer, 80
f.lux, 23
Morpheus (HRV), 139
MyFitnessPal, 80
Archives of Internal Medicine, 5
athlete interviews, 92–139
achievements, 95, 98–99, 101, 102, 106, 107, 109, 111, 114, 117, 119, 122, 124, 127, 131, 133, 135, 139
active living tips

aging well, 99, 108, 109, 118
ethics and beliefs, 128
motivation, 104, 116, 120, 126
self-discipline, 127
sleep, 98, 99, 108, 109, 115, 118, 130–131, 135, 139
spirituality, 95
start slowly, 98, 101, 107, 113, 123, 129, 133, 135
weight loss, 112, 120, 121, 125–126, 138
beginner tips, 94–95, 98, 99–100, 101, 102, 103, 105, 107, 109, 110, 113–114, 116, 124, 125, 129–130, 137–138
challenges faced, 95, 98, 101, 104, 105, 107, 109, 110, 117, 119, 124, 126–127, 129, 133, 135, 138
ethics and beliefs, 95, 96, 98, 106, 110, 115, 118, 120, 125, 134
exercise tips
conditioning, 129
consistency, 101, 107, 116, 129–130, 135, 137–138
enjoyment, 92, 95, 101, 102, 113, 121, 133
goals, 91, 98, 102, 103, 116, 121, 129, 130
habits, forming, 92, 103, 116, 120
pain and injury, 98, 100, 110, 114, 127
personal trainers, 98, 101, 105

balance exercise, 17
Barbisch, Austin, 109–111
basal metabolic rate, 44
beans, 66, 86–87
bear crawl, 30–31
beginner tips. see athlete
  interviews; newbie
  exercises; newbie workouts
belief systems, 96
bench step-up, 31
Berman, Andrea, 112–114
bicycle crunch, 31
biodiversity loss, 8
bird-dog, 31
blenders, 113
blood chemistry, 49, 50, 52,
  58
blood circulation, 20
blood tests, 48, 80–81
blue light, 23
Body Mass Index (BMI), 4
bodybuilding, 109, 110–111,
  125
bodyweight exercise list,
  30–39
  bear crawl, 30–31
  bench step-up, 31
  bicycle crunch, 31
  bird-dog, 31
  burpee, 31
  butt kickers, 31
  close push-up, 32
  crunch, 32
  front kick, 32
  high knees, 32
  hip raise, 32
  inchworm, 33
  jackknife, 33
  jump lunge, 33
  jump squat, 33
  jumping jack, 33
  mountain climber, 33–34
  in-and-out jump squat,
    32–33
  pike push-up, 34

plank, 35
plank with alternating arm
  and leg raise, 35
push-up, 35
reverse lunge, 35
Russian twist, 35
side kick, 35–36
side plank with leg lift, 36
single leg squat, 36
Spider-Man (plank
  position), 36
Spider-Man push-up, 36
split squat, 36
squat, 37
standing bird-dog, 37
stick-up, 38
Superman, 38
Superman plank walk-out,
  38
triceps dip, 38
v-jump, 39
v-up, 39
walking push-up, 39
wall push-up, 39
bodyweight workouts
  Iron Man/Iron Woman, 27
  It's a Bird, It's a Plane, 26
  Kickstarter Strength
    Workout, 24
  Outdoor Park Workout, 25
  Strength Superpowers,
    26–27
  Superhero Abs, 25
bone health, 3, 82
bone strength, 14, 17
bran, 52, 53
branched chain amino acids
  (BCAAs), 91, 121
Brazier, Brendan, 7, 94, 122
breast cancer, 88–89, 114
Brozovich, Dru, 118–119
bulb & stem vegetables, 64
burpee, 31
butt kickers, 31

C

caffeine, 58, 59
calcium, 42–43, 48, 58,
  81–82, 97
calories, 43–45, 80. see also
  athlete interviews
Campbell, T. Colin, 5, 6
Canadian Society for Exercise
  Physiology (CSEP), 16, 17
cancer, 5, 6, 59, 88–89, 114
canned fruit, 52
carbohydrates, 43, 46–47,
  49, 83, 105, 107, 110, 130
Cardio Deck of Cards
  workout, 29
cardio exercises
  burpee, 31
  butt kickers, 31
  front kick, 32
  high knees, 32
  jump lunge, 33
  jump squat, 33
  jumping jack, 33
  mountain climber, 33–34
  in-and-out jump squat,
    32–33
  side kick, 35–36
  v-jump, 39
cardiovascular exercise, 19
casein, 5
cashews, 86
cattle ranching, 8
cereals, 56, 61
Cheeke, Robert, 93–96
chest exercises
  close push-up, 32
  pike push-up, 34
  push-up, 35
  Spider-Man push-up, 36
  walking push-up, 39
  wall push-up, 39
chia seeds, 86
The China Study, 5, 6
cholesterol, 46, 59, 128
circulation, 20

food allergies, 11–12, 40
food diary, sample 4-day,
    68–71
food guides, 5–6
food intolerances, 40, 112
food prep. see planning and
    preparation
food-dependent exercise-
    induced anaphylaxis, 11
four-day food diary sample,
    68–71
fresh fruit, 52
fresh veggies, 51
front kick, 32
frozen fruit, 52
frozen veggies, 51
fruit, 52, 67, 94
fruit sugar, 47
full body exercises
    bear crawl, 30–31
    burpee, 31
fungi, 67

G

Gandhi, Mahatma, 115
gerontology, 11
glucagon, 49
glucose, 49
glutamine, 121
gluten-free diet, 95, 104, 110
glutes exercises
    bench step-up, 31
    bird-dog, 31
    plank with alternating arm
        and leg raise, 35
    reverse lunge, 35
glycemic index, 58, 106
glycogen, 49–50
gold standard guidelines, 16,
    17
Golfman, Jeff, 99–100. see
    also Recipe Index
Goodman, Jonathan, 18
Google Scholar, 49
grain crops, 9

grains, 52–53, 62, 65
green leafy vegetables, 65
green teas, 59
growth hormones, 22, 131

H

habits, forming, 92, 103,
    116, 120
Hackett, Melanie, 49–50,
    195
hamstring exercises
    bench step-up, 31
    reverse lunge, 35
    standing bird-dog, 37
happycow.net, 77, 116, 123,
    137
Harvard School of Public
    Health, 5, 6, 23
health, defined, 2
Health Canada, 6
Healthy Eating Plate
    (Harvard), 6
healthy fats, 45, 56, 128
heart health, 5, 6, 17, 45, 46,
    52, 55, 58, 59
hemp oil, 56
hemp seeds/hearts, 60, 86
herbal tea, 59
high fat/protein diet, 128,
    130
high intensity exercise, 17,
    19, 23
high knees, 32
high protein pasta, 53
high-intensity interval training
    (HIIT), 124
home workouts. see workout
    programs
hormone optimization, 106
hormones, 49–50, 89, 131
Horton, Tony, 113
"How Awake Are You?" test,
    23
human beings, 8, 9, 10, 110
hunger, 80

hydration, 137, 138
hydrogenated oil, 45, 55
hypothyroidism, 89

I

immune system, 50, 59,
    83–84
inchworm, 33
inflammation, 7, 84
ingredient lists, label, 43
Inkster, Karina, 10–12
instant soups, 56
insulin, 49, 50
intensity, of exercise, 15–17,
    19, 139
intermediate exercise list
    bear crawl, 30–31
    bench step-up, 31
    bicycle crunch, 31
    bird-dog, 31
    butt kickers, 31
    crunch, 32
    front kick, 32
    high knees, 32
    hip raise, 32
    inchworm, 33
    jackknife, 33
    jumping jack, 33
    mountain climber, 33–34
    plank, 35
    plank with alternating arm
        and leg raise, 35
    push-up, 35
    reverse lunge, 35
    Russian twist, 35
    side kick, 35–36
    side plank with leg lift, 36
    Spider-Man (plank
        position), 36
    split squat, 36
    standing bird-dog, 37
    Superman, 38
    triceps dip, 38
    v-jump, 39
    v-up, 39

split squat, 36
squat, 37
standing bird-dog, 37
stick-up, 38
Superman, 38
wall push-up, 39
newbie workouts
Kickstarter Strength
Workout, 24
Outdoor Park Workout, 25
N.I.C.E principles, 15–18
North Pole Marathon, 7
novelty, of exercise, 15
nutrient absorption, 80–81
nutrient density, 42, 80, 83
nutrition. see athlete nutrition
nutritional labels,
understanding, 42–43
nutritional yeast, 86, 110
nutritionists, 7, 40
nuts, 67, 86–87, 134

O
Oakes, Fiona, 7
obesity, 4, 116, 120
oils, 45, 55–56, 60, 66
olive oil, 45, 56
Olympics, 132, 133
O'Meara, David, 108–109
omega 3-6-9 oil, 60
omega-3 fatty acids, 60, 82,
101, 257
Ontario Masters Athletics, 7
Ornish, Dean, 5
osteoporosis, 3, 6, 42–43
in-and-out jump squat, 32–33
Outdoor Park Workout, 25
oxidative stress, 6–7

P
Paleo diet, 121
pasta, 53–54
peas, 66
peer reviews, 48–49
performance improvement, 7

personal trainers, 98, 101,
105
physical activity. see exercise;
fitness
physical health, 4–6
Physicians Committee for
Responsible Medicine, 83,
88
phytoestrogens, 88
pierogies, 43
pike push-up, 34
pistachios, 86
plank, 35
plank with alternating arm
and leg raise, 35
planning and preparation,
72–79
advice on, 114
daily food prep tips
grocery delivery, 78–79
make large amounts,
77–78
meal planning, 78
slow cookers, 78
dinner parties, 76
restaurants, 76–77, 100
travel tips
with kitchen,
perishables, 73–74
limited cooking
availability, 75–76
no cooking options,
74–75
nonperishable food list,
73
vegan food prep, 72–73
work meal tips, 73
Plantae system, 10
plant-based diet basics.
see also planning and
preparation; vegan kitchen
cleanses/detoxes, 48–50
dietician advice, 40, 47,
48, 83–84

healthy eating
characteristics, 41
nutrition needs and
individual variances, 40–
41, 44, 47, 126–127
nutritional labels
calorie content, 43–45
carbohydrate content,
46–47
cholesterol content, 46
fat content, 45–46
ingredient lists, 43
laws, 44, 45, 48
protein content, 47–48
serving size, 43
sodium content, 46
understanding, 42–43
vitamins and minerals,
48
sample four-day food diary,
68–71
saturated fats, 45
whole foods, 41–42
plant-based lifestyle
benefits of
animals, environment,
and human beings,
8–9
athletic performance,
6–7
physical health and
disease prevention,
4–6
challenges, 12. see also
athlete interviews
increase in, 1
overall health goals, 2
reasons to choose, 2–4
plant-based milks, 54
plateaus, 15
podcasts, 103, 128
pollution, 8
polyunsaturated fats, 45
powerlifting, 127–128, 131

RECITE INDEX